D0687455

SOURCES FOR
NEW MEXICAN
HISTORY 1821-1848

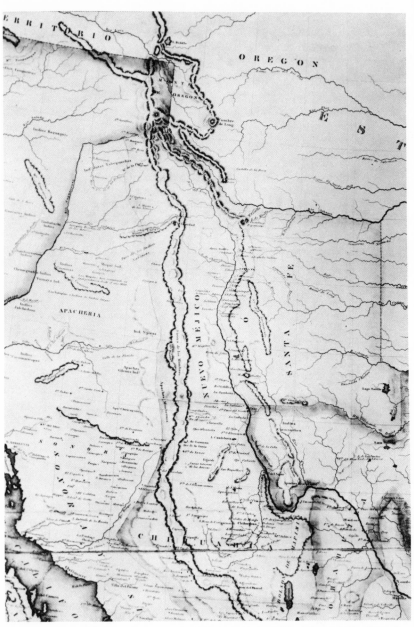

"The Territory of New Mexico in 1828" as outlined by Mapa de los Estados Unidos de Mejico. *Courtesy of the Benson Latin American Collection, The General Library, The University of Texas at Austin.*

SOURCES FOR NEW MEXICAN HISTORY 1821-1848

DANIEL TYLER

MUSEUM OF NEW MEXICO PRESS
Santa Fe, New Mexico

To MY COLLEAGUES: Harry Rosenberg, a Medievalist at home among Westerners; Charles J. Bayard, who first aroused my interest in the West; and James E. Hansen, whose enduring support made this book possible.

This publication was made possible by grants from The Weatherhead Foundation, Colorado State University (Faculty Research Grant), and the National Endowment for the Humanities, a federal agency.

Printed in the United States of America.

Library of Congress Cataloging in Publication Data

Tyler, Daniel.
    Sources for New Mexican history, 1821-1848.

Bibliography: p.
    Includes index.
    1. New Mexico—History—To 1848—Archival resources.
I. Title.
Z1315.T9 1984 [F800] 027   83-27042
ISBN 0-89013-147-3

Museum of New Mexico Press
P.O. Box 2087
Santa Fe, NM 87503

CONTENTS

FOREWORD

Two decades ago, as a beginning graduate student at the University of New Mexico, I first encountered the archives of New Mexico in the Mexican era, 1821–1846. My mentor, Donald C. Cutter (who later served as mentor for Daniel Tyler, too), had pointed me toward the Mexican period as a fruitful area of research. Little had been done in that field, he said, and I soon learned why. In contrast to the orderly archives left by Spanish administrators, the archives of independent Mexico seemed as chaotic as the politics of the young nation. Moreover, the documents themselves were difficult to read. With the removal of Spanish administrators in 1821, the quality of handwriting and orthography had declined on the frontier. Furthermore, years of neglect had resulted in the deterioration or disappearance of many documents.

In preparation for a study that eventually would lead to a book, *The Taos Trappers: The Fur Trade in the Far Southwest, 1540–1846* (1971), I struggled to learn my way through the Mexican Archives of New Mexico. Then, as now, the originals of the MANM, as I soon learned to cite them, were housed at the New Mexico State Records Center and Archives in Santa Fe. In Albuquerque, however, I had convenient access to photoprints of most of the same documents, bound in thick blue volumes that covered much of one wall in the Coronado Room at the University of New Mexico. Accompanying these volumes was a rough finding aid: notes handwritten on the back of used library checkout cards, arranged in bundles held together with aging, brittle rubber bands. For my topic, these cards were of little use, and no better guide existed in Santa Fe. Thus, in search of records relating to the often illicit activities of American trappers, I was forced to read each page in the 158 hefty volumes of photoprints. Reading through documents extraneous to my research, and consuming hours attempting to transcribe and translate poorly written passages, produced frustrations, to be sure, but also offered the frequently fulfilled promise of the researcher's familiar reward—the exhilaration of discovery.

In 1964 I spent the summer searching for traces of American trappers and traders in the archives in Mexico City. There, frustration outweighed exhilaration. Herbert Eugene Bolton's *Guide to Materials for the History of the United States in the Principal Archives of Mexico* (1913) had informed me of the existence of specific documents relating to my subject, but finding them proved far more difficult than I had imagined. At the Mexican national archives, the *Archivo General de la Nación*, Rubio Mané and the patient Beatriz Arteaga explained to me that the collections had been moved many times during and after the Revolution; that some documents were housed in a place inaccessible to researchers, the *Casa Amarilla;* and that low budgets and lack of staff had slowed progress in producing guides. Documents relating to New Mexico were to be found scattered in numerous branches of the archive, often in bundles tied with string, arranged in no particular order. To make matters worse, that summer the archive of the Mexican foreign ministry, *Relaciones Exteriores,* was being moved and was closed to researchers. One archive that Bolton had seen, that of the *Secretaría de Fomento,* eluded me completely, notwithstanding daily visits to every imaginable government office where encouraging bureaucrats told me *mas allá.* A summer of searching, then, yielded little treasure.

A couple of years later, still in search of records relating to American trappers and traders, I visited the principal towns along the Chihuahua Trail—Ciudad Juárez, Parral, and Chihuahua. If archives in the nation's capital were in poor condition, those in the provinces were even worse. Although I was armed with a copy of Manuel Carrera Stampa's *Archivalia Mexicana* (1952), I was not prepared for the complete absence of guides and the short hours that archives were open to researchers. I had better luck at the Huntington and Bancroft libraries in California, and at the Missouri Historical Society in St. Louis, where finding aids were more developed than in Mexico or New Mexico.

Although my initial forays into archives containing materials related to Mexican New Mexico occurred a relatively short time ago, profound changes have since taken place. Daniel Tyler's remarkable *Sources for New Mexican History* makes that clear, as no other source does. Over the last two decades, teams have microfilmed entire archives, such as those in Santa Fe, Juárez, Parral, and Chihuahua. Specialized and once nearly inaccessible collections, such as the official *Gaceta* of the state of Chihuahua, are now on film. A decade ago, the *Gaceta* could be consulted in only one difficult-to-locate government office in the city of Chihuahua. New guides, calendars, and indexes have appeared. Long lost or heretofore unknown documents, such as the notorious Sender Papers or the municipal archives of Carrizal, have surfaced, and the massive *Archivo General de la Nación* and the Mexican national repository of newspapers, the *Hemeroteca,* have been moved to improved facilities.

Just as Tyler provides us with specific information about the rapid progress that has made archival sources more readily accessible to scholars, his guide also represents a major contribution to the very progress that it describes. Thanks to Tyler's work, a researcher now has convenient access to information about the scope, nature, and location of primary sources in Mexico, New Mexico, and other states of the union as well. Tyler has ferreted out pertinent documents from the Huntington Library in California to Yale in Connecticut, and has turned up New Mexico items in such improbable places as Wisconsin and Illinois. Tyler tells us where these sources are, which are on microfilm, what finding aids exist, and how to make the best use of the archives. Prior to the publication of Tyler's guide, the beginning scholar learned about these matters slowly, sometimes painfully, occasionally through serendipity, and usually through conversations with scholars, librarians, and archivists. Even then, none of us had the comprehensive and up-to-date view of the range of the collections that Tyler provides in this single, well-organized volume.

Tyler's *Sources for New Mexican History* is indispensable for beginning and veteran scholars alike. Prepared by a practicing historian, it displays throughout a solid understanding of the researcher's needs and arouses excitement similar to that a bibliophile must feel while browsing through a dealer's rare-book catalog. Tyler's guide piques our curiosity, starts adrenalin flowing, and makes us eager to explore the collections and read the documents.

For my part, I also read Tyler's manuscript with growing gratitude for his hard work at assembling this information, and with a sense of wonder at the progress the profession has made. I also read these pages with a nostalgic and thoroughly irrational regret that I now have convenient access to so many documents on microfilm. When memories of inconveniences and frustrations of research away from home begin to fade, what remains are the pleasant recollections of archival adventures—of untying a dusty bundle of documents that appears to have been unopened by previous researchers; of documents discovered, rather than of pages fruitlessly turned; of exchanging with an archivist some pesos, a meal, and a couple of cervezas for keeping an archive open a few hours longer; and of warm, helpful conversations with Mexican historians, such as the venerable Francisco Almada of Chihuahua.

But I am probably being too sanguine about the effects of progress. There are still documents undiscovered and uncataloged. Even among those documents on microfilm, many remain to be read, understood, interpreted, and reinterpreted.

May Daniel Tyler's guide, then, be as infectious as it is efficacious. May it spark the beginning of an era of vigorous research and writing on one of the most neglected, yet dynamic and fascinating, chapters in the history of the Southwest.

David J. Weber
Southern Methodist University
December 1983

INTRODUCTION

A fter completing a dissertation on the first administration of New Mexico's Governor Manuel Armijo,[1] I spoke with Michael Weber, who was then Chief of the History Division at the Museum of New Mexico. We agreed that the lessons I had learned in the process of locating and translating original sources should be shared with others. Because the Museum was planning to reconstruct a Mexican period room in the Palace of the Governors, and *El Palacio* was planning a special issue on the same theme,[2] Weber suggested applying to the Weatherhead Foundation for a grant that would enable me to prepare a researcher's guide to New Mexico in the Mexican period.

A generous award from the Weatherhead Foundation made it possible to begin work in the summer of 1973. At that time my efforts focused on translation problems. I collected examples of the idiosyncrasies associated with the official language of the Mexican period. By early 1974 I was well into this task, when an opportunity arose to teach in Mexico City with funding provided by the Council for International Exchange of Scholars.

This Fulbright lectureship offered several opportunities, not the least of which was a chance to advance my linguistic and paleographic skills where the most sophisticated problems could be addressed by resident experts. While teaching at the Universidad Nacional Autónoma de Mexico, I persuaded several Mexican graduate students to study the Mexican period using microfilm I had brought with me from New Mexico.[3] As their projects developed, the class began looking for additional documentation in public and private archives of Mexico City. As a result of these searches, I realized that the Mexican period was as challenging to the Mexicans as it had been for me during my dissertation research. I concluded that a good researcher's guide should list and describe all extant resources in both Mexico and the United States.

Returning to the United States in 1976, I resumed work on the guide with priorities reordered. Instead of continuing the section on translation, I began to collect information on document collections. The high cost of travel required additional financial assistance, and this time the National Endowment for the Humanities granted a substantial sum to the Museum of New Mexico so that I could travel in Mexico and the United States looking for materials not included in the microfilmed archives of New Mexico. As project director, working for and with the Museum, my goal was to complete a finder's guide, after which I expected to prepare glossaries and paleographical rules designed to assist translators of Mexican period documents once they had been found.

Gathering and organizing descriptive material consumed far more time than had been anticipated in the grant proposal. News of the award from the National Endowment for the Humanities actually arrived while I was on a second Fulbright lectureship in Argentina, and although I was still on sabbatical leave when I returned to Colorado in 1980, the time remaining for research was insufficient to prepare a guide with both descriptive and mechanical sections. Even with the assistance of a Faculty Research Grant from Colorado State University, delays caused by major archival changes in Mexico and the dispersed condition of collections in the United States quickly led to the expenditure of resources. In addition, reorganization of the Mexican archives during the *sexenio* of President José López Portillo turned up collections previously off limits or unknown even to Mexican period specialists. Identifying these materials consumed more time and produced a greater body of information than had been anticipated. All of these factors led me to the conclusion that a researcher's guide would be sufficient unto itself even if it served only to point out where collections are located and what they contain. Readers should know that this volume generally represents the state of affairs as of 1982. Some corrections have been made to reflect changes made in 1983.

Coincidentally, the University of New Mexico Press published David Weber's *The Mexican Frontier, 1821–1846,* at the same time I ended my research. When this book appeared, I suffered the momentary fear that the cart had arrived before the horse; that Weber's outstanding work would make my guide superfluous. A careful look at the unevenness in Mexican period scholarship shows that much is yet to be done on the Mexican Southwest, however.[4] Weber indicates that little has been done on social history, the role of the militia, and the activities of Mexicans in the Santa Fe trade. Similarly, Elizabeth A. H. John, in her review of Weber's book, argues the case for further research on the life of the Indians and the impact of religion on the lives of the *nuevomexicanos.*[5] To these suggestions should be added a number of additional themes such as land and water rights, farming and livestock raising, and the judicial system. Indeed, much remains to be done.

Two other books merit comment because of their relationship to this guide: Henry Putney Beers, *Spanish and Mexican Records of the American Southwest,* and Richard E. Greenleaf and Michael C. Meyer, *Research in Mexican History.*[6] The former is an exceptionally fine bibliographic guide to archive and manuscript sources. Beers' enviable experience and thorough scholarship are evident in this tour de force. The difference between his work and what is presented herein is one of scope and methodology. The parameters for my study are based on the geographical limits of New Mexico as this area was understood by the Mexican government during the first twenty-five years after independence. Beers includes Texas, Arizona, and California, and his narrative description of sources for each area includes both the Spanish colonial and Mexican periods. As Beers notes, however, his findings are based primarily on published finding aids. Additionally, he concluded his research prior to the archival revolution that occurred in Mexico under the presidency of José López Portillo. By contrast, I have tried to incorporate already published information with my own findings after examination of materials in most of the archives and libraries described. I have also identified a significant number of collections in the United States and Mexico for which no finding aids exist.

Greenleaf and Meyer's *Research in Mexican History* is an excellent primer for anyone beginning research in Mexico. As Greenleaf mentioned to me at the *Archivo General de la Nación* in the summer of 1981, however, the book is due for a revision. Undoubtedly, the revised edition will correct errors that have crept in with the passage of time.

The purpose of this volume is to identify manuscript and contemporary printed materials dealing with New Mexico from 1821 to 1848. The dates are somewhat flexible to accommodate scholars pursuing themes beyond the parameters of this study. Consequently, some materials have been noted whose contents touch only tangentially on the Mexican period but still provide perspectives on the people or institutions of New Mexico during an adjoining era.

The guide also is directed toward making research activity more efficient. In most cases the location of each repository is mentioned, along with the best procedures for gaining access to the documents and other pertinent information. Given the cost of travel and per diem support necessary for sustaining research distant from home, planning and careful preparation before departure are essential. Finding aids, both published and unpublished, are listed in the narrative and at the end of each chapter so that researchers will be able to avail themselves of this literature prior to perusing the documents. In several footnotes, I have included the names of key people if they appeared likely to remain in their posts for some time, or will be available for consultation in years to come.

A third objective has been to provide a background on the creation of Mexican period records, what has caused them to be so dispersed, and where they might be found through diligent exploration. I have taken this approach in the hope that some of the "lost" material will be encountered through the rational detective work of those who understand the distribution channels for official documents during the Mexican period. As is evident in this volume, many finds have been made during the past ten years due to an understanding of the history of Mexican bureaucracy.

Finally, this guide is intended to promote further study of the Mexican period. Both Hispanos and Anglo-Americans should profit by digging into the record. The former will be able to focus more sharply on their sense of identity by tracing roots back to a period when the Far North was one of Mexico's dynamic regions.[7] The latter will find evidence of frontier heroism similar in many ways to feats lauded by admirers of pioneers in the trans-Mississippi West. They will find that the Mexican population grew by fifty percent between 1821 and 1846,[8] that expansion took place to the east and west of the more sheltered reaches of the Rio Grande, and that laws and customs were invented on the frontier to deal with conditions ignored by the central government in Mexico City. Even the attitudes toward Indians, the environment, and their own livelihood paralleled many of the characteristics associated with the saga of westering pioneers. Additionally, study of the Mexican period holds promise of a more sophisticated treatment of the several Indian cultures. Not all Comanches, Apaches, and Navajos terrorized the Rio Grande communities. Many lived in peaceful settlements adjacent to Mexican villages, while others became integrated in Mexican society. Answers need to be found regarding the role of indigenous peoples during a period of cultural change in New Mexico. If this brief epoch can be examined as an era of change, as opposed to a time of barbarism between Spanish and North American sovereignty, great profit will be gleaned from further study. In many ways, the 1821–1848 period is a missing link in studies about the West, the frontier, Chicanos, Mexico, and Native Americans.

Chapters in this book are organized with two ideas in mind. First, most of the source material on New Mexico is located in New Mexico, so New Mexico is the first priority. The New Mexico Historical Society, the Museum of New Mexico, and, since 1969, the New Mexico State Records Center and Archives have accomplished a great deal in collecting and organizing sources relevant to the state's past. Second, the author hopes that this volume will encourage students outside of New Mexico to research the Mexican period. For this reason, the second chapter is an attempt to identify the outstanding collections in other states so that preliminary investigations can be made in local institutions. The third chapter on the National Archives and related federal centers rounds out the coverage of the United States. The final chapters explain the situation in Mexico. A bibliography of printed sources lists those primary materials created by soldiers, sojourners, and entrepreneurs whose views of New Mexico and Mexicans provided North Americans with their first images of this new and challenging land. It also includes printed documents, articles containing reprinted or translated source materials, and some government publications.

Readers should be warned that the contents of this volume are neither complete nor definitive. Furthermore, because of unevenness in available information, or the range in size of many listed collections, some are included in detail while others are represented only by sample citations. This latitude can be noted in the Franciscan records, which are only partially cited, and in the *Hacienda* archives in the *Archivo General de la Nación,* which have been located and are now available for consultation. Other examples of such unevenness abound. Perhaps the reader will remember that this is only a guide.

Inconsistencies exist in the citation of documents. As much as possible, I have tried to retain the system used by each archive, believing that users of this volume will enjoy greater success if entries herein are similar to those encountered in finding aids, indexes, and card catalogs. In a few cases I have taken liberties with punctuation and spelling in order to prevent confusion over the variety of ways in which collections are cited by different finding aids and/or institutions. Readers will also note the duplication of information, especially background information, among the several chapters of this book. This was done in the belief that readers often will refer only to a specific chapter. Although the book is written to have greater significance if read from beginning to end, each chapter can stand alone.

I have incurred a great many debts in the course of my work on this book. A large folder of correspondence attests to the many letters I have received from archivists, librarians, and historians kind enough to respond to my endless questions. All have provided me with information that forms a vital part of the book, and some have provided me with direction and guidance far beyond what I had any expectation of receiving. Vivian Fisher, Head of the Microfilm Division at the Bancroft Library, read part of the manuscript and assisted me in identifying those materials at the Bancroft which have relevance to this study. Janet Fireman also read the manuscript, combed out the rough spots, streamlined the prose, and helped salvage what must have seemed incoherent ramblings. Although I am fully responsible for the final version of this text, the credit for stylistic refinement is strictly hers. David Weber and Myra Ellen Jenkins also provided me with encouragement and support. At the New Mexico State Records Center and Archives, I was warmly welcomed and unfailingly attended by Mike Miller, Richard Salazar, and Stan Hordes. Sherry Smith-Gonzales aided me in the preparation of the book's bibliography, and Tom Chávez, Associate Director for History of the Museum of New Mexico, fought most of the battles for me so this volume could go to press. At the University of New Mexico I worked several long days at the Coronado Room, where I was allowed special privileges by Tom Farren, then Head of Special Collections. His assistants, Jan Barnhart and Marianne Spores, were equally solicitous in attending to my requests and providing me with information that I was unable to dig out on my own. I must also acknowledge a debt to Simeon H. (Bud) Newman, John Wilson, W. Michael Mathes, Ron Swerczek, Winston (Chuck) DeVille, and Janet Lecompte, all of whom aided me with information and encouragement when I was most desperate.

In Mexico, my debts are many. I feel particularly grateful for the many kindnesses of Alfonso Escarcega Domínguez, *un caballero chihuahuense*, who opened doors all over the state of Chihuahua for me. In Mexico City, I found the *Archivo General de la Nación* in the process of moving, but the hospitality of its directors, Dr. Alejandra Moreno Toscano and Lic. Leonor Ortiz Monasterio, made it possible for me to work with the various departments even though everything was in a state of flux. In particular, I wish to thank Gilberto Martínez Bribiesca, Miguel Civeira Taboada, Jorge Garibay Alvarez, Stella Gonzales, and Gerald McGowan for their great helpfulness. Roberto Beristáin also made my work in the *AGN* much simpler. The individuals who aided me in other archives in Mexico are legion, but I wish particularly to name María Eugenia López de Roux, Gloria Grajales, Luis Garfias, and Felipe Colomo Castro. These professionals and many others like them taught me the meaning of Mexican hospitality and generosity.

Two others stand out among the many who supported me in the preparation of this guide. Mike Weber, who was the first to recognize the merits of the project and the one most responsible for acquiring funding, was always interested in the progress of my research and ever patient when the results were delayed. I am equally indebted to my wife Silvia. She not only helped me gain access to records where *norteamericanos* are sometimes suspect, but she disciplined herself to stick with me during long hours of tedium, paging documents in dusty archives. She helped me with most of the research and may have learned something about her own country in the process.

Since the typing and retyping of this manuscript proved to be something of a chore for someone who does not read Spanish, I want to express a special word of thanks to Deborah Clifford. She managed to meet my deadlines with admirable good humor, professionalism, and a keen eye for my lapses.

Daniel Tyler
Fort Collins, Colorado

NOTES

1. Daniel Tyler, "New Mexico in the 1820s: The First Administration of Manuel Armijo" (Ph.D. diss., University of New Mexico, 1970).

2. *El Palacio* 80 (Fall 1974).

3. One of these students published her findings in the first volume of a series launched by the Universidad Iberoamericana. See Lourdes Lascuráin Orive, "Reflexiones sobre Nuevo Mexico y su integración a los Estados Unidos de Norteamérica," in *El Destino Manifiesto en La Historia de La Nación Norteamericana*, Serie Estudiantil, No. 1 (Mexico: Universidad Iberoamericana, 1977).

4. By way of introduction to his bibliographical essay, Weber notes that "Massive archival collections, both in Mexico and the United States, have yet to be examined in detail, and exciting challenges and new discoveries await the serious researcher." See David J. Weber, *The Mexican Frontier, 1821–1846: The American Southwest under Mexico* (Albuquerque: University of New Mexico Press, 1982), p. 377.

5. Elizabeth A. H. John, "Good News and Bad News on the Mexican Frontier," *New Mexico Historical Review* 57 (July 1982), pp. 289–93.

6. Henry Putney Beers, *Spanish and Mexican Records of the American Southwest* (Tucson: University of Arizona Press, 1979); Richard E. Greenleaf and Michael C. Meyer, *Research in Mexican History: Topics, Methodology, Sources, and a Practical Guide to Field Research* (Lincoln: University of Nebraska Press, 1973).

7. Weber, *The Mexican Frontier*, p. xviii.

8. Ibid., p. 195.

ABBREVIATIONS

AGN	*Archivo General de la Nación*
BIA	Bureau of Indian Affairs
BLM	Bureau of Land Management
M	Letter designation for NARS microfilm which has high research value because it represents the filming of an entire series.
MANM	Mexican Archives of New Mexico
NARS	National Archives and Records Service
NMHR	*New Mexico Historical Review*
NMSRCA	New Mexico State Records Center and Archives
SANM	Spanish Archives of New Mexico
T	Letter designation for NARS microfilm which does not usually represent a complete series of documents. T film was often reproduced in response to a particular request.
UNAM	*Universidad Nacional Autónoma de Mexico*
UTEP	University of Texas at El Paso

SOURCES FOR
NEW MEXICAN
HISTORY 1821-1848

New Mexico State Records Center and Archives, Santa Fe, New Mexico. Photograph by Art Taylor.

Entrance to the History Library, History Unit, Museum of New Mexico, Santa Fe. Photograph by Art Taylor.

CHAPTER I
RECORDS IN NEW MEXICO

1. UNDERSTANDING WHERE THE RECORDS ARE AND WHY:

The search for Mexican period documents in New Mexico should take two factors into account: (1) the administrative framework of the Mexican period, and (2) the history of official Spanish language documents of New Mexico from 1846 to the present. Understanding these elements will make it easier to spot gaps in the written records, to know how to search for extant copies, and to understand the fate of these official records since the occupation of New Mexico by the United States.

Mexican period documents continue to appear. A good example of an unexpected windfall occurred in the early 1970s when the University of Texas at El Paso was offered several sacks of documents for sale by a Mexican "entrepreneur." The sacks contained records of the municipality of Carrizal, a small town one hundred miles south of El Paso. They had been discovered in a barnyard by a Texan who came to Carrizal looking for an old hacienda door. After purchasing and microfilming the documents, the University of Texas returned them to officials in Chihuahua where the forty *cajas de folletos* are awaiting a permanent home in the Casa de Gobierno.[1] A more recent example concerns the archives of the Villa de Santa Cruz de la Cañada. These records, representing the official business of the Northern District (Rio Arriba) with its administrative center *(cabecera)* at Santa Cruz de la Cañada, are mostly from the Mexican period. On June 21, 1982, they were sold at auction.[2] Another collection, the Alice Scoville Barry Papers, came to the New Mexico State Records Center and Archives (NMSRCA) after having fallen into the hands of

3

a bookdealer who may have acquired them from W. W. H. Davis. Years before, these papers had been auctioned and purchased by Jack Sparhawk. Alice Scoville Barry of New Hope, Pennsylvania, discovered the documents in her aunt's trunk in 1976 and donated them to the NMSRCA in June of that year.[3] Records of the Rio Abajo have also disappeared, and many hope they will soon be found in private collections.[4] Whatever happens, the search for Mexican period documents will continue to be surrounded by mystery and intrigue because of their monetary value, their utilitarian use in land claims, and the unfortunate manner in which they were neglected during the first years of North American occupation of New Mexico.

A. CREATING RECORDS IN NEW MEXICO; THE BUREAUCRACY BEFORE 1837.   When the Plan of Iguala was proclaimed to the country on February 4, 1821, New Mexico formed part of the *Provincias Internas de Occidente*. The governor was subordinate to a commandant general and to an adjutant inspector in Chihuahua.[5] For the next two years New Mexico functioned with almost complete autonomy[6] while the government of Agustín de Iturbide floundered. Ten days after he abdicated (March 19, 1823), Congress declared itself constituted. In the fall of that year, the number of states in the nation was reduced to sixteen, and New Mexico was combined with Durango and Chihuahua as the *Estado Interno del Norte*.[7] The three provinces failed to agree on a capital, and on May 22, 1824, Durango succeeded in gaining statehood; two months later, on July 6, 1824, Chihuahua was accorded the same status, and El Paso, "historically part of New Mexico, was transferred to Chihuahua."[8] New Mexico's territorial status was endorsed in the Constitution on October 24, 1824, and remained unchanged until 1835.

During these eleven years, the territories of Mexico came directly under congressional supervision, but Congress failed to draw up regulations for internal government. This meant that New Mexico followed some of the administrative reforms promulgated at Cádiz in 1812–14 and continued throughout the Mexican period with a system which included limited elections, representative institutions, revitalized municipal government, and a voice in Congress.[9]

Governed by a *jefe* (or *gefe) político*[10] in civil matters and a *comandante principal* in military affairs, the people of New Mexico lived under a political hierarchy that placed a great deal of power in the hands of a few individuals. Most governors were citizens of New Mexico, picked from a *terna* (list) provided to Congress by the territorial legislature. Their length in office varied with national and local events, but theoretically, they were expected to serve eight years. By the Constitution of 1843 this was reduced to five years.[11]

The governor wore several hats, and in searching for documentation, it must be kept in mind that he was generally involved in every aspect of territorial administration. He corresponded with the various secretariats of the central government, responding to decrees, requests for information, and circulars.

He responded to local petitions from ordinary citizens, priests, and Indians, many of whom recognized him as the embodiment of justice, capable of overriding the arbitrary rule of powerful alcaldes. He was president of the territorial (departmental) legislature *(diputación, junta, asamblea)*, thus effecting a strong control over territorial laws. He monitored activities of the territorial treasury *(comisaría)* and supervised the distribution of revenue earned from taxing the Santa Fe trade. He served occasionally as *comandante principal* (after 1839 *comandante general)*, thus influencing defense and Indian policies as well as militia activities. He even dealt with the alcaldes, enforced the collection of tithes, and enjoyed close, but not always friendly, relations with some of the priests who actively sought his assistance or challenged his authority in the political arena.

Military authorities also generated records. According to a law of March 21, 1826, New Mexico was supposed to have three presidial companies, each made up of six officers and one hundred men.[12] They were to be stationed at Santa Fe, Taos, and San Miguel del Bado. From time to time, troops from the Santa Fe presidio did bivouac at Taos and San Miguel, but when Indian problems moderated or traders no longer came, they returned to Santa Fe. The central government failed to provide sufficient funds for the establishment of the three presidios. Furthermore, the Santa Fe unit itself rarely was able to muster more than fifty soldiers *presentes para formar* (fit for duty). This situation, repeatedly revealed in the monthly reports of the *Compañía de Santa Fe,* indicates the importance of the militia.

The same law that authorized three companies of regular troops in New Mexico provided for the organization of *milicia rural* and *milicia urbano*. Both were military units comprised of local citizens that had existed somewhat like a national guard since colonial days. Appointed by the governor and made up of volunteers, they participated in most military engagements in the Mexican period. On occasion the militia was joined by a group of retired soldiers *(tropa veterana* or *inválidos),* when military circumstances dictated the maximum use of all men under arms. The *inválidos* were assigned to escort and maintenance duties. They received some form of rations in return for their services.

Administratively, New Mexico was under a *comandante principal* whose relationship to the governor depended on the personalities involved. His authority was supposed to be clearly separated from civil and ecclesiastical affairs, but lines of authority in New Mexico tended to merge under the auspices of the *jefe político,* who occasionally received a double appointment as both civil and military leader. The *comandante principal* reported to the *comandante general* in Chihuahua until New Mexico was elevated to a separate *Comandancia General* in 1839. Some correspondence was directed to the war department *(Secretaría de Guerra y Marina),* but in theory, New Mexico was expected to use the chain of command, communicating directly with Chihuahua regarding supplies, salaries, and permission to engage in military activities.

The Santa Fe troops elected a *comandante económico (habilitado)*, whose job it was to requisition needed items from the *Comisaría General* in Chihuahua. As the record reveals, however, similar requests were often made to the *comisario substituto* in Santa Fe, who obliged by providing food and money to troops that received very little of each. The *habilitado* sometimes purchased stores directly from Santa Fe traders. Since civil authorities needed military assistance to enforce tax laws and protect the citizens, a situation evolved in which ad hoc arrangements were made in spite of guidelines established by Mexican laws.

Searching the military records of New Mexico reveals the extent to which military matters affected most other activities. Even alcaldes became involved in their occasional role as captains of militia units. Indian policy is evident in reports of campaigns launched against New Mexico tribes, and pacification measures appear in documented efforts to keep interpreters on the payroll and funds in the gift account *(fondo de aliados)*. Service records *(hojas de servicio)*, fighting strength *(estado de fuerza)*, and militia reports contain detailed information on the personal lives of New Mexican citizens. Military records, therefore, can be searched profitably for a great variety of data which may have little to do with defense.[13]

The territorial *diputación* was another creator of written records. Although its initial organization was illegal, this body functioned normally through the Iturbide years.[14] In 1823 it officially divided the territory into *partidos* headed by Santa Fe, Albuquerque, Santa Cruz de la Cañada, and El Paso.[15] Each administrative center of the *partidos* was governed by an *ayuntamiento*, while the smaller pueblos and villages were ruled by an alcalde.

Although the *diputación* often acted as a rubber stamp for the territorial governor, it had the right to apportion taxes among the towns, supervise expenditures of funds, and approve local regulations. With the governor's consent, it could launch public works projects, enact measures affecting education, agriculture, commerce, and industry, supervise the progress of church missions, approve land grants, and submit proposals to New Mexico's deputy to Congress.[16] Members *(vocales)* of the *diputación* (usually seven) sometimes met in secret session and sometimes not at all when funds were insufficient to pay their salaries.[17] This situation partially explains why the journals of New Mexico's legislative body are fragmented in the NMSRCA (April 22, 1822–February 15, 1837, and January 1, 1845–August 10, 1846). Legislative minutes for the years 1837–1839 and 1843–1846 are to be found in the MANM.[18]

The shortage of money in New Mexico and the closely knit circle of *ricos* who administered the territory created a situation in which the territorial treasurer *(comisario)* enjoyed considerable power. Before the administrative centralization effected throughout Mexico in 1836, the *comisario* and *subcomisario* drew money from the *Comisaría General* in Chihuahua to pay salaries of public officials and to address other financial obligations. The *Comisaría General*, in turn, received directives from the *Secretaría de Hacienda*, which, with its various departments *(mesas)*, was the fiscal agent of the national government. The sudden increase in available funds resulting from taxation of Santa Fe caravans and the confiscation of contraband created tempting conditions for all kinds of fraud and collusion. The *comisario* had to work closely with the *administrador de rentas* (senior customs official), who might even be the *comisario* himself. He also had to watch the local alcaldes, who could offer the traders "protection" in return for a *mordida* paid at some point on the trail before the wagons arrived in Santa Fe. In addition, he was aware of the governor breathing down his neck, because the income from taxes was frequently the basis for the governor's salary. And most important, he had to consider the needs of the military, without which he could not enforce the collection of taxes and fees which the traders were required to pay.

With these many considerations, the *comisario* corresponded frequently with both local and national officials. He made out reports for the *Comisaría General* in Chihuahua; he received instructions from the *Comandancia General* regarding the imposition of forced loans; he reported to the *jefetura* and handled expenses of that office; he received tithes collected by the *diezmero;* and he communicated on occasion with *Hacienda* and *Relaciones Exteriores* regarding various matters of interest to the central government. His was a keystone position in territorial administration, and the records reveal a definite concern on the part of federal authorities that all was not completely honest in the execution of his duties.[19]

Although *ayuntamientos* (town councils) had been dissolved in the late colonial period, in 1820 the King of Spain was forced to restore the Constitution of 1812 and recall the Cortes. In so doing, the *ayuntamiento* system was reestablished, and by 1821, most New Mexican towns and Indian Pueblos had their own *ayuntamientos*.

The *ayuntamiento* governed at the local level. Comprised of at least one alcalde, several elected *regidores* (municipal magistrates), and a *síndico procurador* (attorney), the *ayuntamiento* adopted ordinances for governing the jurisdiction it represented, supervised local elections, verified land exchanges, and served as a court of first resort for civil and criminal cases. Towns with a population of over one thousand were supposed to have *ayuntamientos*, but even though New Mexico had fifteen places that would qualify in 1821, few had the full complement of officials.[20] In Santa Fe, the *ayuntamiento* was presided over by the *jefe político*.[21]

Records of *ayuntamiento* activities are incomplete. Some collections were destroyed during the Mexican War and subsequent uprisings, but the general carelessness of officials in the Mexican and early territorial periods resulted in lost records.[22] In some places, records were not even kept because of the illiteracy of the officials, the high cost of paper, or infrequent meetings. Although Governor Armijo listed sixteen *ayuntamientos* in 1828, a few years later Antonio Barreiro counted only four and noted that the majority of towns and pueblos were under the control of an alcalde.

The institution of alcalde was well established in New Mexico by 1821. Records were kept pertaining to the management and administration of the *alcaldías,* and when elections took place, the archives were formally delivered to incoming officials. In this way, the orderly process of government was maintained.

Although the alcalde's role in public administration varied from place to place, he was essentially the governor's representative to the people.[23] In his name, the alcalde could give possession of lands, collect taxes, and lead the militia in military campaigns. His relationship to the *diputación* was that of executor of the laws passed by that body and approved by the governor. He was also the court of first resort for petty quarrels, ditch disputes, truancy, and a host of social problems, both civil and criminal. All these matters required satisfaction. Appeals went directly to the governor.

In legal matters, New Mexico once more revealed the gap between what was desired by the central government and what was possible on the frontier. Some courts existed, but most justice was dispensed at the local level. By a decree of May 20, 1826, a circuit court was established at Parral for Durango, Chihuahua, and the territory of New Mexico. The same decree provided for a district judge at Santa Fe, but none was appointed until the 1830s.[24] Another decree of 1829 provided New Mexico with an *asesor* who was expected to be consulted on civil and criminal cases and who was, in fact, the legal adviser representing the central administration.[25] Antonio Barreiro arrived in 1831 to act in this capacity, but two years later the position was vacant.

In retrospect, the administration of justice reflected social, economic, and demographic realities. Lacking sufficient professionals trained in the law, local alcaldes handled the lion's share of the work. Inconsistencies in the execution of laws appeared arbitrary to outsiders and territorial officials, but New Mexican justice reflected years of abandonment by the central authorities and, as a result, custom and precedent often superseded the national laws. Extant documents, especially those organized as "Judicial Proceedings" in the Mexican Archives of New Mexico (MANM), constitute an important source for understanding the daily struggles of the people.

Another source of information on the life cycle of New Mexicans is the church records. Here, again, gaps exist in the records. The decline of the mission on the frontier, the expulsion of Spaniards, many of whom were men of the cloth, and financial problems which the Church experienced while missions were being secularized caused hardship for those charged with the task of recording ecclesiastical events. But many of the daily records of births, deaths, marriages, confirmations, and occasional censuses *(padrones)* were maintained by individual parishes. Most of what was recorded in New Mexico was later collected and organized for researchers in Fray Angélico Chávez, *Archives of the Archdiocese of Santa Fe, 1678–1900*.[26] The ninety reels of microfilm, for which the Chávez work serves as a guide, were filmed in 1969 by the NMSRCA.

The Mexican period in New Mexico coincides with the secularization of the mission system. As of 1821, New Mexico had twenty-three Franciscans, but the secularization process had already begun.[27] Five years later, the number of Franciscans had dropped to nine, reduced in part by the expulsion of Spaniards. By 1832 only five missions had resident priests, and as of 1840 the few remaining Franciscans had died off.[28] Secular priests did not fill the gap with great rapidity. Whereas five priests served New Mexico in 1826—the largest number on the frontier at that time, by 1846 their numbers had only increased to eleven.[29]

The Church in New Mexico was under the jurisdiction of the Bishop of Durango. This post was vacated when Juan Francisco Castañiza died in 1825. Not until 1831 was it again occupied, when José Antonio Laureano de Zubiría was appointed to fill the vacancy. Bishop Zubiría made three visits to New Mexico (1833, 1845) and appointed a vicar at Santa Fe to serve as his representative with power to issue permits to build chapels, administer confirmations, and serve as ecclesiastical judge.[30] But the Church was not an institution of leadership in New Mexico, and many of its priests were accused of abandoning their responsibilities in favor of a life of hedonism.

In searching beyond the records of the Archdiocese of Santa Fe for information on New Mexico's religious, the political activities of the Church should not be ignored. The Bishop of Durango corresponded with the governor of New Mexico and several priests regarding civil matters that threatened stability in the territory. Until 1833, collecting tithes was the responsibility of civil authorities who collected what they could and paid the priests a stipend from gross receipts. When North Americans began arriving to trade in New Mexico, they stirred up the political pot and took sides against the priests, who retaliated by organizing political factions against the foreigners.

In sum, the priests were few, but their influence surpassed their numbers. They ran for elected office, represented New Mexico as territorial delegates in Mexico, and challenged the civil authorities on matters which had little bearing on their ecclesiastical profession. Some may have sympathized with the newly organized Brothers of Our Father Jesus, popularly known as the Penitentes, but the lack of written records by the Brothers prevents us from knowing much about the nature of their activities during the Mexican period.[31]

B. CREATING RECORDS IN NEW MEXICO AFTER 1837. After the loss of Texas in 1836, the conservative faction gained control in Mexico City and drew up a centralist constitution (December 30, 1836) which abolished the autonomy of the states and territories and divided the nation into twenty-four departments. New Mexico became one of these departments. The departmental system was designed to maintain closer contact with all parts of the nation and to tighten up the administration of local affairs. The president of Mexico named the departmental governors, who now reported more to him than to Congress. The old territory was reorganized into districts, or *prefecturas*, over which ruled prefects appointed by the governors.[32] The prefects, in turn, named the subprefects and *jueces de paz;* the latter designation replaced the old *alcalde constitucional.* Prefects were supposed to act as little governors in their own sphere before passing on unresolved problems to the departmental authorities. At the same time, they communicated directly with the ministries of the central government.

Responding to this reorganization, Governor Albino Pérez ordered the Department of New Mexico organized into two *prefecturas* on May 22, 1836. Each *prefectura* was further divided into *partidos* as follows:[33]

District 1:
Partido 1: Santa Fe, Bado, San Ildefonso
Partido 2: Cañada, Taos, Abiquiú, Ojo Caliente, San Juan, Chama, Trampas.

District 2:
Partido 1: Cochití, Jemez, Sandía, Albuquerque
Partido 2: Isleta, Valencia, Tomé, Belén, Sabinal, Socorro, Laguna, Zuñi, Acoma.

By a law of June 11, 1844, New Mexico was again reorganized. This new structure, which was in effect at the time of the North American occupation of Santa Fe in 1846, had a profound effect on the establishment of the first New Mexican counties. It also reflected the uniqueness of a Northern District. Record-keeping centers of the prefects are shown in parentheses:[34]

District of the North or Rio Arriba: (Santa Cruz de la Cañada), Chimayó, Truchas, Trampas, San Juan, Taos, Mora, Abiquiú, Rito Colorado, Ojo Caliente, Río de Chama and Chamita.
Central District: Santa Fe, San Ildefonso, Sierra Blanca, Jemez, Algodones, Angostura, Santa Ana, Zía, San Felipe, Santo Domingo, Chile, Cochití, San Miguel del Bado, Tecolote, Las Vegas.
Southeastern District or Rio Abajo: Bernalillo, Corrales, Alameda, Ranchos (Albuquerque), Padillas, Valencia, Tomé, Laguna, Belén, Sabinal, Socorro.

The advent of the departmental system weakened popular interest in political affairs. The *diputación* appears to have become less effective with the change. Renamed the *junta* in 1837 and the *asamblea* in 1843, it met only sporadically under the administration of Governor Manuel Armijo (1837–44), while a corresponding strength seemed to develop in the military branch of the administration.[35] *Ayuntamientos* were supposed to be located in the urban centers, and were referred to as *cabeceras de partido*. But the smaller units administered by the *jueces de paz*, still called *alcaldías*, maintained their function as the real centers for the administration of laws and justice.[36]

Other officials experienced minor changes. The *comisaría* was reorganized with a new *jefe superior de hacienda* so that New Mexico's fiscal decisions would be made through direct contact with the *Secretaría de Hacienda* in Mexico City. No longer did Chihuahua serve as intermediary. The court system remained as primitive, even though each district was supposed to gain a district court from which appeals were to be made to a *tribunal superior* in Santa Fe. Money was not available to establish these courts, and trained lawyers were almost totally absent. On September 10, 1844, the *asamblea departamental* passed a resolution asking the supreme government to establish a court of second and third resort in Chihuahua, but nothing was done. Courts of first resort were established at Santa Fe, Los Luceros, and Valencia,[37] but for all practical purposes, the *jueces de paz* exercised the same role they had enjoyed before the Constitution of 1836.

Consistent with the national government's objective of preventing additional outbreaks of rebellion or attempted secession, the military arm of New Mexico's government became increasingly powerful. Not only were the governors often given military as well as civil authority during the last ten years of the Mexican period, but some efforts were finally made to address shortages in order to prepare a proper defense. In 1839, New Mexico was made a *Comandancia General*[38] whose military lines of communication now stretched directly to the President of Mexico and the *Secretaría de Guerra y Marina*. Two sections of militia were organized in each of the three *prefecturas*, commanded by a colonel and reporting directly to the *Comandante General* of New Mexico.[39] An *inspector de milicias rurales* tied these units together under a central command that worked closely with the governor.[40] All this, combined with the assignment of the Fifth Division on March 15, 1845, to protect Chihuahua, Durango, and New Mexico, suggests the military emphasis which characterized New Mexico's government between 1836 and 1846.

C. THE STATUS OF MEXICAN ARCHIVES, 1846 TO THE PRESENT. When North American troops arrived in Santa Fe on August 18, 1846, the official archives of New Mexico were in the hands of Juan Bautista Vigil y Alarid, Secretary of the Government. General Stephen W. Kearny had given no instructions regarding these archives when he appointed Donaciano Vigil Secretary of the Territory of New Mexico. The appointment was a good one, at least in the sense that Vigil had worked with the archives as military secretary to Governor Manuel Armijo. With dispatch, he took the documents into his custody.[41]

During the next few years, the archives remained in the Governor's Palace in Santa Fe. In 1849–50, Vigil prepared a chronological list of the documents entitled *Indice General de Todos los Documentos del Tiempo de los Goviernos de España y de Méjico hasta el año de mil ochosientos cuarenta y seis.* This is an important document, because it reveals the extent of Vigil's inventory before land records were segregated by the Surveyor General.[42] In 1850 New Mexico became a territory, but the documents were neglected. During the next decade, they were shunted back and forth between the librarian and the territorial secretary while the Palace underwent various stages of remodeling.

Meanwhile, by terms stipulated in the Treaty of Guadalupe Hidalgo, the United States was bound to respect the property of all former citizens of Mexico. To effect this obligation, Congress established the post of Surveyor General for New Mexico, whose responsibility it was to segregate documents relating to land titles from the official archives for the purpose of ascertaining the legality of Spanish and Mexican land claims. William Pelham, the first Surveyor General of New Mexico, occupied his post in January 1855.

Governor David Meriwether allowed Pelham to take two wagonloads of documents to his office to make the necessary selections. From 168,000 papers, Pelham chose 1,715 documents. These were placed under his control and later put in the custody of the General Land Office of the Department of the Interior.[43] They remained in the custody of the Surveyor General until that office was abolished in 1925, at which time they were transferred to the district cadastral engineer in charge of the Public Survey Office at Santa Fe. The Civil Works Administration prepared transcriptions and translations of the Spanish land grant records, copies of which were supplied to the Historical Society of New Mexico. Between 1955 and 1957, these records, along with Pueblo land grant documents and Vigil's list of the Spanish archives and his register of land titles, case files, and correspondence related to the adjudication of land titles were also filmed. Copies were distributed to the Bancroft, Huntington, and New York Public libraries as well as to the National Archives in Washington. The originals finally came to rest in the NMSRCA in 1972. The Bureau of Land Management (BLM) inspects them annually and retains some control over the entire collection. A new publication prepared by Richard Salazar will facilitate use of the microfilmed documents (SANM I).[44]

Administrative records not dealing with land title had remained in the custody of the governor of New Mexico since the 1850s. They did not receive equal treatment. When Governor William A. Pile entered the Governor's Palace in 1869, he ordered the removal of some documents from a room he wished to occupy. Several wagonloads were dumped into the streets, where they were picked up by Eleuterio Barela, a wood hauler from Cieneguita. Several years after Pile's departure when the newspapers blasted Pile for his vandalism of the archives, Barela brought back some of the documents. In 1886, he turned over the remainder to territorial librarian Samuel Ellison.[45]

In October 1880, Ellison had taken custody of the archives. After several appeals to the territorial legislature, he was finally awarded a small sum sufficient to arrange the documents by subject and file them in 144 pasteboard boxes. Ellison knew his work. As interpreter and translator for several New Mexico governors, he understood the importance of the archives, and as territorial librarian, he was able to assist Hubert Howe Bancroft and Adolf F. A. Bandelier by providing transcripts of documents requested. In 1900, after one attempt had failed because of a fire in 1892, the archives of New Mexico were placed in a special vault in the capitol under the supervision of the territorial secretary.

Arguing that the Spanish and Mexican archives of New Mexico were federal property, the Library of Congress launched a campaign in 1902 to have them transported to Washington. Against the objections of members of the New Mexico Historical Society, four packing cases filled with documents were turned over to the Library of Congress on May 14, 1903. For twenty years they remained in the Library's Division of Manuscripts, where they were arranged chronologically, flattened, and cleaned. In 1923, the State Museum of New Mexico, established in 1909 with its home in the Palace of the Governors, asked for the return of the documents. When it was ascertained that they could be properly cared for, they were shipped to Santa Fe and stored at the Museum in a concrete vault.

In 1927, the state legislature passed an act making the Historical Society of New Mexico the official repository for public archives. The Museum of New Mexico administered the funds appropriated by the legislature for this purpose, but it lacked facilities and staff to care for, organize, and inventory the official records being generated by state agencies. Between 1938 and 1941, the Historical Records Survey of New Mexico, with equipment and film supplied by the University of New Mexico, microfilmed the Spanish and Mexican archives. Enlarged photoprints were deposited in the Special Collections Department of the University of New Mexico Library. A copy was sent to the Bancroft Library. Of the 238 volumes of photoprints, 154 relate to the Mexican period. This collection is more fully discussed in this chapter in the section dealing with the Special Collections Department of the University of New Mexico Library.

In 1959 the state legislature addressed the problem of noncurrent public records which were being stacked on shelves or piled on floors in the basement of the Fine Arts Museum and in the Hall of Ethnology. A Public Records Act was passed creating a new agency, the State Records Center (now the NMSRCA), as the official depository for all public records. This act, amended in 1963 to include specifically those records created by Spain and Mexico, made the new agency the custodian for all public records and those private records acquired through use of public funds. Although some of the Museum officials referred to the transferal of documents as a "daylight bank robbery,"[46] the Public Records Act clearly gave the NMSRCA authority to archive official materials created by New Mexico since the Spanish colonial era. After a short hiatus the Museum and the NMSRCA restored friendly relations.

To house its records, the state selected the recently purchased Ilfeld & Co. warehouse on Montezuma Street in Santa Fe. The 464 cubic feet of records from the Museum of New Mexico came under control of the Archives Division, headed by Dr. Myra Ellen Jenkins. In addition to these materials, Jenkins sought out official documents in the recesses of public buildings all over the city. In less than ten years, she succeeded in bringing in 1,933 cubic feet of public records and 193 cubic feet of private papers and historical documents donated to the state. When it became apparent that the fragile Spanish and Mexican documents would have to be restricted because of their condition, the NMSRCA applied for and received grants from the National Historical Publications Commission to reorganize, calendar, and microfilm records through the territorial period. The results are as follows: Spanish Archives of New Mexico (SANM II, 22 reels); Mexican Archives of New Mexico (MANM, 43 reels);[47] and the Territorial Archives of New Mexico (TANM, 189 reels). Calendars and guides are available for each publication.

By the mid-1970s the administrative structure governing the public records of New Mexico was functioning smoothly. To a great extent this resulted from the Herculean efforts of Dr. Jenkins. Although she often attracted controversy, her search for missing records and her professional approach to scholarly research established the NMSRCA as an example to other records centers in the nation.

Since Santa Fe and Albuquerque are the principal centers for archival research in the Mexican period, the following guide to collections is arranged by cities. With both the NMSRCA and the Museum of New Mexico located in the capital, Santa Fe is the obvious beginning point.

2. SANTA FE; NEW MEXICO STATE RECORDS CENTER AND ARCHIVES (NMSRCA):

The NMSRCA is located at 404 Montezuma within easy walking distance from Santa Fe's central plaza. Two card catalogs provide initial assistance in locating archival holdings: (1) a name index showing private collections and historical film collections; and (2) a subject index including special drawers entitled "Land Grants" and "Land Conveyances." Collections which have inventories are included in two blue notebooks arranged alphabetically. Researchers should be careful to check both the index cards and the inventories in the event that a private collection has been accepted and is in the process of being inventoried. Although the MANM collection is by far the richest source for

Mexican period research, the following auxiliary collections may prove particularly useful on subjects not emphasized in official documents.

(1) Alvarez, Manuel. Papers, 1830–1856.

Correspondence received by Alvarez from North Americans such as Charles Bent, Josiah Gregg, S. Houck, Daniel Webster, etc., in the 1840s. Includes some letters sent by Alvarez, business papers, and Alvarez's petition for naturalization and passports. A chronological index provides dates and names of correspondents.

(2) Archuleta Family Papers. See entry under Twitchell Collection.

(3) Armijo, Valentín. Papers, 1831–1835.

Settlement of estate of Juan Antonio Cabeza de Vaca. Includes petition for construction of a *capilla* at Peña Blanca, land conveyance, and inventory of the estate. These are copies of originals in the possession of Valentín Armijo, Santa Fe.

(4) Bandelier, Adolf (Hemenway Southwest Collection), 1604–1845.

Transcripts of miscellaneous documents made by Bandelier and photocopied for the NMSRCA. One item, dated 1845, is a decree of the *asamblea departamental* regarding a loan by citizens to maintain sufficient troops to fight the expected invasion of Texans. A complete analysis of the Hemenway Southwestern Collection was made by John P. Wilson in 1974.

(5) Barry, Alice Scoville. Papers, 1674–1863.

Includes several transmittals of decrees and orders from Mexico City to the *jefe político* and *comandante principal* of New Mexico in 1821, 1826, and 1828. A letter from the *jefe político* to the *comandante principal* orders the dispatch of soldiers and a cannon to accompany the *ciboleros* leaving from San Miguel del Bado, November 30, 1830. Additional communications between Mexico City and New Mexican officials.

(6) Bent, Charles. Governor's Papers, 1846–1847.

One of the collections noted under "Miscellaneous New Mexico Documents" in the "Collections" card file, these papers should be used along with "Records of the Territorial Governors" (Reel 98 of the Territorial Archives of New Mexico). Eight folders contain letters to and from Bent regarding matters of local justice, Navajo depredations, and a complaint from Trinidad Gabaldón, wife of Manuel Armijo, who protests that Diego Archuleta is bothering her about a debt. The final item documents the payment of salary to Bent's estate received by the administrator, Ceran St. Vrain.

(7) Bergere Family Papers, 1829–1967.

One item in these family papers is an 1829 land conveyance of Domingo Peralta, Los Lentes, to Vicente Otero, Tomé, executed before the *alcalde constitucional,* Jacinto Sánchez.

(8) Bibo, Mrs. Arthur. Papers, 1689–1904.

This is a collection of documents relating mostly to land matters in the vicin-

ity of Acoma and Laguna. The entire collection is restricted.
(9) Blackmore Papers, various dates.

This collection of papers dealing with William Blackmore's land grant interests between 1856 and 1878 are in large part records from the Surveyor General's office. Most are from the Mexican period. A very detailed 5 x 8 card index is available. Some records are in the NMSRCA; others are in the Museum of New Mexico.

(10) Bloom-McFie Papers, 1846–1938.

Two items of interest to the Mexican period are a typed copy of Kearny's Proclamation of August 19, 1846, and the response in Spanish (also a typed copy) by Juan Bautista Vigil y Alarid.

(11) Borrego-Ortega Family Papers, 1706–1892.

Mostly copies of family papers, wills, land conveyances, etc., in the Santa Cruz area. Names include Beronica González (1828), Francisco Vigil, Pascuala Romero (1830), María Consesión Lujan-(1835), Pedro Asencio Ortega (1837–1844), Manuel Pablo Ortega (1839–1840), María Rosa Agostina Chacón (1840, 1841), Candelaria Mondragón (1844), María Pascuala de los Dolores Romero (1846, 1848), etc.

(12) Boyd, E. Collection, 1822–1960s.

This collection includes the Peralta Family Papers, among which are a number of land conveyances and *hijuelas* (estate inventories). The following places are mentioned: La Joya de Sevilleta, Los Padillas, San Miguel del Socorro, and Corrales. Other historic documents, not in the Peralta Papers, include a typescript of a letter from William Workman to his brother in 1826; a transcript of a loose document from the Archdiocese of Santa Fe (1827, #10) in which the citizens of Rio Chiquito promise to observe the patronage of the Virgin Mary in her title of Nuestra Señora de San Juan; copies of various baptismal entries, 1836–1901; and the Martín Family Papers, 1780–1876, dealing with events in the Santa Cruz de la Cañada area.

(13) Ina Sizer Cassidy Collection, 1828–1850.

Contains photostatic copies of items in the Ritch Collection, Huntington Library (RI93 to RI96). Includes reports and proclamations by Manuel de Jesús Rada, Manuel Armijo, Juan Andrés Archuleta, and Donaciano Vigil.

(14) Chávez, Amado (Museum Collection), 1698–1888.

This collection primarily contains land grant papers which refer to approximately twenty-two different grants.

(15) Chávez, Felipe. Papers, 1810–1901.

Two items bear on the Mexican period: an August 24, 1843, debt of Samuel C. Owens (Isaac Lightner), to Manuel and Ambrosio Armijo; and a November 14, 1846, acknowledgment of a receipt from Andrés P. Henderson to José Chávez.

(16) J. F. Chávez. Papers, 1707–1920. See entry under Twitchell Collection.

(17) Chávez, Mariano. Papers, 1796–1943.

Various items include family papers and matters relating to the Piedra Lumbre and Tierra Amarilla grants.

(18) Church Records: From collection entitled "Miscellaneous New Mexico Documents."

Some originals but mostly copies of records from the Archdiocese of Santa Fe regarding the licensing of the church at Las Trampas de Taos, including inventories of church property. Other documents deal with the Santuario de Chimayó, the *capilla* at Santa Cruz de la Cañada, etc.

(19) Collier, Adella Collection, 1836–1974.

Contains the papers of Frederick Muller, an Indian fighter, businessman, and politician in Rio Arriba. One document is a March 24, 1836, land conveyance in Rio Arriba from Juan Angel Leiba to José Antonio Romero.

(20) Conveyances.

Another of the collections listed under "Miscellaneous New Mexico Documents," this one includes land conveyances (some copies) in the vicinity of Chimayó, Algodones, Santa Cruz de la Cañada, Santo Domingo de Cundiyo, Rancho San Ildefonso, Chama, Santa Fe, and San Miguel del Bado.

(21) Cordova Family Papers, 1774–1912.

Land conveyances in San Antonio de Padua del Pueblo Quemado (Cordova area), plus a water rights decision in Pueblo Quemado, a conveyance of a house lot in the plaza of La Cañada, and the partition of an estate.

(22) Cragin, Francis Whittemore. "Papers." From the collection entitled "Miscellaneous New Mexico Documents."

This is an index of names to be found in the oral history section of the Cragin Collection in the Pioneer Museum, Colorado Springs. Some of the names are of people active in the Mexican period.

(23) Delgado Family Papers (Jenkins Collection), 1740–1886.

Includes three conveyances of land (1825, 1830, 1832) and a sale of livestock in 1833 in the San Miguel del Vado and Real de Dolores areas.

(24) Delgado Family Papers (Dingee Collection), 1740–1890.

Miscellaneous accounts of soldiers stationed at San Miguel del Bado and the mine Real del Oro, Tuerto, and records of a livestock purchase and a letter from José Zubía on behalf of Mariano Chávez urging legal action against the "estrangero León."

(25) Delgado, Felipe. Papers, 1704–1912.

These personal papers include a genealogy chart of the Delgado family compiled by Fabiola C. de Baca Gilbert.

(26) Durán, María G. Collection, 1785–1846.

Family papers relating to the Abiquiú area include an acequia dispute, will and protest, *hijuelas,* circular from Governor Armijo establishing penalties for buying livestock from Apaches and Navajos, litigation over land ownership, an 1845 circular establishing districts for justices of the peace, and 1846 circulars ordering the people to defend their homes and calling up the militia to defend the Northern District against the invasion by the United States.

(27) Extranjero/Anglo Traders Collection, 1823–1848.

One of the collections listed under "Miscellaneous New Mexico Documents," it primarily contains photocopies and typescripts of documents, including permission from the Superintendent of Indian Affairs to pass through Indian country; letters from William Becknell and the Workmans; naturalization papers of Matthew Kinkead; various manifestos; and a few items regarding prisoners of the Texan Santa Fe expedition.

(28) Gardesky, Martin. Collection, 1612–1912.

Collection includes two documents on the Valenciana Mines, 1827–1836, and two communications from Mexico City regarding the pay and promotion of Blas Antonio Magaña (1826 and 1842).

(29) Getty Family Papers, 1846–1870.

One document is an unidentified letter from a soldier in Kearny's army containing a description of the march into Las Vegas and the march to and peaceful capture of Santa Fe.

(30) Griffin, W. W. Papers, 1836–1901.

Two documents, 1836 and 1845, deal with the donation of land in the city of Santa Fe.

(31) Hinojos Family Papers, 1785–1902.

Photostats of original documents including wills, land conveyances, and divisions of property in the city of Santa Fe. Montoya, Trujillo, and Ortiz families are most frequently named.

(32) Historical Society of New Mexico, Miscellaneous Collection, 1680–1930.

Materials on the Mexican period include several printed decrees from the *secretarías* of *Estado* and *Hacienda;* judgment quieting title to lands belonging to Antonio Armijo in San Miguel del Bado (1822); and a letter from Diego Archuleta to Doña Dolores Lópes in Abiquiú, December 2, 1846.

(33) Jaramillo-Bent-Scheurich Family Papers, 1834–1952.

Papers of these three interrelated families refer to property and events in Taos, 1829 to 1900s. Among conveyances of houses and land is a handwritten account by Teresina Bent describing the assassination of her father, Charles.

(34) Jones, Robert. Collection, 1824–1960.

These papers consist of documents concerning the Dixon area. One item is the sale of land by Manuel Martín, a Picurís Indian, to José Antonio Pacheco, March 4, 1824.

(35) Kelly, Booker. Family Papers, 1767–1835.

Papers of the Mestas family in the Chama area and the Sena family in the Tesuque area. Also included is an inventory of church possessions of San Francisco de Nambé.

(36) Land Grant Documents, 1704–1858. See entry under Twitchell Collection.
(37) Lente Family Papers, 1764–1834. See entry under Twitchell Collection.
(38) López Family Papers, 1819–1908.

These papers pertain to the Baca family of Cienega, 1805–1915. Communications include promissory notes, orders for account audits, and acknowledgment of payment of sheep involved in a *partido* contract. Other business papers, an acequia dispute, and livestock purchases make up the balance of this collection.

(39) Magoffin Papers. See entry under Twitchell Collection.
(40) Marquéz y Melo Papers, 1819–1824.

These are the papers of a prominent Chihuahua-Santa Fe trader. They include his account books, business correspondence, and letter books.

(41) Cesarita Sandoval Martínez-Alonso C. Martínez Family Papers, 1829–1982.

One item relevant to the Mexican period is a conveyance of land by Lorenzo Córdova to Antonio Martín, Arroyo Hondo, November 11, 1829.

(42) Henry McGavran Collection (Charles Beaubien), 1825–1914.

Collection includes copies of the field notes of the Sibley Survey, verification of the marriage dispensation of Carlos H. Beaubien to María Paula Lovato, July 30, 1827, given by Antonio José Martínez, and a copy of a letter dated June 5, 1856, from Beaubien to Manuel Alvarez concerning Padre Martínez.

(43) Martínez Family Papers, 1790–1908.

These are copies of papers dealing with land conveyances in the Santa Cruz area. Two places mentioned in the Mexican period documents are Barrio de La Cuchilla and La Cieneguita.

(44) Martínez Family Papers (Minge Collection), 1827–1888.

Distinct from the above entry, these papers contain the will of Antonio Severino Martínez (the original, a copy, and translation) plus other wills and family papers. See Ward Alan Minge, "The Last Will and Testament of Don Severino Martínez," *New Mexico Quarterly* 38 (1963): 33–50. Also included in this collection is the first book on Martínez printed on New Mexico's first press. An autobiography dated 1838, it is titled *Relación de méritos del presbítero Antonio José Martínez, domiciliario del obispado de Durango. Cura encargado de Taos en el departamento de Nuevo Mexico.* This same volume is available at the Huntington and Newberry libraries.

(45) Miranda, Guadalupe. Family Papers, 1800–1910.

Photocopies of a collection belonging to John M. Fenn, descendant of Guadalupe Miranda, which pertain to land petitions, conveyances, registration, etc. Also included are a contract awarded to Miranda for teaching school in Santa Fe in 1832 and a commission as captain in the militia conferred on Miranda by Antonio López de Santa Anna.

(46) Miscellaneous Conveyances. See entry under Twitchell Collection.

(47) Miscellaneous Letters and Diaries, 1807–1893.

One of the collections listed under "Miscellaneous New Mexico Documents," these materials include the La Joya de Sevilleta Record Book with information on Socorro, La Joya, Indian campaigns, a smallpox epidemic, etc. (1807–1849).

(48) Miscellaneous New Mexico Documents.

These are separate collections which have not been filmed and are not included in the MANM. Each collection is listed separately in alphabetical order in this section if it contains Mexican period material. Those listed are:

> Northern New Mexico Documents (Marc Simmons Collection)
> University of New Mexico Library Collection
> Extranjero/Anglo Traders Collection
> Cragin Papers (Oral History Index)
> Miscellaneous Spanish and Mexican Archives
> Donaciano Vigil. Governor's Papers, 1847–1848
> Conveyances
> Church Records
> Wills and Estates (hijuelas)

(49) Miscellaneous Papers, 1610–1924. See entry under Twitchell Collection.

(50) Miscellaneous Spanish and Mexican Archives. One of the collections listed under "Miscellaneous New Mexico Documents." These are photocopies of a variety of circulars, letters, municipal ordinances, proceedings, plans, etc. Included in the collection are circulars from Facundo Melgares and José Antonio Vizcarra, a printed Mexican peso, correspondence of George C. Sibley, an *ayuntamiento* plan to populate San Miguel del Bado, Las Vegas, Sapello, Ocate, and other places in 1832 (typescript), proceedings of the *ayuntamiento* of Santa Fe in 1833 (typescript), a list of Santa Fe property owners in 1836 (also listed as document 1314, SANM I), typescript copy of a letter from Manuel Alvarez to Daniel Webster complaining about the corruptness of Mexican officials (also found in microfilm M199 from State Department Records, RG 59), and an 1845 (?) index of official correspondence sent by the departmental secretary of New Mexico to various secretariats of the Mexican government.

(51) Northern New Mexico Documents (Marc Simmons Collection).

Documents in this collection representing the Spanish, Mexican, and Territorial periods are included as one of the collections listed under "Miscellaneous New Mexico Documents." They are photocopies of originals owned by Rex Arrowsmith of Santa Fe. Mexican period materials include sale deeds for land conveyances in the Taos area, an IOU signed by Carlos Beaubien, a printed court docket for June 1832 in Chihuahua, a receipt for funeral expenses, and several legal statements involving different matters.

(52) Otero, T. Collection, 1772–1845.

This is the collection of the Bernardo Vásquez-Franco Papers which contains a substantial record of the life of a soldier in the Mexican period. Included in the many official and personal papers are promotions, reports, inventories, receipts, and accounts. In addition to the military documents are a hand-written copy of tables of weights and measures, collections of maxims and moral lessons, and the diets and medication prescribed for dropsy.

(53) Ortiz Family Papers, 1726–1841.

Not to be confused with the Ortiz Family Papers in the Twitchell Collection, these documents came to the NMSRCA from the Museum of New Mexico. They were probably created as a result of litigation over the Caja del Rio Grant. The papers include various wills, an 1830 contract for sale of lambs, and an accusation by Fernando Ortiz of La Cienega in 1832–33 that Antonio José Martín is a "vago" and a "picarro."

(54) Perea Family Papers, 1697–1897.

Consisting primarily of land conveyances, disputes, and *partido* contracts in the Bernalillo-Albuquerque area, this collection of documents refers to the activities of several families: Romero, García, Chávez, and Perea.

(55) Price, Sterling. Governor's Papers, 1847–1848.

Three documents make up this collection: (1) a military permit issued to José Manuel Vigil in the Mora-Las Vegas area (1847); (2) a letter (and translation) from Antonio José Martínez to Price appealing to him as governor to consider the plight of fifty-nine prisoners condemned to death, or awaiting sentence, for their involvement in the Taos uprising; and (3) a photocopy of a letter from Price to the Governor of Chihuahua regarding the evacuation of Rosales by North American troops. Also see item 199, Reel 98 (TANM) for additional documentation on Price's term as governor.

(56) Prince, Le Baron Bradford. Papers. Various dates.

In the section of these papers entitled "Historical Notes and Events," item 11 includes Mexican period notes and "clippings" collected by Prince. In another section entitled "Historical Documents," a number of items deal with affairs at Santa Cruz de la Cañada. Miscellaneous items are listed in the calendar.

(57) Pueblo Indians Collection, 1789–1933.

Not included as one of the "Private Collections," these papers contain several documents from the cases of the Court of Private Land Claims regarding the Pojoaque River and San Ildefonso grants.

(58) Read, Benjamin M. Collection, 1804–1854 (Series I) and 1704–1926 (Series II).

Series I: Organized according to Read's own numbering system, the official records in this collection were filmed in the MANM. They include various decrees and instructions of the governor regarding Indian depredations, passports, and the official recognition of Manuel Alvarez as U.S. Consul. Correspondence between Guadalupe Miranda and Juan Bautista Vigil y Alarid concerns the problems of foreigners in New Mexico. Personal items, not filmed in the MANM, include many letters between Alvarez and others (Bent, Gregg, etc.) who sought the consul's aid.

Series II: These records include wills, land litigation, Manuel Alvarez Papers (a letterbook, 1839–1846, and a diary, 1840–1841), Pedro Quintana Papers, and the Martínez Papers, the latter including the five publications of Padre Martínez. These Alvarez Papers should not be confused with a similar entry title on this list.

(59) Renehan-Gilbert Papers. Various dates.

This collection consists largely of papers dealing with land grant matters. From the records of the Galisteo Grant, there are a number of land conveyances relative to the Mexican period. Other land exchange documents relate to the El Rancho area, lands within the Pueblo of San Ildefonso, disputes between the Pueblo of Laguna and citizens of Cubero, and several Mexican period documents pertaining to the Santa Cruz de la Cañada area. The papers can be used with permission of the NMSRCA.

(60) Romero, Frank. Papers, 1825, 1852.

Two items of note: (1) an 1825 selection of José Manuel Mestas from the Santa Cruz de la Cañada area for service in the *milicia civil;* and (2) on the reverse side of this document, settlement of an acequia dispute.

(61) Salazar, Silvania. Papers, 1806–1850.

These papers concern land and water rights in Santa Rosa de Lima de Abiquiú and Santo Tomás Apostal de Abiquiú. The Mexican period documents are land conveyances.

(62) Saracino, Francisco. Family Papers, 1839–ca. 1874.

Copies of original documents dealing with the Cebolleta area. Papers have not been inventoried.

(63) Seligman Collection, 1803–1910.

Several documents involving Manuel Armijo include a promissory note to him for two hundred pesos, a report from Juan Andrés Archuleta giving Armijo the line of march of the Texan Santa Fe expedition, and a letter from Armijo to Donaciano Vigil, June 25, 1843, asking for interrogation of the soldiers attacked by Texans on the Arkansas River. A few additional documents touch on the Mexican period.

(64) Sena Family Papers, 1781–1858. See entry under Twitchell Collection.

(65) Simmons, Marc. Collection. See "Northern New Mexico Documents." (Item 51 above.)

(66) Suaso Family Papers, 1751–1826.

These are miscellaneous papers relating to the Embudo area. One fragmented document dated April 18, 19, and 25, 1826, relates to a squabble over land which had been abandoned during the time of Indian troubles.

(67) Twitchell, Ralph Emerson. Collection. 1610–1924.
This extensive collection includes many documents on the Mexican period. It also includes private papers of several individuals important to this period. The official papers were included in the MANM. They include military matters discussed in correspondence between Santa Fe and Chihuahua, legal proceedings, citizens' complaints, correspondence from the *secretarías* of Mexico, and miscellaneous matters of local interest. A revised calendar, April 1, 1968, replaces the original descriptive list. It corrects previous errors and lists documents chronologically with a cross-reference to the old "Twitchell Number," the latter appearing on the inventory and document folders. Other papers included in this collection are as follows:

(a) Territorial Papers (Magoffin Papers of correspondence with the Secretary of War, 1846–1849).
These are typescript copies of correspondence between James W. Magoffin and Secretary of War W. L. Marcy. The papers contain Magoffin's itemized accounting of expenses incurred while effecting the "Bloodless Conquest" of New Mexico. The file includes testimonial letters from William Connelley, Philip St. George Cooke, and others.

(b) Land Grant Documents, 1704–1858.
Various land petitions.

(c) Miscellaneous Conveyances, 1706–1843.
Sales of land in the Bernalillo, Vallecito, and Cuyamungue areas.

(d) Wills and Estates, 1804–1856.
Includes wills, powers of attorney, and *hijuelas*.

(e) Archuleta Family Papers, 1747–1909.
Various papers of Diego Archuleta including a certificate of education, Seminary at Durango, 1838; Cross of Legion of Honor Award, 1841; Commission as Indian Agent, 1857; Commission as Brigadier General of Militia, 1861; and an undated Act to change counties in Mexico introduced by him. A letter from Manuel Armijo, July 7, 1841, to Juan Andrés Archuleta, *Subinspector de Armas*, deals with land conveyances in Pojoaque and Cuyamungue.

(f) J. M. Chávez Papers, 1707–1920.
These papers deal with the Ute War of 1845. Included are letters from Juan Andrés Archuleta to José Martín Chávez, appointed commanding officer of the Ute expedition, instructions to Chávez regarding how to fight the enemy and divide up the spoils of victory, a letter from Chávez asking for permission to cross over to the left bank of the Arkansas in pursuit of the enemy, and other letters discussing arms, soldiers, and instances of cowardice among the troops.

(g) Ortiz Family Papers, 1726–1841.
Many of these papers relate to the Indian campaigns of Matías Ortiz in 1821 and 1822. A summary of his thirty-four years of public service is included. Other documents are wills, land petitions and sales, correspon-

dence involving the expulsion of Spanish priests, and a power of attorney given by Manuel Armijo to D. Gaspar Ortiz on August 14, 1846.

(h) Lente Family Papers, 1764–1834.
These documents include an exchange of lands in Los Lentes and San Fernando and the sale of land in Los Lentes, both transactions taking place in 1822. A copy of a will of Pedro Antonio Lente and an updated declaration of land division are part of this collection.

(i) Sena Family Papers, 1781–1858.
This collection contains an appointment of Tomás Sena *"para colectar limosnas,"* land exchanges, a plan of the *ayuntamiento* of San Miguel del Vado to place settlers at Las Vegas, Sapello, Ocate, etc., land conveyances in Ancón de los Trigos (1841), a sale of lands at Los Trigos (1845), and a copy of an order by Governor Manuel Armijo regarding militia organization at San Miguel del Vado.

(j) Miscellaneous Papers, 1610–1924.
A few items for the Mexican period include an 1831 promissory note, a fragment of a *diligencia matrimonial,* 1835, a bill of sale, 1839, and the properties of Josiah Gregg, 1844, as found in *Commerce of the Prairies.*

(68) University of New Mexico Library Collection. Various dates.
One of the collections noted under "Miscellaneous New Mexico Documents," this contains photocopies of originals in the Zimmerman Library, University of New Mexico. Described later in this chapter, these copies include the José Martínez Papers, Spanish and English Language Manuscripts, 1826–1827, Spanish Language Manuscripts, 1811–1867, L. Bradford Prince Papers, Louis D'Armand Papers, Miguel Antonio Lovato Papers, and Julius Seligman Papers.

(69) Vigil, Donaciano. Papers, 1766–1873.
The official papers in this collection were filmed in the MANM. They include military records for the companies of Santa Fe and San Miguel del Bado, 1826, a peace treaty with the Comanches, land petitions, conveyances and proceedings, correspondence related to the uprising of 1837, various communications from the governor, and some decrees from the central government. In the unfilmed private papers are an assortment of biographical and autobiographical notes, wills, vital statistics, land sales, and miscellaneous correspondence.

(70) Vigil, Donaciano. Governor's Papers, 1847–1848.
As one of the collections noted in "Miscellaneous New Mexico Documents," this one contains a number of queries from local officials asking for clarification of laws, boundaries, and other matters. Printed decrees outline voting districts and call for the population to vote. Other communications to Vigil describe difficulties with Indians. Additional records dealing with Vigil's term as territorial governor can be found in Reel 98 of the TANM.

(71) Wills and Estates *(hijuelas),* 1804–1856. See entry under Twitchell Collection.

(72) Wallace, Lew. Papers. Various dates.
One item dated October 30, 1829, is a handwritten translation of a docu-

ment having to do with an expedition among the Comanche and discussions with these Indians regarding the possibility of finding minerals.
The following microfilm publications deal with the Mexican period.

(1) Mexican Archives of New Mexico (MANM). 43 reels. These are the official records of the Mexican period as they were received by the NMSRCA in 1960 plus those documents from other collections known to exist within the state which contained official records. The originals have been retired, but may be viewed by scholars on request.
(2) Spanish Archives of New Mexico (SANM I). 66 reels. These are the papers relating to New Mexico land grants, housed in the U.S. Bureau of Land Management in Santa Fe and arranged and microfilmed by the University of New Mexico in 1955–1957. Reel 1 is an alphabetical listing of these archives as they appear in Volume I of Twitchell's *The Spanish Archives of New Mexico*.[48] Reels 2–6 are the documents described by Twitchell. Reel 7 includes the grants to Pueblo Indians as described by Twitchell. Reels 8 and 9 are Miscellaneous Archives and Reel 10 is Vigil's index. Richard Salazar has completed a new index to SANM I which will facilitate more efficient use of these ten reels. His index includes the Twitchell number, a description of the document(s), the date, and a frame number. Reels 11 through 63 contain the records of old land titles, grant dockets, and private land claims as collected by the Surveyor General and the Court of Private Land Claims. The total of 66 reels is arrived at by totaling the "A," "B," and "C" parts of Reel 31.
(3) Spanish Archives of New Mexico (SANM II). 22 reels. These are the documents listed by Twitchell in Volume II of *The Spanish Archives of New Mexico*. They are numbered in chronological order, 1–3097, and include the years 1621 to 1821.
(4) Spanish Archives of New Mexico (SANM I), translations. 4 reels. These are 16 mm copies of translations done by the WPA from records in the Bureau of Land Management. The documents coincide with Twitchell Numbers 1–1384.
(5) Territorial Archives of New Mexico (TANM). 189 reels.
(6) Archives of the Archdiocese of Santa Fe. 90 reels. Filmed in 1969 by the NMSRCA, these records comprise a variety of ecclesiastical materials from the Spanish colonial period to 1900. Julián Josué Vigil has prepared a microfiche and microfilm *Guide to the Archives of the Archdiocese of Santa Fe*, both of which are available at the NMSRCA. This *Guide* is a supplement to the work of Fray Angélico Chávez and facilitates research through cross-referencing names, locating fragmentary materials, and aiding in abbreviations used in official documents. Vigil has also prepared a microfiche guide, *Early Taos Censuses and Historical Sources*.
(7) Census Records by County, 1850. 5 reels. Bernalillo, San Miguel, Taos, Rio Arriba, and Valencia counties are included. These records should be used

in conjunction with the publications of Virginia Langham Olmstead.[49]
(8) Deed Books. 49 reels. Part of the records of Bernalillo and Rio Arriba (33 reels), Taos (4 reels), Santa Fe (9 reels), Socorro (2 reels), and Valencia (1 reel) counties. These Deed Books contain copies of wills, land transactions, and business affairs during the Mexican period.[50]
(9) Bishop Zubiría's Visitation of New Mexico, 1833. 1 reel. This *Libro de Visita Pastoral* is made up of 213 pages and an *anexo* of thirteen pages dealing with Zubiría's visitation to Mexico's northern departments. A typed page at the beginning dated November 23, 1940, indicates that the filming was done by the *Secretaría de Hacienda y Crédito Público*.
(10) Armijo Papers, Beinecke Library. 1 reel. Not listed in the published catalog to the Beinecke Collection, this film is made up of official records, 1823–1878, contained in three folders (116 pages). Most deal with Governor Manuel Armijo.[51]
(11) Villa de Santa Cruz de la Cañada Archives (Sender Papers; Restricted). 3 reels. This film was made by the NMSRCA in the late 1960s while the Sender Papers were in litigation. The film quality is poor. Three hundred and thirteen separate communications relate to every conceivable problem associated with local government. Two lists (indexes) are available. The first was made by the NMSRCA in the late 1960s when the documents were remanded to its custody for a brief period. A more recent list was drawn up by the marshall of Kansas City prior to the auction of all the Sender documents on June 21, 1982. This second list is far more complete, although its accuracy cannot be attested to until the documents are available for inspection. *(See also* footnotes 2 and 42 of this chapter.)
(12) Newberry Library, Abiquiú Documents (restricted). 3 reels. These documents are made up of the William Greenlee Papers, Pablo Gonzáles Papers, Joseph Chávez Papers, and Espinosa-Quintana Collection. The microfilm is restricted in order to prevent duplication without permission from the Newberry Library.
(13) Historical Society of New Mexico. 2 reels. These are the records of the Historical Society of New Mexico from its beginning in 1859 to 1959.
(14) Ritch Collection. 11 reels. These are copies made of the microfilm at Highlands University, Las Vegas, which is a copy of the originals in the Huntington Library, San Marino, California. Reel 1 is a photocopy of the Huntington's index cards filed chronologically, each of which contains an identifying number plus document description.
(15) Our Lady of Guadalupe at Peña Blanca. 1 reel. These records were not included in the original Archdiocese of Santa Fe film. They were filmed by Vance Golightly Microfilm and include baptisms, 1841–1909.
(16) Bancroft Library, *Archivo Militar* film. 2 reels. This collection consists of reels 11 and 14 from the Bancroft Library's ninety-three reels filmed in

Mexico on 16 mm film in 1954–1955. These two reels contain *expedientes* of special interest to students of the Mexican period: Reel 11: Exp. XI 481.3/1714; 2474; 1710; 2567; 2580; 2588; 2590; 2663; 2713; 2725; 3150; 3151; 3154; 3156. Reel 14: Exp. XI 481.3/329; 2199 (5 *tomos*); 1297.

(17) U.S., National Archives, RG 46, Territorial Papers of the United States Senate, Reel 14, New Mexico, 1840–1854. A few items pertain to the Santa Fe trade.

(18) U.S., National Archives, RG 59, M199, Reel 1, Despatches from U.S. Consuls in Santa Fe, 1830–1846.

(19) Huntington Library, Various Newspapers. 2 reels. Newspapers included in this publication are the *Santa Fe Republican* (December 11, 1847, to August 8, 1849—some missing), and the *Santa Fe Republican* (January 1, 1847, to September 23, 1848).

3. SANTA FE; MUSEUM OF NEW MEXICO:

The Museum of New Mexico was founded in 1909. The core of its manuscript and document collection was assembled by the Historical Society of New Mexico, to which extensive additions have been made in the fifty years since the founding of the Museum. Between 1960 and 1962, the official documents contained in these collections were transferred to the newly created NMSRCA. Many private collections were also donated on a long-term loan basis. The remaining manuscript and printed source materials, microfilm collection, maps, and secondary sources make the Museum an excellent resource center, however. The History Library is located on Washington Avenue just north of the plaza and adjoining the Palace of the Governors. *A Guide to the Museum of New Mexico History Library,* although dated, is useful for reference to manuscript and printed materials as well as newspaper holdings.[52] Some materials are available by request on Interlibrary Loan. The following manuscript collections contain material on the Mexican period of New Mexico:

(1) Abeyta, Mrs. Andrea S. Family History, 1807–1948.

In this handwritten family record, the Abeyta family of Abeytas, New Mexico, has accumulated a record of child rearing, devotional customs, home medicinal remedies, family lineage, and education. The book served as a primer for successive generations of Abeytas. In this 1908 copy of the original text, researchers can find reference to folk customs practiced in nineteenth-century New Mexico.

(2) Bureau of Indian Affairs. Collection, 1689–1859.

These are photocopies of a collection located by John P. Wilson and Bruce Ellis beneath the stairway leading to the basement of the Bureau of Indian Affairs Southern Pueblo Agency in Albuquerque. Wilson was on the quest for some Santa Clara documents, which A. Bandelier had seen, when he stumbled on these materials by accident.

The BIA has forty-five original autograph documents plus photostat negatives and typescript English translations. Early in the 1970s, Wilson made positive photostat prints from the negative copies and deposited these prints, along with an English translation, in the History Library of the Museum of New Mexico. He then prepared a catalog.[53]

The bulk of these documents deal with land matters involving the pueblos of Laguna, Isleta, Santa Clara, Santo Domingo, Zía, Santa Ana, Jemez, and Taos. Other materials include various kinds of personal suits, election matters, water controversies, personal property inventories, orders from the governor, wills, and property inventories. Items of significance to land matters also include abstracts of deeds prepared by Pueblo Lands Board personnel which document transfers between Indians and non-Indians in the Mexican period.

(3) Webb, James J. Memoirs, 1844.

James Josiah Webb was a merchant involved in the beginning of the Santa Fe trade. Before he died in 1899, he wrote about his first trip to New Mexico in 1844 and his first two years as a businessman in Santa Fe. His son had the memoirs typed and bound, and the 210-page manuscript was secured by Chief Justice William J. Mills for the Historical Society of New Mexico. It was edited by Ralph P. Bieber and published as *Adventures in the Santa Fe Trade, 1844–1847*, Vol. I of the Southwest Historical Series (Glendale, Calif.: The Arthur H. Clark Co., 1931).

NOTE: The following items do not appear in *A Guide to the Museum of New Mexico History Library*.

(4) Miscellaneous Land Transfer Documents, 1837–1845.

These transfer documents are dated January 5, 1837, February 6, 1843, September 22, 1845, May 12, 1829, and July 20, 1842. They deal with Cuyamungue between 1837 and 1908 with the exception of the document dated September 22, 1845, which refers to La Joya, a town forty-seven miles north of Socorro on the Rio Grande.

(5) Conver, Conaiegerine Marie. Collection, 1830–1850.

This collection is comprised of one photostatic copy of Deed Book No. 2 of Rio Arriba County. In 446 pages, it records land conveyances dating from the 1830s to the 1850s. In the back of the journal appears a list of those parties mentioned in the journal.

(6) García, Ruth. Collection, 1846–1908.

This is a set of eighteen documents proving title to a parcel of land near Santa Cruz de la Cañada. Included in the documents are titles, *hijuelas,* and bills of sale from the Mexican and territorial periods.

(7) Walter, Paul A. F. Collection, 1712–1845.

This collection consists of six photostatic copies of original manuscripts dating from the Spanish and Mexican periods. The two Mexican period documents, originals of which are at the NMSRCA, include a proclamation on the maintenance of order and good government presented to the *ayuntamiento* of Santa Fe in 1833 by Lic. D. Antonio Barreiro in 1833,[54] and a decree of Mariano Martínez, governor and commanding general of the Department of New Mexico, placing assessments on leading citizens for defense against the ''Texans,'' February 15, 1845.

The following microfilm publications contain material on the Mexican period and are available through Interlibrary Loan:

(1) M-15 (1 reel): Bent, Charles. Correspondence, 1839–1846, with Manuel Alvarez, U.S. Consul. 54 letters, the originals of which are in the Benjamin M. Read Collection at the NMSRCA.

(2) M-17, 18, 19, 20 (4 reels): Alvarez-Vigil Papers. These are copies of originals in the NMSRCA.

(3) M-34 (1 reel): Gilmer, Jeremy Francis (Lt.). Letters of Lt. Gilmer to Captain George Lewis Welcker, 1846–1847. Twelve letters from July 4, 1846, to February 16, 1847, describing life in New Mexico, the New Mexicans, war-related matters, gold-mining, and the Bent murder.

(4) M-145 (1 reel): Nelson Parraga, Charlotte Marie, ''Santa Fe de Nuevo Mexico: a study of a frontier city based on an annotated translation of selected documents (1825–1832) from the Mexican archives,'' Ph.D. dissertation, Ball State University, 1976.

(5) M-152 (1 reel): U.S. Surveyor General, New Mexico. This is Reel 22 of the Records of Private Land Claims, 1855–1890, the originals of which are stored in the NMSRCA. Reel 22 is part of the 66-reel publication produced in 1955–1957 by the University of New Mexico. The entire microfilm collection is available at the NMSRCA and the Special Collections Department, University of New Mexico.

(6) M-172, 173, 174, 175 (4 reels): U.S. Census Office. 7th Census, 1850. These four reels are copies of the National Archives and Records Service publication M–467 to M–470 taken from RG29. Census data are from Bernalillo, Rio Arriba, Santa Fe, Santa Ana, San Miguel, Taos, and Valencia counties.

(7) M-180 (1 reel): Sandoval, David Alex, ''Trade and the *Manito* Society in New Mexico, 1821–1848,'' Ph.D. dissertation, University of Utah, 1978.

4. ALBUQUERQUE; UNIVERSITY OF NEW MEXICO LIBRARY (ZIMMERMAN LIBRARY), SPECIAL COLLECTIONS DEPARTMENT (CORONADO ROOM):

Located on the second floor at the west end of the Zimmerman Library, the Special Collections Department is second only to the NMSRCA in archives, manuscripts, and microfilm publications useful for Mexican period research. Materials checked out from Special Collections can be left at the main circulation desk of the Zimmerman Library for use when the Coronado Room is closed.

The following collections contain information on the Mexican period of New Mexico. Most have inventories and are also indexed in a card file (3 drawers) by personal and corporate name as well as by geographic reference. In addition to a collection number, a letter suggests the nature of material in the collection.[55] Summaries of contents are available for most collections acquired prior to 1957 in Albert J. Díaz, *Manuscripts and Records in the University of New Mexico Library.*[56]

(1) Alvarez, Manuel. Memorandum Book, ca. 1834–1844.

On the first page of this photoprint of the original volume of 153 pages, the author has written, *"Este libro contiene algunos discursos, frases, sentencias . . . y notas sacadas de varias obras que pienso ser util tener presentes . . . 28 Diciembre 1834."* The original of this item is supposed to be located either in the NMSRCA or in the Museum of New Mexico, but searches in both places have been unproductive.[57]

(2) Armijo, Antonio. X, 1830, Coll. No. 203.

Photocopies from seven pages of Armijo's journal. The typed material in French shows the itinerary and route of Armijo from New Mexico to California plus a cover letter written by José Antonio Chávez.

(3) Bryan, Richard William Dickinson. P, M, 1844–1939, Coll. No. 1.

The first of two boxes of material contains the *escritura de venta* (bill of sale) on the sale of thirty varas of land in *"esta demarcación de Sandía punto de Bernalillo"* for seventy-nine pesos. The sale is from José Antonio Lujan for his brother in favor of Miguel Antonio Gonzáles and is dated January 29, 1844.

(4) Cañon del Agua Grant. X, 1843–1860. Coll. No. 190.

This is a sixteen-page report copied from Reel 17 of the Land Grant Records. It is the same as Report 40, File 70, of the Surveyor General's Office records and includes a request from José Serafín Ramírez to the governor on February 12, 1844, to work a mine: *"fundir y moler metales."* Other letters in this collection are from Ambrosio Armijo (1844) and Governor Mariano Martínez (1844). English translations appear at the end of the folder.

(5) Catron, Thomas Benton. P, M, 1704–1934, Coll. No. 29.

In addition to personal letters and records of his legal firm, this large collection includes notebooks, press books, and land grant papers from the Las Animas, Anton Chico, Tierra Amarilla, Mora, Gervacio Nolan, Ojo Caliente, Antonio Armijo, Guadalupe Miranda, and José Sutton grants.[58]

(6) Chávez, José Felipe. P, 1739–1936, Coll. No. 10.

Chávez was a merchant and an agent for other mercantile establishments in Belén and Santa Fe. His papers include the donation and sale of land, a promissory note, a request from Felipe Sena in 1838 to Governor Manuel Armijo asking the latter for his intervention in a matter of debt, a list of furniture belonging to Felipe Sena, Sena's request for compensation for what was taken from him during the suppression of the Taos uprising in 1847, and an IOU in favor of Manuel Armijo for four hundred pesos at twelve percent annual interest.

(7) D'Armand, Louis. P, 1721–1871, Coll. No. 121.

Two items, both of which have been collated in the MANM microfilm publication, pertain to the Mexican period. The first is a booklet listing the members of the permanent company of Santa Fe certified by José Caballero and dated December 31, 1837. The second item, dated December 21, 1841, from Antonio López de Santa Anna, confers the grade of captain on Donaciano Vigil for meritorious services.

(8) Dreesen, Donald S. P, 1846–1912, Coll. No. 290.

This project, entitled "Founders of Albuquerque," is a genealogical guide to families in Bernalillo County and the Rio Abajo in the seventeenth and eighteenth centuries. The results of this research, begun in 1974 and contained in blue loose-leaf notebooks, may prove useful for the study of families who lived in these areas during the nineteenth century. The Pecos River and El Paso areas are not included, and the northern boundary of the study area is defined by a line from Jemez through Cochití to Cerrillos and Galisteo.

(9) Elam Theft Collection. P, M, 1600–1975, Coll. No. 330.

Box B contains a statement to the governor of New Mexico from the Pueblo of Santo Domingo asking for additional land to graze cattle, sheep, and horses. This is a copy of the original request made on March 8, 1841.

(10) Fergusson, Erna. P, F, Y, 1846–1964, Coll. No. 45.

Comprised mostly of notes, newspaper clippings, photographs, and pamphlets used in writing her books, this collection also contains letters and notes about old Albuquerque families (Box VI, Folder 4), and a printed copy of the family tree of James Wiley Magoffin (Box VII, Folder 5).

(11) Field, Mary Lester. Y, F, 1600–1900, Coll. No. 132.

Several Mexican period artifacts include photographs of copper pots from Mora, Manuel Armijo's necklace, and many photographs of silver pieces and santos.

(12) Gay, John L. P, 1841–1887, Coll. No. 193.

These eighty-four items, donated by Mrs. Gertrude M. Gay through W. A. Keleher in 1961, are photocopies of records relating to the business affairs of Rafael and Manuel Armijo, who had stores in Albuquerque and Mesilla. Most of the material deals with the Armijo connection to the South during the Civil War and reveals how they provisioned the Confederate troops invading New Mexico in 1862. Documents also attest to their purchase of slaves in 1865.

(13) Huning, Franz. P, 1812–1906, Coll. No. 194–1.

One undated item which appears to be from the Mexican period is a last will and testament of María Catarina Padilla, resident of the Plaza de San Andrés de las Padillas, Jurisdicción de la Misión de San Agustín de la Isleta. Another item, dated June 6, 1831, relates to the appearance of Manuel Armijo, Rafael

Mestas, and others before the alcalde of Albuquerque (Ambrosio Armijo) regarding a debt of two hundred pesos which Antonio Otero had promised to pay Armijo.

(14) Lovato, Miguel Antonio. P, 1790–1849, Coll. No. 137.

This collection consists of seven documents relative to or written by Lovato, a citizen of Galisteo and Santa Fe. One item is a twelve-page report to the president of Mexico in 1835 regarding the several Indian nations surrounding New Mexico. Other documents include various accusations regarding planting in someone else's property and seizing territory belonging to the Pueblo of Sandía. A six-page document (1838–1839) expounds on social, economic, and military problems. Since they are official records, these documents have been collated in MANM.

(15) Martínez, Antonio José. M, 1835–1859, Coll. No. 188.

One item is a two-page folio sheet entitled, *"Religión,"* with additional comments dated September 24, 1859. The other item is a copy of a book entitled *Aritmética,* pages 3–40, Taos (?), 1835 or 1836.

(16) Martínez, José. M, 1769–1845, Coll. No. 105.

Out of a total of nine Spanish language documents from the Spanish and Mexican periods, three deal with the 1821–1848 period: a *compra venta* (trade contract) between José Antonio Martín and Juan Dionicio García, November 30, 1836; the relating of a miracle which occurred in Rome on April 5, 1839; and a loose page from a notarial book, January 27, 1845.

(17) New Mexico Archives Collection. P, 1600–1875. No collection number.

This collection is best described as a photoprint collection of the Spanish and Mexican archives of New Mexico. Prepared during 1938–1941 by the Historical Records Survey of New Mexico, the collection is made up of 240 volumes which contain prints made from the microfilm publication produced by the Historical Records Survey. The blue and red volumes are organized as follows:

Twitchell II documents (1621–1820)	84
Documents, 1821–1846	145
Militia Papers, 1774–1843	1
Indian Depredations, 1847–1853	1
Martínez Papers	2
Military Account Book, 1805–1836	1
Miscellaneous	6
TOTAL	240

The difference between this photoprint collection and the SANM/MANM microfilm publication is that the latter was reorganized to include official documents found by the NMSRCA in private collections. The photoprints are more difficult to read than the 1960s microfilm publication due to technical problems of reproduction. The volumes are a handy reference tool when the microfilm cannot be used, however. For the 1822 to 1828 period, a typed index is available on 3 x 5 cards for each document. A hand-written index was done for the 1828 to 1832 period. Both are the work of Enrique Cortés.

Researchers who are confused by references to a New Mexico Archives Collection containing 684 volumes should be aware that this includes the 240 volumes of New Mexico documents plus photoprints collected from various repositories throughout the world, i.e., the *Archivo General de la Nación, Biblioteca Nacional, Museo Nacional*, Catholic Church, etc.

(18) New Mexico. University. Library Collection, Y, F, 1784–1955, Coll. No. 113.

Mexican period items include two broadsides of Donaciano Vigil, January 25, 1847, and February 12, 1847, plus a manifesto of Mariano Martínez of September 8, 1844, issued when he was governor of New Mexico.

(19) New Mexico Documents (rare), P, 1770–1886, Coll. No. 146.

This collection is comprised of legal documents including many conveyances of land and personal property, wills, powers of attorney, IOUs, account books, and a receipt for funeral expenses. Most matters relate to exchanges in Taos and Abiquiú and involve a number of familiar names.

(20) New Mexico Imprints. X, Y, 1835–1853, Coll. No. 197.

This collection contains several pedagogical tracts such as the *Aritmética* (1836) of Antonio José Martínez; the *Ortografía* (1837) of the *Academia Española;* and the *Retórica* (1835) of Padre Martínez. In addition, one can find two pages of José María Alvarez' *Instituciones,* and three pages of the *Leyes del Territorio de Nuevo Mejico* (1846).

(21) New Mexico Passport Records. X, Y, 1835–1853, Coll. No. 184.

One item is a photoprint of a document listing immigrants from other states to New Mexico dated July 8, 1827, and July 31, 1827. The second item is a set of sixteen photoprints for the year 1828 including a list of 248 immigrants to Santa Fe from Mexico, Chihuahua, and other states.

(22) Ortiz y Pino. P, 1750–1981, Coll. No. 336.

The collection contains various papers relating to the life of Don Pedro Bautista Pino and his descendants.

(23) *Padrón General de El Rito.* X, 1839, Coll. No. 295.

This is a general census for El Rito showing the number of persons, their sex, age, marital status, and professed trade as of the year 1839.

(24) Reeve, Frank Driver. P, M, F, X, 1610–1968, Coll. No. 158.

Most of the materials relevant to the Mexican period in this collection are copies from photoprints or microfilm publications at the Bancroft Library. The general subject matter treats Indian affairs, such as Apache willingness to make peace with the North Americans (1825, 1826); plans to create protected settlements for Faraones, Mescaleros, and Gileños (1826); military actions of the Company of El Bado against the Apache (1832, 1834); a decree of the Sonoran congress authorizing interstate cooperation and settlement by Mexicans among the Apaches living between the Gila River and the Sierra del Cobre (1838); expeditions against the Comanche and the Mescalero (1825); *fondo de aliados* (friendship fund) for the Gileños; and plans to join the Apaches de Paz to units of Mexican soldiers in order to pursue a common enemy. Actual documents in this collection deal with land sales in the Truchas area.

(25) Romero, Secundino. P, 1824–1911, Coll. No. 287.

The first folder of this collection contains a number of legal documents including suits for debt, subpoenas, and other legal matters in San Miguel del Bado.

(26) Prince, Le Baron Bradford. P, M, 1800–1922, Coll. No. 109.

These documents, some of which have been collated and filmed in MANM, reflect a variety of activities related to Santa Cruz de la Cañada, Santa Fe, San Ildefonso, San Juan, and Santa Clara. Among items mentioned are a complaint of the *ayuntamiento* (corporation) of La Cañada regarding contradictory laws (1826); a contemporary copy of a peace treaty made between Mexico and the Comanche nation (1827); a list of alcaldes and *regidores* from Albuquerque (1829); a warning from the government in Santa Fe to the alcalde of La Cañada not to withhold service which he is expected to perform (1837); a circular warning of the uprising of Navajos (1839); an undated letter from William Bent to Manuel Alvarez commenting on how a certain Taos priest has been stirring up the people against North Americans; and a circular of June 4, 1843, warning that a party of 400 Tejanos had been seen in the vicinity of the Rio Colorado. Other items included in this collection are mentioned in Albert J. Díaz, *Manuscripts and Records in the University of New Mexico Library.*

(27) Santa Fe, New Mexico. P, 1822–1934, Coll. No 76.

Item 2–5 is made up of photoprints of the March 1822 articles regarding the celebration of independence in Santa Fe. Item 1–33 is comprised of several leaves of the Journal of the Corporation of Santa Fe *(ayuntamiento)*, 1829–1836. This original manuscript includes the following dates: May–July 1829; April 8, 1830; April 12, 1832–July 27, 1833; March 29, 1833; April 27, 1833; May 4 and May 11, 1833; April 27, 1833; March 30, 1833; March 1836; and fragments from the month of May in an unidentified year. This journal, translated by George P. Hammond of the Bancroft Library, contains discussion of water control, distribution and cleaning of irrigation ditches, damage done by animals running loose, morality in the community, and a general lack of respect shown by North Americans.

(28) Seligman, Julius. M, 1791–1872, Coll. No. 157.

The majority of these documents deal with land exchanges in Albuquerque, Algodones, Angostura, Bernalillo, and other places in the Rio Abajo. Included in the collection are *escrituras de venta, testimonios* relating to land and water claims, oaths, petitions, and other legal documents having to do with land sales. This collection is collated in MANM.

(29) Spanish and English Manuscripts. M, 1791–1887, Coll. No. 106.

Three items from the Mexican period include an 1826 sale of land to Julián Armijo in Albuquerque; a petition to reclaim land, probably in the same area; and an *escritura de venta*, July 19, 1846, in favor of Juan C. Armijo.

(30) Spanish Language Manuscripts. M, 1811–1867, Coll. No 342.

This collection includes a copy of the broadside of Donaciano Vigil entitled, *"Triunfo de los Principios Contra la Torpeza,"* January 25, 1847 (from the Prince Collection), and another broadside dated February 12, 1847, issued by Donaciano Vigil. A third item related to the Mexican period is a manifesto by Mariano Martínez dated September 8, 1844.

(31) Women of New Mexico. P, 1598–1975, Coll. No. 303.

Part of this collection is a list of names of women in New Mexico history. The list includes María Gertrudis Barceló (Doña Tules), Ignacia Jaramillo Bent (Mrs. Charles Bent), Josefa Jaramillo Carson (Mrs. Kit Carson), Susan Shelby Magoffin, and Luz Beaubien Maxwell.

The Coronado Room has a good collection of microfilm for research on the Mexican period. The following references have been excerpted in the same order as they appear on a typed list of microfilm holdings. Additional notations are taken from the card catalog.

(1) The Béxar Archives at the University of Texas Archives. 1727–1890. 17 reels. References to New Mexico are scarce in the printed general guides[59] and more detailed document calendars. Painstaking research may turn up significant items.

(2) United States. Bureau of Indian Affairs. Letters Received by the Office of Indian Affairs, 1824–1881. Arizona Superintendency (27 reels), New Mexico Superintendency (37 reels). Both sets are from Microcopy M234 (NARS).

(3) Prince, LeBaron Bradford, 1840–1922. This is the same as Collection No. 109 listed above plus the papers of Antonio Salazar originally in Collection No. 122. 1 reel.

(4) United States. Adjutant General's Office. Compiled Service Records of Volunteer Union Soldiers Who Served in Organizations From the Territory of New Mexico. Microcopy M427. 46 reels.

(5) United States. Adjutant General's Office. Index to Compiled Service Records of Volunteer Union Soldiers Who Served in Organizations From the Territory of New Mexico. Microcopy M242. 4 reels.

(6) United States. Congress. Senate. Report of the Commissioners on the Road from Missouri to New Mexico, 1827. This item was filmed in 1950 by the General Service Administration. Since it was most likely a private order, no ''M'' or ''T'' number is available.

(7) New Mexico. Early State Records. 1580–1915. For contents, refer to William S. Jenkins' *A Guide to the Microfilm Collection of Early State Records* (Washington: Library of Congress, 1950), with references to the Journal of the Provincial Deputation (1824–1837) and the Journal of the Departmental Assembly (January 1845–August 10, 1846). 40 reels.

(8) United States. Census Office. 7th Census, 1850. Population schedules of the seventh census of the United States for New Mexico appear as follows: Reel 1 (Bernalillo and Rio Arriba counties); Reel 2 (Santa Ana and Santa Fe counties); Reel 3 (San Miguel and Taos counties); Reel 4 (Valencia County). 4 reels.

(9) Ritch Papers, 1539–1885. This microfilm copy of the Huntington Library manuscript portion of the Ritch Papers is made up of eleven reels. In addition to official correspondence, reports, and circulars, the Ritch Papers contain some unique items. The first two reels consist of miscellaneous Spanish language documents from the Spanish and Mexican periods in New Mexico. Reel 8 is the *Biografía del Rev. P. José Antonio Martínez, cura párroco de Curato de Taos,* by Santiago Valdez. Reel 11 contains the catalog cards of the entire collection with six cards to a frame. Special Collections also has a card catalog file organized alphabetically by name which allows researchers to find the reel and frame number of a specific subject.

(10) California University. Bancroft Library, New Mexico Originals (Pinart Papers). This microfilm copy of the Pinart Papers was made by the University of California, Berkeley. 3 reels.

(11) Alvarez, Manuel. Papers, 1833–1862. The first reel of this publication contains the fifty-four letters exchanged between Charles Bent and Manuel Alvarez.[60] Originals form part of the Read Collection located at the NMSRCA. The other three reels contain correspondence, official reports, and business records. 4 reels.

(12) Appointment Papers. Confirmations and Rejections Regarding James W. Magoffin. In 1957, the Special Collections Department requested microfilm from the State Department records in the National Archives. This reel includes: (1) Appointment papers: Confirmations and Rejections, 1820–32, attested Senate Resolution, January 10, 1825 (2 pages); (2) Appointment papers: Applications and Recommendations for Office, 1817–25 (Letter dated December 13, 1824) (4 pages); (3) Pardons, Volume 25, p. 11; (4) Amnesty Oaths, Texas (Individuals), Box 139 (5 pages); (5) Instructions to Consuls, Volumes 2 (pp. 344–45), 3 (pp. 148–50, 181–84, 318, 328), 5 (pp. 181–84, 265), 6 (pp. 3,5). 1 reel.

(13) Texas-Santa Fe Papers, Texas Archives. Arrott Roll No. 17. Contains official correspondence among Texas, Santa Fe, and Washington officials on the disposition of Santa Fe after its acquisition from Mexico. 1 reel.

(14) Abiquiú, New Mexico. Santo Tomás Church. Baptismal register, May

1832–December 1861. The three books of originals were loaned to the University of New Mexico for microfilming by J. D. Ortiz. 1 reel.

(15) Pueblo of Acoma. Records, 1777–1925. Baptismal, marriage, and death records from the mission of San Esteban de Acoma, 1777–1872, plus correspondence between territorial and U.S. officials, 1828–1925. An inventory of the mission is included. The first reel contains an 1841 petition to the court at Cebolleta by the principal men of Acoma and a petition to the governor by Román Gallegos in 1829. Other items include inventories and contracts not related to the Mexican period. Reel 2 contains portions of Roman Missals and related religious material not from the Mexican period. Reel 3 includes Baptismal Records (1819–72), Marriage Records (1777–1872), Death Records (1819–33), and Miscellaneous Documents (1777–1925). 3 reels.

(16) Maps of New Mexico, Mexico, North America, and the World, 1507–1900. Contents are listed in a folder in the Coronado Room. 1 reel.

(17) United States. Congress. House Committee on Private Land Claims, 1856–1890. This is a collection of Congressional documents concerning private land claims in New Mexico. Filmed by the University of New Mexico in 1969, the documents represent various kinds of maps and legal papers used by the House Committee on Private Land Claims. 2 reels.

(18) Bork, Albert William, *Nuevos Aspectos del Comercio entre Nuevo Mexico y Misuri, 1822–1846.* "Tesis que presenta AWB para obtener el grado de doctor en letras." (Mexico, 1944).

(19) New Mexico Land Grants. Spanish Archives of New Mexico (SANM I). These are the documents described in Twitchell's *The Spanish Archives of New Mexico,* Vol. I, which were filmed by the University of New Mexico, 1955–1957. Reels 1–6. See Díaz, *A Guide to the Microfilm of Papers Relating to New Mexico Land Grants,* for a more detailed description.

(20) New Mexico Land Grants. U.S. Bureau of Land Management.
This is the continuation of the previous citation and includes Reels 7 to 63. The records include various indexes and record books kept prior to the establishment of the Surveyor General's Office including the Vigil Index and books in which land titles were recorded in accordance with the Kearny Code, Records of the Surveyor General's Office, and Records of the Court of Private Land Claims. The best entry to this collection is through Díaz, *A Guide to the Microfilm of Papers Relating to New Mexico Land Grants.* The sixty-six reels mentioned by Díaz take into account the fact that Reel 31 also has parts "A," "B," and "C."

(21) Father Martínez Papers. This is Reel No. 8 of the Ritch Papers. 1 reel.

(22) Archives of the Archdiocese of Santa Fe, 1678–1900. Includes baptisms, marriages, burials, accounts, patents, *diligencias,* and assorted loose documents. 90 reels.

(23) United States. Consulate, Santa Fe, New Mexico. Despatches from U.S.

Consuls in Santa Fe, August 28, 1830–September 4, 1846. NARS Microcopy M199. 1 reel.

(24) United States. Surveyor General of New Mexico. Letters Sent and Received, 1854–1893. This material is from RG 49, Records of the Bureau of Land Management, and is microcopy M27 of the NARS. 8 reels.

(25) United States. Treasury Department. Letters Received by the Secretary of the Treasury from collectors of customs, 1833–1869. This is NARS publication M174, Reel 60, series G. 1 reel.

(26) Mexico. *Secretaría de la Defensa Nacional. Departamento de Archivo.* These are reels (16 mm) copied from the collection at the Bancroft Library. Special Collections has the following reels: 1, 3–7, 9–11, 15, 16, 19, 21, 23, 26, 31–34, 36, 41, 48, 61, 68, 72, 80, 90.

(27) New Mexico. NMSRCA. MANM. 43 reels.

(28) Rio Grande land case papers: Santa Fe, Land document No. 1 with summary of translation. 1843–1848. Deals with Santa Ana Pueblo. 1 reel.

(29) Steck, Michael. Collection No. 134. This collection contains material on Santo Domingo and the Navajos in October 1844, and a document written by Charles Bent providing a census of Indians in New Mexico in November 1846. 7 reels.

5. ALBUQUERQUE; ARCHIVES OF THE ARCHDIOCESE OF SANTA FE:

During the colonial period in New Mexico, ecclesiastical records first were kept in the custodial archive in Santo Domingo Pueblo and then in Santa Fe, when the Custody of the Conversion of St. Paul began to fade away due to deaths and departures of the old friars.[61] During the Mexican period, similar materials were accumulated by the secular vicar and pastor of Santa Fe together with the records of official acts of the vicarate and visitations from Durango. Some ecclesiastical documents remained at the missions; others were lost during the last half of the nineteenth century because of a lamentable failure on the part of Church authorities to gather the available records for organization, classification, and preservation.

Beginning in 1934 the problem was addressed by Archbishop Rudolph A. Gerken, who assembled the extant records of the missions, the Custody of the Conversion of St. Paul, the vicarate of New Mexico, and the parishes of New Mexico to the middle of the nineteenth century.[62] The documents were organized by bound volumes and loose documents, but the real job of classification was addressed by Fray Angélico Chávez, who divided the loose documents into three categories: (1) *Diligencias Matrimoniales* (prenuptial investigations); (2) Loose mission documents to 1850; and (3) Diocesan papers, 1850 to 1900. The bound volumes were divided into five classes: (1) Books of *Patentes* (copied letters from Franciscan superiors); (2) Books of Accounts (local inventories and accounts); (3) Books of Baptisms; (4) Books of Marriages; and (5) Books of Burials.[63]

After completing his work, the archives were placed in a vault in the chancery of Santa Fe. Permission was granted in 1969 to the NMSRCA to make a microfilm copy.[64] An eighty-page index to this microfilm publication entitled *Guide to the Archives of the Archdiocese of Santa Fe* was recently prepared by Julián Josué Vigil at New Mexico Highlands University. A copy is available at the NMSRCA. The originals, now located in the chancery across from the Masonic Lodge in Albuquerque at 200 Morningside Drive, have been retired.[65] Supplemental filming was carried out in the 1950s–60s by the Texas firm of Vance Golightly Microfilm.[66] Except for some Peña Blanca baptisms (1841–1909), these materials from parishes in Santa Fe, Albuquerque, Taos, Santa Cruz de la Cañada, Peñasco, Ribera, Mora, and Peña Blanca are of the period following the Mexican War.

For Mexican period research, the Archdiocesan records have great value. Prenuptial investigations to legitimize marriages include genealogical history, which is not always easy to find in church registers. A bound volume of tanned bison skin from San Miguel del Vado provides this kind of information for the years 1829 to 1834. Similar examples exist. In the loose documents, in addition to the drafts of marriages, baptisms, and burial entries, diligent researchers will find information on Indian depredations, battle casualties, land donations and transfers, irrigation disputes, education, censuses, citizen meetings, brotherhoods, and much more.The books of *Patentes* contain information on Church business, such as problems with flocks, construction of new buildings, visitations, licenses and permits for special functions, circulars from the Bishop of Durango, and the resettlement of priests from one place to another. In short, the Archdiocesan records, used in conjuction with the official civil records of New Mexico (MANM), offer a reasonably complete picture of the social and religious life of the people. The Chávez calendar and Vigil index provide excellent finding aids for scholars interested in this collection.

6. ALBUQUERQUE; BUREAU OF INDIAN AFFAIRS SOUTHERN PUEBLOS AGENCY:

In addition to the documents indexed by John Wilson for the Museum of New Mexico, the BIA has abstracts of deeds showing land transfers between Indians and non-Indians during the Mexican period. The notes prepared by Pueblo Lands Board personnel were taken from deeds in county courthouses. They constitute an important source for research on Pueblo land tenure.

7. A SUMMARY OF DESCRIPTIVE REFERENCES AND FINDING AIDS EXCLUDING UNPUBLISHED INDEXES AND INVENTORIES:

(1) Beers, Henry Putney. *Spanish and Mexican Records of the American*

Southwest. Tucson: University of Arizona Press, 1979.

Part I, entitled "The Records of New Mexico," is a particularly useful survey of official records, documentary publications, land grant material for both New Mexico and Colorado, records of local jurisdictions, ecclesiastical records, and a history of how the several records-creating agencies evolved.

(2) Chávez, Fray Angélico, O. F. M. *Archives of the Archdiocese of Santa Fe, 1678–1900*. Washington: Academy of American Franciscan History, 1957.

This is a calendar of the religious and secular Church records of New Mexico to 1900. The author was responsible for arranging and classifying the documents.

(3) Díaz, Albert J. *A Guide to the Microfilm of Papers Relating to New Mexico Land Grants*. Albuquerque: University of New Mexico Press, 1960.

This guide describes how the land grant papers were microfilmed by the University of New Mexico and discusses the arrangement of the collection, which is now located in the NMSRCA.

(4) ———. *Manuscripts and Records in the University of New Mexico Library*. Albuquerque: University of New Mexico Library, 1957.

Díaz was in charge of the library's Special Collections Department. This publication reflects the author's desire to organize manuscripts and printed records for use by scholars. Though dated, it is useful for quick references to collections on deposit at that time.

(5) ———. "University of New Mexico Special Collections." *New Mexico Historical Review* 33 (July, October 1958): 235–51, 316–21.

A list of collections at the University of New Mexico Library made when Díaz was Special Collections Librarian.

(6) Jenkins, Myra Ellen. *Calendar of the Microfilm Edition of the Mexican Archives of New Mexico, 1821–1846*. Santa Fe: NMSRCA, 1970.

Arranged by reels (1 to 43), this calendar lists each document by date and includes information sufficient for identifying the sender and the subject treated. Scholars should be aware that the forty-third reel containing miscellaneous documents from 1822 to 1829 was not included in the original calendar.

(7) ———. *Guide to the Microfilm Edition of the Mexican Archives of New Mexico, 1821–1846*. Santa Fe: NMSRCA, 1969.

This small booklet supplements the *Calendar* by providing an historical background to the Mexican period, the institutions which created records, and a brief history of what happened to the documents after New Mexico was captured in 1846. "Roll Notes" contains brief descriptions of the contents of each reel of MANM.

(8) Jenkins, William S., comp., and Hamrick, Lillian A., ed. *A Guide to the Microfilm Collection of Early State Records*. Washington: Library of Congress, 1950. Self-explanatory.

(9) Kielman, Chester V. *Guide to the Microfilm Edition of the Béxar Ar-*

chives, 1822–1836, Vol. 3. Austin: University of Texas Archives, 1971.
Self-explanatory.

(10) Olmstead, Virginia Langham, comp., *Spanish and Mexican Censuses of New Mexico, 1750–1830.* Albuquerque: New Mexico Genealogical Society, Inc., 1981.

In addition to the census records, the author has included a list of abbreviations of baptismal names that were frequently used by enumerators.

(11) ———. *New Mexico Spanish and Mexican Colonial Censuses: 1790, 1823,1845.* Albuquerque: New Mexico Genealogical Society, Inc., 1975.

This is the first of the author's two volumes dealing with New Mexican censuses. A wealth of family information is contained in the listing of names taken from MANM Reels Nos. 3 (1823) and 40 (1845). One of the uses of the Census of 1845 is to make a comparison by name with that of the Census of 1850 to determine which families chose to return to Mexico after the war.

(12) Reeve, Frank D. "The Charles Bent Papers." *New Mexico Historical Review* 29 (1954): 234–39, 311–17, 30 (1955): 154–67, 252–54, 340–52; 31 (1956): 75–77, 157–64, 251–53.

This is the most accessible version of original letters in the Benjamin M. Read Collection at the NMSRCA. These letters have also been included in the first reel of a four-reel microfilm publication entitled, "The Manuel Alvarez Papers, 1833–1862."

(13) Stone, Jess H. *A Guide to the Museum of New Mexico History Library.* Santa Fe: Museum of New Mexico, 1973.

This is an annotated guide to manuscript collections and selected printed sources for Spanish and Indian histories of the Southwest.

(14) Twitchell, Ralph Emerson. *The Spanish Archives of New Mexico.* Vol. I. Cedar Rapids, Iowa: The Torch Press, 1914.

Referred to as "Twitchell I," this compilation of documents is a listing of land grant records collected by the Surveyor General's Office and the Court of Private Land Claims. Twitchell prepared this volume when the archives of New Mexico were under control of the Library of Congress. The first six reels of the publication, "New Mexico Land Grants. Spanish Archives of New Mexico" (total of sixty-six reels), are identical to what Twitchell lists in this volume.

(15) Vigil, Julián Josué. *Guide to the Archives of the Archdiocese of Santa Fe.* Microfilm edition, 1982.

Available in film or fiche from the NMSRCA, this *Guide* was designed to be used with Chavez's *Archives of the Archdiocese.* Its cross-referencing of names and documents and explanations of official abbreviations are only a few of the aids provided by the author.

NOTES

1. Daniel Tyler, "The Carrizal Archives: A Source for the Mexican Period," NMHR (*New Mexico Historical Review*) 57 (July 1982): 257–67.
2. These documents, referred to as the Sender Papers, are named after Kenneth D. Sender, who offered them for sale to several institutions in the 1960s and 1970s for approximately $50,000. The State of New Mexico initiated litigation against Sender, claiming the collection belonged to the state, but Sender won on a technicality. When he was unable to pay his legal fees, however, the law firm of Catron, Catron and Sawtell, which held a half interest in the collection, forced a sale, and on June 21, 1982, their representative in Kansas City, Missouri, offered the highest bid at auction ($24,000) and took possession of the documents. During the brief period that the documents were in the hands of the NMSRCA, they were microfilmed (poorly) and indexed. Although the Sender Papers are presently unavailable for research, the NMSRCA is attempting to raise money to buy the documents from Catron, Catron and Sawtell.
3. Letter from Stanley M. Hordes, State Historian, Santa Fe, July 23, 1982.
4. Some contemporary printed materials have been located in the church of San Felipe de Neri in Albuquerque. The exact contents remain unknown. Another collection that might contain Mexican period material belongs to Bill Griffith of Albuquerque, an avid collector of New Mexicana for many years. Griffith prefers not to divulge what he owns and has indicated that he wants the collection destroyed at the time of his death.
5. Marc Simmons, *Spanish Government in New Mexico* (Albuquerque: University of New Mexico Press, 1968), p. 48.
6. Nettie Lee Benson, *La Diputación Provincial y El Federalismo Mexicano* (Mexico: El Colegio de Mexico, 1955), p. 121.
7. Ibid., p. 204.
8. David J. Weber, *The Mexican Frontier, 1821–1846* (Albuquerque: University of New Mexico Press, 1982), p. 25.
9. Ibid., pp. 22, 27. Weber notes that a committee of the *Cámara de Diputados* approved a plan in 1828, but no plan was ever approved by the entire Congress. A printed thirty-one page copy of the committee document can be found in Governor's Papers, 1828, Communications Received from Authorities Within Mexico, January 21–December 1, Communications from *Congreso General, Mexico*, MANM, Reel 7, frames 1002–31.
10. This title was used as early as 1820. See Simmons, *Spanish Government*, p. 48n. 27.
11. Lansing Bartlett Bloom, "New Mexico Under Mexican Administration, 1821–1846," *Old Santa Fe* II (January 1915): 225. Manuel Armijo occupied

the governor's post for the longest term, 1837–1844. Researchers who use *Old Santa Fe* may become confused by the irregularity which appears in the numbering system. The editors changed from a consecutive numbering system (1–6) to one which corresponded to the accepted practice of limiting each volume to four serial editions. Bloom's articles appear as follows:

"The Country; Its Resources, The People; Their Economic Activities; The Provincial Government" . . . . Vol. I, No. 1 (July 1913), pp. 3–49.
"Independence Established; First Steps; Province Waiting Upon Nation; New Mexico Becomes a Territory" . . . . . Vol. I, No. 2 (Oct. 1913), pp. 131–75.
"Economic Matters; Two Years of Quiet Development; Evidences of Weakness; Hampered Growth; Contemporary Opinions on New Mexico in 1832" . . . . Vol. I, No. 3 (Jan. 1914), pp.235–87.
"A Turbulent Year; Reaction: Army and Church Against Liberalism" . . . . Vol. I, No. 4 (Apr. 1914), pp. 347–68.
"Changing to the Department System; The Insurrection of 1837; New Mexico in 1838; Slavery and Texas" . . . . . Vol. II, No. 5 (July 1914), pp. 3–56.
"Commerce and New Mexico; A One Man Administration, 1838–1844; Texan Aggressions, 1841–1843; Constitutional Government Reestablished, 1843–1844" . . . . Vol. II, No. 6 (Oct. 1914), pp. 119–69.
"A Year Under an Alien Governor; Six Months Under the Senior Deputy; A Third and Last Chance for Manuel Armijo; The Texan Crisis in the United States and in Mexico" . . . . Vol. II, No. 3 (Jan. 1915), pp. 223–77.
"The Closing Months of Mexican Administration; Passing from Mexico to the United States" . . . . Vol. II, No. 4 (Apr. 1915), pp. 351–80.

Letter from Nancy Brown, Office Manager, NMHR, July 27, 1982.
12. No. 5, *Estados Adjuntos,* Law of March 21, 1826, and February 3, 1826, *Bandos y Comunicaciones Oficiales,* University of London, Reel 2.
13. See Chapter IV, "Military Organization, Function, and Capability," in Daniel Tyler, "New Mexico in the 1820s; The First Administration of Manuel Armijo" (Ph.D. diss., University of New Mexico, 1970), pp. 159–233.
14. Benson, *La Diputación Provincial,* p. 70. See also Weber, *The Mexican Frontier,* in which the author notes that the electors of fourteen municipal *alcaldías* (districts), including El Paso, met in Santa Fe and chose seven *vocales* (representatives) to serve in the *diputación* (p. 19). The fourteen *alcaldías* were Cochití, Jemez, Alameda, Belén, Laguna, Albuquerque, Santa Cruz de la Cañada, Isleta, Santa Fe, San Juan, Bado, Taos, El Paso del Norte, and Abiquiú. See Military Records, 1822, Miscellaneous Soldier's Receipts, MANM, Reel 1, frame 1403.
15. Bloom, "New Mexico Under Mexican Administration," *Old Santa Fe* I (October 1913): 157–58.
16. Henry Putney Beers, *Spanish and Mexican Records of the American Southwest* (Tucson: University of Arizona Press, 1979), pp. 28–29.

17. Bloom, "New Mexico Under Mexican Administration," II: 131, 146.

18. Beers, *Spanish and Mexican Records,* p. 29.

19. See Chapter III, "Points of Economic Stress," in Daniel Tyler, "New Mexico in the 1820s: The First Administration of Manuel Armijo," pp. 77 –159.

20. Bloom, "New Mexico Under Mexican Administration," I: 44. By 1830, official communications mention four *ayuntamientos:* Santa Fe, Albuquerque, Santa Cruz de la Cañada, and Taos. See Legislative, 1830, Ayuntamiento Proceedings, MANM, Reel 11, frames 164–240. Antonio Barreiro agrees, listing the following *ayuntamientos* and *alcaldías:* Santa Fe (San Miguel del Vado; Cochití, Jemez, Sandía); Cañada and Taos (San Juan, Abiquiú); Albuquerque (Isleta, Tomé, Belén, Sabinal, Socorro, Laguna). See Lansing B. Bloom, "Barreiro's Ojeada Sobre Nuevo Mexico," NMHR III (April 1928): 150.

21. Miscellaneous, 1822, MANM, Reel 1, frame 1147.

22. Beers, *Spanish and Mexican Records,* pp. 64–65.

23. For a discussion of several local institutions, including the alcalde, see Lynn I. Perrigo, "New Mexico in the Mexican Period, as Revealed in the Torres Documents," NMHR 29 (January 1954): 28–40.

24. Beers, *Spanish and Mexican Records,* pp. 7–8.

25. Decree of August 29, 1829, *Justicia,* Vol. 48, p. 69, *Archivo General de la Nación;* unsigned letter from *Justicia y Negocios Eclesiásticos,* November 15, 1833, *Justicia,* Vol. 28, p. 186, *AGN.*

26. Fray Angélico Chávez, *Archives of the Archdiocese of Santa Fe, 1678–1900* (Washington: Academy of American Franciscan History, 1957). Julián Josué Vigil prepared a microfilm and microfiche *Guide to the Archives of the Archdiocese of Santa Fe* which supplements Chávez's work. It is available at the NMSRCA.

27. Santa Fe, Santa Cruz de la Cañada, Albuquerque, and El Paso already had secular priests by 1820. One year later, Tomé had a priest. Weber, *The Mexican Frontier,* p. 57.

28. Ibid., p. 59.

29. Ibid., pp. 59, 74.

30. Beers, *Spanish and Mexican Records,* p. 70.

31. Their churches *(moradas)* in New Mexico and Colorado contain artifacts such as artwork and musical instruments which date back to the Mexican period and help tell the story of New Mexicans who were experimenting with religious changes at this time.

32. Prefects were elected for four years, subprefects for two. *Ayuntamientos* and justices of the peace held office for one year. Bloom, "New Mexico Under Mexican Administration," I: 9.

33. Governor's Proclamation, May 13, 1837, Governor's Papers, Communications Sent by Governor, MANM, Reel 23, frames 570–78.

34. Letterbook, April 27, 1846, Communications Sent by Governor and Secretary of Governor, Letterbook of Communications Sent by Governor to Authorities Within New Mexico, MANM, Reel 41, frames 175ff.

35. Bloom, "New Mexico Under Mexican Administration," II: 132.

36. Weber, *The Mexican Frontier*, p. 39.

37. Bloom, "New Mexico Under Mexican Administration," I: 45, 155n., 119, 259; II: 12, 227n.,571.

38. This post was vacated in August 1845 but was reestablished by Governor Armijo in March 1846.

39. Governor's Proclamation, April 13, 1846 (copy), Governor's Papers, Communications Sent by Governor and Secretary of Government, MANM, Reel 41, frame 273.

40. Armijo to Alvarez, July 5, 1841, Santa Fe, Governor's Papers, Communications Sent by Governor and Secretary, Miscellaneous Communications Sent to Authorities Within New Mexico, MANM, Reel 28, frame 1586. In 1841 this position was held by Don Juan Andrés Archuleta, "Teniente Coronel Subinspector de las Milicias Rurales," who led the militia against the Texan Santa Fe expedition.

41. Dr. Myra Ellen Jenkins, former Deputy for Archives at the NMSRCA, is the expert on these records. Some of her views on what happened to the records after 1846 were presented at the annual meeting of the Arizona Historical Society in Yuma, Arizona, May 8, 1970. Other parts of the story are discussed in Beers, *Spanish and Mexican Records*, pp. 9–27.

42. The Vigil Index is available in SANM I, Reel 10. Regarding specific documents, many were already missing by 1850. The archives of the Northern District (Santa Cruz de La Cañada), for example, which Governor Charles Bent had apparently taken into his custody on his way to Taos on January 14 or 15, 1847, were already lost. These documents fell into private hands when Bent was assassinated, and eventually found their way to Kenneth D. Sender. See Myra Ellen Jenkins, "Background of the Sale of the Archives of the Villa of Santa Cruz de la Cañada (Jurisdiction of the North)," typescript dated May 16, 1966, NMSRCA; and above, n.2.

43. Numerous inventories were prepared. The Surveyor General completed a "Schedule of documents relating to grants of land by the Spanish and Mexican governments, forming the archives of the Surveyor General of New Mexico." This was followed by a list of Spanish and Mexican governors and an alphabetical list of land grants arranged by name of grantee. Additional lists of private land claims were compiled and published by the Department of the Interior. See Beers, *Spanish and Mexican Records*, p. 48, and notes 18–23 on the same page.

44. The contents of the land grant microfilm are explained in Albert J. Díaz, *A Guide to the Microfilm Papers Relating to New Mexico Land Grants* (Albuquerque: University of New Mexico Press, 1960). Salazar's publication is a reel-by-reel listing of documents in the first ten reels of SANM I. The resulting calendar includes a document description, corresponding Twitchell Number, date, and frame number. He is presently preparing a second calendar for the remainder of SANM I.

45. Beers, *Spanish and Mexican Records*, p. 12. See also *Santa Fe Daily New Mexican*, March 4, 1886, p. 4, col. 3.

46. Myra Ellen Jenkins, ''The Historical Society of New Mexico and the Museum,'' paper given for the Museum of Albuquerque Lecture Series, August 10, 1979.

47. Complete microfilm copies of the MANM are located at the University of Arizona, University of California (Berkeley), California State College (Hayward), California State College (Long Beach), University of California (Santa Barbara), Denver Public Library, Colorado State University, Library of Congress, Tulane University, University of New Mexico, New Mexico Highlands University, College of Santa Fe, New York Public Library, Abilene Christian College, University of Texas (Austin), Texas A and M University, Southern Methodist University, University of Texas (El Paso), Midwestern University, University of Utah, and University of Virginia.

48. Ralph Emerson Twitchell, *The Spanish Archives of New Mexico*, 2 vols. (Glendale, Calif.: The Arthur H. Clark Co., 1914).

49. Virginia Langham Olmstead, *New Mexico Spanish and Mexican Colonial Censuses, 1790, 1823, 1845* (Albuquerque: New Mexico Genealogical Society, Inc., 1975), and *Spanish and Mexican Censuses of New Mexico, 1750–1830* (Albuquerque: New Mexico Genealogical Society, Inc., 1981).

50. Queries regarding original deeds should be sent to county clerks as follows: Bernalillo (P. O. Box 542, Albuquerque, NM 87103); San Miguel (Court House, Las Vegas, NM 87701); Taos (P.O. Box 676, Taos, NM 87571); Rio Arriba (P.O. Box 158, Tierra Amarilla, NM 87575); Valencia (P.O. Box 969, Los Lunas, NM 87031). The Santa Ana records are missing. Valencia County is the only one which admits to having Mexican period records (letter to the author from Debbie Ridley, Deputy Clerk of Valencia County, July 20, 1982). The other counties say that their Mexican period records are in the NMSRCA.

51. The Beinecke Library citation is as follows: ''N.M. (Province) Governador, 1835–1846 (Armijo). Official documents and reports signed by Armijo and other officials, 1823–1878, Mexico.'' The Beinecke call number is W.A./Ms/ S–986/N421.

52. Jess H. Stone, *A Guide to the Museum of New Mexico History Library* (Santa Fe: Museum of New Mexico, 1973).

53. Letter from John P. Wilson, Las Cruces, New Mexico, July 6, 1980. A copy of the catalog is available at the Museum of New Mexico and at the

NMSRCA. The University of New Mexico Law Library has applied for a grant to film this collection.

54. See the English translation by Marc Simmons, "Antonio Barreiro's 1833 Proclamation on Santa Fe City Government," *El Palacio* 76 (Summer 1970): 24–30.

55. B (Business records); D (Documents); F (Photographs); M (Manuscripts, Typescripts, Holographs); P (Papers); X (Photoprints, Xerox Copies, etc.); Y (Pamphlets).

56. Albert J. Díaz, *Manuscripts and Records in the University of New Mexico Library* (Albuquerque: University of New Mexico Library, 1957). See also "University of New Mexico Special Collections," NMHR 33 (July, October 1958): 235–51, 316–21, by the same author.

57. According to Tom Chávez, Associate Director for History of the Museum of New Mexico, the Coronado Room copy is the only extant edition of the Memorandum Book. Chávez prepared a dissertation on Alvarez, "The Life and Times of Manuel Alvarez, 1794–1856" (Ph.D., University of New Mexico, 1980).

58. In addition to a 106-page inventory prepared in 1972, these records are accessible by referring to a typed index divided as to case number and grant name. Case numbers refer to the U.S. Court of Private Land Claims.

59. See Chester V. Kielman, *Guide to the Microfilm Edition of the Béxar Archives, 1822–1836,* vol. 3 (Austin: The University of Texas Archives, 1971).

60. See also Frank D. Reeve, "The Charles Bent Papers," NMHR 29 (1954): 234–39, 311–17; 30 (1955): 154–67, 252–54, 340–52; 31 (1956): 75–77, 157–64, 251–53.

61. Chávez, *Archives of the Archdiocese,* pp. 3–4.

62. Beers, *Spanish and Mexican Records,* p. 71.

63. Chávez, *Archives of the Archdiocese,* pp. 4–5.

64. In the preface to his *Archives of the Archdiocese,* Chávez states that both the Utah Genealogical Society and the Huntington Library were given permission to microfilm the documents. The Genealogical Society completed its work in 1956. The NMSRCA gained permission to refilm the records in 1969. Eighty reels were filmed at this time, and ten more were added at a later date, making a total of ninety. Complete sets of the 1969 edition can be viewed at NMSRCA, the Special Collections Department of the University of New Mexico Library, the Golden Library at Eastern New Mexico University, and the Donnelly Library at New Mexico Highlands University. Other copies are in private hands, some complete, some not. Because additional copies will not be made, those in existence will prove increasingly valuable to researchers. The 1969 edition contains 80 reels. Ten reels were added at a later date, including Reel 82 which contains miscellaneous records of the 1811–1873 period. Letter from Mike Miller, Archivist, NMSRCA, September 24, 1982.

65. The Chancery is not open to the public, but researchers may call on Thursdays (505 268-4572) for consultation. A microfilm copy of the Archdiocese of Santa Fe records is on deposit here along with the original registers. In addition, the Chancery holds copies of the reels filmed by Vance Golightly Microfilm for the Genealogical Society of Utah. None of this material is available for loan. Registers B–40 and B–41 from the Church of Santa Cruz de la Cañada are also stored at the Chancery awaiting filming. Both registers are "Baptisms," the first covering the years 1844–50, and the second 1853–54.

66. Golightly is now out of business. Some of its negative microfilm was purchased by Southwest Microfilm, 2601 E. Yandell Drive, El Paso, TX 79903.

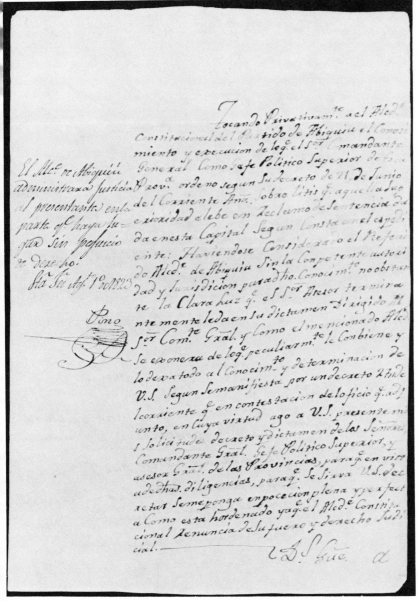

Order to the Alcalde Constitucional *of Abiquiu to administer justice according to the decree of June 21, 1823. Marginal notation by Juan Estevan Pino, August 1, 1823.* (Mexican Archives of New Mexico, *Governors Papers, Communications Received from within New Mexico. New Mexico State Records Center and Archives.) Photograph by Daniel Martinez.*

Bancroft Library, University of California, Berkeley. Photograph by Michael Mathes.

CHAPTER II

RECORDS IN OTHER STATES OF THE U.S.A.

Since the main purpose of this volume is to provide researchers with a general understanding of Mexican period source materials, it seems appropriate to identify collections in other states which pertain to this topic. Some microfilm publications and contemporary printed materials may have been overlooked, but all known manuscript collections have been included in the survey of states with which this chapter deals. It is hoped that students who do not live in New Mexico will be able to take advantage of libraries and archives close to home so that the high cost of out-of-state research can be put off as long as possible.

Outside of New Mexico, California and Texas have the best collections of manuscript and printed materials on the West and Latin America. The exceptional library and archive facilities in these two states, combined with a distinguished tradition of private collecting, have created excellent resource facilities such as the Bancroft and Huntington libraries and the multifaceted University of Texas libraries with their specialized segments. Readers who seek assistance through correspondence with professionals in these institutions will find them willing to clarify matters not sufficiently explained in this guide.

Other states mentioned herein have a few collections of less significance. The objective of this survey of sources is to locate primary materials, copies of primary materials, and contemporary printed materials such as broadsides, pamphlets, and other printed decrees. The reader should not expect to encounter references to the many published works of North American travelers and traders to New Mexico which are also valuable for comments on life and customs in New Mexico. These works, including some government reports, will

51

be found in a bibliography at the end of the book.

1. CALIFORNIA:

A. THE BANCROFT LIBRARY.   Hubert Howe Bancroft's failure as a miner proved to be a boon for historians interested in the West and Mexico. Beginning in 1860 when he brought together seventy-five volumes dealing with California, Oregon, Washington, and Utah, until 1905, when his vast collection of manuscripts and printed materials was purchased by the University of California, Bancroft worked continuously to gather materials and publish histories of the western United States and Mexico.[1]

The Bancroft Library is located at Berkeley in the middle of the University of California campus. A two-volume guide describes the manuscript collection. Volume I covers the entire West "from Alaska to Arizona and from Texas to Hawaii, with the exception of California."[2] It is arranged by geographic regions, essentially states, and within these divisions alphabetically by creator of the document(s). Volume II references manuscripts relating chiefly to Mexico and Central America. It is arranged alphabetically by author. Both of these volumes provide date and subject matter of the document(s), a brief description of contents, and an indication (HHB) if the materials belonged to the original Bancroft collection. The following collections pertain to New Mexico in the Mexican period.

(1) New Mexico Originals: In an article prepared for the *New Mexico Historical Review* by Fray Angélico Chávez, the author notes that the "New Mexico Originals" (NMO) consist of documents belonging originally to the "Spanish Archives of New Mexico."[3] In fact, the basis for this collection is the work of Alphonse Louis Pinart, a French scholar, who seems to have acquired original documents from the archives in Santa Fe during the 1870s.[4] Pinart loaned the collection to Bancroft for use in preparing his *History of Arizona and New Mexico, 1530–1888.*[5] Bancroft later acquired the collection, which, along with additional purchases, came to be known as the "New Mexico Originals." A few of the ninety-nine items in this collection pertain to the Mexican period:

(a) P-E 59: A list of *alcaldías* and collections made therefrom for the expenses of deputy Pedro Bautista Pino, signed by José Antonio Vizcarra and José Caballero, 1821–22.
(b) P-E 60: A listing of the officers of the presidial company of Santa Fe, including a statement of provisional salary adjustments for 1823.
(c) P-E 61: A letter from Juan Nepomuceno Almonte to Manuel Armijo, Aug. 9, 1841, acknowledging receipt of a communication of June 12, 1841.

(2) Other references for the Mexican period in New Mexico as cited in *A Guide*

to Manuscript Collections in the Bancroft Library:[6]

(a) P-E 223: Photocopy of a diary of Antonio Armijo of a journey from New Mexico to California and back, November 7, 1829, to April 25, 1830. Included in a letter dated May 14, 1830, from José Antonio Chávez to Lucas Alamán, Minister of Relations, this diary was originally found in the *Archivo General de la Nación (AGN), Fomento: Caminos,* vo. 8.

(b) P-E 238: A collection of letters, diary, and sketches reflecting the travels and business dealings of Alexander Barclay, an Englishman who worked at Bent's Fort from 1838 to 1842 before locating at the Hardscrabble settlement in 1844. His correspondence with Charles Bent, Thomas Fitzpatrick, Eugene Leitsendorfer, and others gives some insight into developments along the upper Arkansas River.

(c) P-E 30: Dictation of Thomas Oliver Boggs to H.H. Bancroft providing reminiscences of his business associations with Bent, St. Vrain, and Company during the 1844–1860 period.

(d) P-E 225: A typed transcript of Kit Carson's story as told by himself. The original is in the Newberry Library. This dictated autobiography tells how Carson came to New Mexico in 1826 and worked for Ewing Young as a cook, then as a guide and interpreter traveling through parts of New Mexico and Chihuahua. It describes his trapping adventures, battles with the Indians, travels to California, and other experiences of a full life.

(e) P-E 32: Dictation of Francisco López, a native New Mexican who participated in the revolution of 1837.

(f) P-E 203: This is a photoprint collection made of the Spanish Archives of New Mexico. The enlarged prints were copied from microfilm made by the Historical Records Survey of New Mexico during 1938–41.[7] Eighty-four volumes of documents pertaining to New Mexico during the Spanish period (1621–1820) are sometimes referred to as "Twitchell II documents" because of the calendar located in Ralph Emerson Twitchell's *The Spanish Archives of New Mexico,* Vol. II.[8] This collection has been supplemented by purchase of the Mexican Archives of New Mexico (MANM), which contains other official documents as well as those which were on deposit with the New Mexico State Records Center and Archives (NMSRCA) at the time of filming.

(g) P-E 204: These are photocopies of Mexican period documents collected and filmed by the Historical Records Survey of 1938–41. Only the first four of 154 volumes are calendared in Twitchell's *The Spanish Archives of New Mexico.* This collection is identical to that contained in the Zimmerman Library of the University of New Mexico with the exception that the latter includes two additional volumes of the Martínez Papers. In 1969, the Archives Division of the NMSRCA completed forty-two reels (there are now forty-three) of the official Mexican period records, including official documents from the holdings of the Zimmerman Library.

(h) Film P-E 231: Microfilm copy of the Benjamin M. Read papers. The originals belonged to the Historical Society of New Mexico before being transferred to the NMSRCA in 1961. Official records are filmed with the MANM (forty-three reels). This collection contains various decrees and instructions of the governor, dealings with Consul Manuel Alvarez, and letters to Alvarez from Charles Bent, Josiah Gregg, and others. Also included are papers of Donaciano Vigil and Read's own historical notes, correspondence, and clippings.

(i) P-E 233: Typed translation by George P. Hammond of the *diario* of the *ayuntamiento* of Santa Fe during the years 1829–36. The record is incomplete, but it contains discussions of water control, distribution, and ditch maintenance; damage done by animals running loose; the morality of the community; and the North American disrespect for Mexican laws. The original of this document is in the Zimmerman Library, University of New Mexico.

(j) P-E 230: Photocopies of baptisms, marriages, and deaths from the Iglesia de Nuestra Señora de Guadalupe, Taos. Extracts were made from the Santa Fe Archdiocesan Archives. They include the baptism, marriage, and burial of Kit Carson and his wife, Josefa Jaramillo.

(k) Film P-E 205: Records pertaining to land titles microfilmed by the University of New Mexico. Some are described in Twitchell's *Spanish Archives of New Mexico*. Others contain indexes and record books kept prior to the establishment of the Surveyor General's Office, including Donaciano Vigil's index and books; records of the Office of Surveyor General for New Mexico; and records of the U.S. Court of Private Claims. Formerly housed in the Bureau of Land Management, the originals are now in the NMSRCA.

(l) M-M 1735: Typescripts of papers relating to the trial, imprisonment, and damage suit of William G. Dryden, a U.S. citizen charged by the Mexican Government with being an accomplice in the 1841 Texan Santa Fe expedition. The file contains correspondence dating back to 1839. This is the only entry in Volume II of *A Guide to the Manuscript Collections of the Bancroft Library* which bears on New Mexico in the Mexican period. It is available on microfilm.

(3) Herbert E. Bolton Papers: Not included in the two-volume *Guide,* these materials, mostly typescripts, contain several items of interest.[9] Vivian Fisher's *Key to the Research Materials of Herbert Eugene Bolton,* available only at the Bancroft Library, is an excellent guide to this collection. It provides a brief description of each document as well as its source *(AGN, Archivo Militar,* etc.). The following selections pertain to New Mexico in the Mexican period:

(a) No. 343: Transcript of correspondence (19 pages) among Mexico, New Mexico, and Chihuahua (1826–27) regarding the penetration of North Americans into Mexico. Governor Antonio Narbona of New Mexico laments his shortage of troops, notes that Taos is a principal avenue of access, and decries the North American practice of seeking passports for the purpose of carrying on commerce in other regions of the frontier. Letters from Mexican ministers of state to the North American ambassador in Mexico, Joel Poinsett, indicate that this matter was of concern to both countries *(AGN: Gobernación).*

(b) No. 470: A typescript (1 page) of Governor Bartolomé Baca's response to news that an overland party from Kentucky was outfitting an expedition for New Mexico with the objectives of mining and selling contraband merchandise in the interior *(AGN: Gobernación).*

(c) No. 471: A transcribed text (24 pages) of documents from the *Archivo Militar* in Mexico City regarding encroachments of North Americans into Texas and New Mexico territories (1839–42). Correspondence includes letters from Manuel Arista, Refúgio de la Garza, John Morris, C. Van Ness, Manuel Armijo, and others.

(d) No. 472: Typescript of documents (6 pages) expressing the Mexican government's fear of North American encroachments *(AGN: Gobernación).*

(e) No. 688: Letters relating to the activities of Texans and Texas prisoners in central Mexico. This typescript of 164 pages includes letters from New Mexico's governor, Manuel Armijo *(Archivo Militar).*

(f) No. 690: Typescript of documents relating to military operations on the Mexican border prior to and at the beginning of the Mexican War. This 132-page text covers the years 1841–46 and includes correspondence of Manuel Armijo, Juan N. Almonte, and Isidro Reyes *(AGN: Relaciones Exteriores).*

(4) Microfilm Collections, *AGN:* When Herbert Eugene Bolton searched the *ramos* of the *AGN* for material relevant to the history of the United States, he was guided more toward the colonial period. This area was better organized, but Mexicans have also ignored the Mexican period because the loss of territory and other disturbances generated by war with the United States did not inspire research. Recently, scholars have shown more interest in these events. (See Chapter V.)

The Bancroft Library has microfilmed some of the same materials which Bolton copied. In the filming process the library did not attempt to correlate with what Bolton copied, but chose instead to film entire volumes. Even though there is no correlation between Bolton's Papers and the Bancroft's microfilm collection, the microfilm notebooks provide a reference (ex., *"BG,"* p.—) to additional descriptive information in Bolton's *Guide to Materials for the History of the U.S.*[10]

To use the microfilm, researchers should first consult the "Shelf List of Archival Film of Mexico" in the Microforms Division Office. The next step is to review the microfilm notebooks (binders), which provide more detailed document description. In most cases, compilers of these notebooks used the same description provided by Bolton in his *Guide,* but in the case of *Historia* and *Expulsión de Españoles* no description or calendar existed when the filming was being done.

Three *ramos* which include some material on New Mexico in the Mexican period are *Archivo Histórico de Hacienda, Expulsión de Españoles,* and *Gobernación.* Bolton's Guide, and some of his labeling, are to be used with caution due to the recent reorganization of the *AGN.* (See Chapter V.)

(a) *Archivo Histórico de Hacienda: Temporalidades, Legajo* 117: Pages 89–112 deal with the establishment of *aduanas* at Taos and San Miguel del Bado. Documentation deals with the temporary existence of an *aduana* at Santa Fe and concludes with remarks on the flow of contraband in the years 1836–44. Pages 113–16 contain additional information on contraband in New Mexico as well as other *noticias curiosas* (1839). *Legajo* 176: Includes information on the accounts of New Mexico's *aduana fronteriza y territorial* from July 1, 1834, to June 30, 1835. Other notebooks, manifestos, and a manual discuss accounting entries of the *aduana.*

(b) *Explusión de Españoles:* As noted above, there are no binder sheets guiding the researcher into the seventy-two volumes (65 reels) of this *ramo.* Fortunately, the *AGN* has published a two-volume guide (No. 26) which lists the volumes in numerical order and provides a brief description of the documents.[11] Several items relating to New Mexico in the 1827–30 period are to be found in both volumes.

(c) *Gobernación:* Formerly classified as *Casa Amarilla, Vol.* 120, this collection is made up of nineteenth-century documents dealing with both California and New Mexico. The New Mexico materials include information on the founding of a patriotic society in Santa Fe in 1832; fur trading and the perceived threat from North Americans; elections in New Mexico, 1830–31; the appointment of Santiago Abreú in 1832 as the *jefe político* of New Mexico, and various papers concerning the position of the *jefe político* in California and New Mexico in 1833.

(5) Microfilm Collections, Miscellaneous: In addition to the previously mentioned MANM and Spanish Archives of New Mexico (SANM), the library has a complete set of the microfilmed records of the *ayuntamiento* of Chihuahua, 1711–1890 (717 reels), the *Archivo Municipal* of Juárez (91 reels), and selected documents from the *Archivo Franciscano* of the *Biblioteca Nacional,* 1634–1826 (1 reel). It also has a three-reel collection entitled, "Mexico. Laws, Statutes, etc. *Bandos y comunicaciones oficiales, 1744–1843.*" This is a very useful assortment of printed decrees collected by the University of London.

Most important for New Mexico in the Mexican period is the collection of ninety-three reels of 16 mm film from the *Secretaría de la Defensa Nacional.* These documents were filmed by permission of the Mexican government in 1954–55. Selections were made with primary emphasis on California and the

American Southwest from the 1820s to the 1850s. The microfilm is available for consultation only in the Bancroft Library. It is not available for sale or Interlibrary Loan. The library also has three guides to the *Archivo Militar* where the documents were filmed. Volume I, the only published guide, covers the years 1821–47. Volumes II and III are carbon copies of typescripts and cover respectively the years 1848–55 and 1855–59.

(6) Miscellaneous: One of the finest libraries for students of the West, the Bancroft Library contains a number of rare books and secondary sources useful to researchers of the Mexican period. In addition, a number of typescript and manuscript sources dealing with the history of California hold promise of material germane to New Mexico. Since the fiscal year 1970–71, however, the library has added manuscript materials to only two of its collections: the papers of Alexander Barclay, and the diary and accounts of M.M. Marmaduke.[12] Because Marmaduke traveled through New Mexico in 1824–25 and commented on New Mexico and its inhabitants, his impressions are especially significant to this study.[13]

B. THE HUNTINGTON LIBRARY.   The Huntington Library, San Marino, is a complex composed of an art gallery, botanical gardens, and a superb research library for the study of British and American history and literature. The Research Library is divided into three areas: manuscripts, rare books, and reference books. The library's collections include many priceless works, such as Benjamin Franklin's *Autobiography* and Henry Thoreau's *Walden*. It also administers a publications program, resulting in the *Huntington Library Quarterly* and a number of scholarly books. Since it is such an active place for research, prospective users should write prior to a planned visit in order to ascertain the availability of needed materials. Letters should be directed to the Reader Services Librarian.

New Mexican materials for the Mexican period will be found either in the William G. Ritch Papers or the "Imprint File." Both contain primary sources, but the Ritch Papers are by far the best known and most useful. The chronological catalog of Americana should also be consulted.

(1) William G. Ritch Papers: Consisting of 2,274 pieces (folders containing one or more sheets), the Ritch Papers were acquired by the Huntington Library in 1928 from the estate of William G. Ritch, Secretary of the New Mexico Territory in the 1870s and president of the New Mexico Historical Society in 1880. Dealing chiefly with official life in New Mexico from 1539 to 1890, the collection is particularly good for official communications of the 1840–84 period, covering North American penetration of New Mexico, the Civil War, and Indian Affairs. Since the Ritch Papers contain a substantial number of official documents and have not been filmed in the MANM, they constitute an important source for the Mexican period.

In addition to correspondence, the papers include court records, church inventories, passport lists, decrees, censuses, and proclamations. Access to specific documents is through two card files organized alphabetically and by individual documents. A microfilm copy of the Ritch Papers (10 reels) is available in the Special Collections Department of the University of New Mexico Library. An additional eleventh reel includes the catalog cards prepared by the Huntington Library. The Special Collections Department of New Mexico has a separate index file which is identical to that filmed in San Marino except that it is arranged alphabetically while the filmed cards are arranged chronologically.[14]

Although the Ritch Papers contain too many documents for a complete listing in this guide, the following sampling will suggest the variety of information available on New Mexico in the Mexican period:

(a) 1823: Permission given by William Clark, Superintendent of Indian Affairs, St. Louis, to Carlos Beaubien and fifteen others to pass through Indian Country to Council Bluffs.

(b) 1824: Permission given by the commander of the Sixth Infantry Regiment, Ft. Atkinson, to Antoine Robidoux and party to pass through Indian Country to the border of Mexico.

(c) 1824: Letter to the Governor of New Mexico, Bartolomé Baca, from William Becknell, St. Louis, saying that he is not associated with other North Americans at Taos, but that he will take notes on their activities and will report to the governor when he next returns to Santa Fe in June.

(d) 1825: Record book (80 pages) listing the trade goods brought into New Mexico by various North Americans. Their value and the taxes paid are also mentioned. Included among the manifestos are those of Ewing Young, Richard Campbell, and the Robidoux brothers (Isidore, Antoine, and Michel).

(e) 1826: Letter from Santiago Abreú, New Mexico's delegate to the National Congress in Mexico City, to the *Diputación* of New Mexico warning that body to be suspicious towards any North Americans asking permission to travel through the territory. He asks for a list of all North Americans then residing in New Mexico as well as information on whether they have bought lands, married, or otherwise settled down as residents.

(f) 1826: Correspondence from George Sibley to the deputy alcalde of Taos explaining that he is on government business to survey a road to the Arkansas River with permission of the governor of New Mexico. He declines the alcalde's request to present himself for further instructions.

(g) 1827–77: Family record of Donaciano Vigil giving vital statistics and other information (six pages).

(h) 1828: Applications for a passport from John Pearson, Richard Campbell, Julian Greene, Ewing (Joaquin) Young, and Luke Murray, who say in their petition that they have done everything required of them by the law of June 6, 1826, and request the alcalde's approval so that the governor will provide them with passports.

(i) 1828: Book of passport registry. Among the 172 names mentioned are James (Santiago) Glen, David Waldo, Ceran St. Vrain (Sambrano), Richard Campbell, William Walker, and Strother Remick.

(j) 1829: A petition by Gervacio Nolan to the *Ayuntamiento de Taos* asking for a naturalization as a Mexican citizen. The petition notes that Nolan entered New Mexico in 1824, that he is an armorer by trade, that he is a good Roman Catholic, and that he is married to a Mexican. The petition is approved.

(k) 1829–31: Naturalization papers approved for the following: Charles Beaubien, Gervacio Nolan, John Rowland, Antoine Robidoux, Louis Robidoux, Richard Campbell, Joseph Thomas Boggs, William Wolfskill, Ceran St. Vrain, David Waldo.

(l) 1834–36: Custom House record book (thirty-seven pages) showing the traffic in imported goods and taxes paid on these items.

(m) 1835: An edict from Governor Albino Pérez including eleven articles concerned with the prohibition of arms sales to the Indians.

(n) 1837: Several documents having to do with the uprising of this year include a translated version of Manuel Armijo's *"Pronunciamiento"* of September 8, 1837, and an inventory of goods belonging to Santiago Abreú, who was killed in the fighting.

(o) 1838: Depositions and certificates testifying to the loyalty of Donaciano Vigil during the uprising of 1837 (seventeen pages).

(p) 1839: Manifesto presented to the *aduana* of Santa Fe by the merchant James (Santiago) Magoffin.

(q) 1845–46: Several documents having to do with Donaciano Vigil, including a certificate on his good conduct, a speech of 1846 to the legislature in Santa Fe, and his appointment as territorial secretary in the same year. Other drafts of letters and memoranda constitute twenty-eight pages of material.

(r) 1848–50: Correspondence between Manuel Armijo and Donaciano Vigil concerning the future of New Mexico and Armijo's personal status.

(s) 1877: Biography of P. Antonio José Martínez, the Taos *cura*, written by Santiago Valdez. This manuscript constitutes Reel No. 8 of the microfilm edition of the Ritch Papers.

(2) Huntington Library Imprint File: Newspapers, printed items, and some reports form part of this collection. The imprints are rare items printed through the year 1875 and arranged in the file according to place of publication, publisher, and date. Some rare book facsimiles of early titles are also included.[15] Several titles are noted here to suggest the value of this source:

(a) No. R127389: *Cuaderno de ortografía*. Dedicado a los niños de los Señores Martínez de Taos. Santa Fe: Imprenta de Ramon Abreú a cargo de Jesús María Baca. 1834. 11 unnumbered leaves.

(b) No. 119779: *El Payo de Nuevo-Mejico*. Periódico del gobierno del departamento . . . *Tomo* 1. Sábado 5 de Julio de 1845. Santa Fe: Imprenta del gobierno a cargo de J.M.B. Año de 1845. 2 leaves.

(c) No. 107962: *La Verdad*. Periódico del Nuevo-Mejico (Weekly). Santa Fe (?), 1844. *Tomo* 1, no.32 (12 Septiembre 1844).

(d) No. 206073: Martínez, Antonio José. *Cuaderno de cuentas que contiene las principales reglas de aritmética, especulativas y prácticas faciles a instruirse, aun con sóla su lectura y una poca de meditación, los jovenes aplicados a esta facultad.* Por el presbítero Antonio José Martínez cura de Taos. Impresa en la oficina del mismo a cargo de Jesús María Baca, 1836.

(e) No. 206072: R. Academia Española, Madrid. *Ortografía de la lengua castellana*, compuesta por la Real Academia Española. 9 edición notablemente reformada y corregida. Taos, reimpresa en la oficina del Sr. Cura D. Antonio José Martínez a cargo de Jesús María Baca, 1837. 99 pages.

(f) No. 127397: Martínez, Antonio José de, 1793–1867. *Relación de méritos del Presbítero Antonio José Martínez, domiciliario del obispado de Durango, cura encargado de Taos en el departamento de Nuevo Mexico.* Impresa en su oficina a cargo de Jesús María Baca, 1838. 34 pages.

(g) No. 206358: *Tramites de los jusgados inferiores en las materias que se siguen a solicitud de parte.* Taos, Nuevo Mexico, a cargo de J.M. Baca, 1838. 10 pages. Suplemento de 10 paginas, 1839.

(h) No. 436868: *Manualito de parrocos, para los autos del ministerio mas precisos y auxiliar a los enfermos.* Tomado del de él P. Juan Francisco López. Imprenta del Presbítero Antonio José Martínez a cargo de J.M. Baca, 1839. 52 pages.

(i) No number (not available): *Corto compendio que contiene ciertas advertencias de las letras, como se deletrean, leen, juntan a que se dice decorar, se pronuncian y escriben . . .* Imprenta del P.A.J.M. a cargo de J.M.B. año de 1841. 10 pages.

(j) No. 206359: Para de Phanjas, Francois. *Algunos puntos de lógica, tomados de la del autor Para, traducidos de Latín al castellano por el señor presbítero D. Antonio José Martínez para iniciar a sus discípulos en la forma silogística.* Imprenta del mismo a cargo de J.M.B. año de 1841. 12 pages.

(k) No. 206071: Alvarez, José María. *Instituciones de derecho real de Castilla y de Indias.* Por el Dr. D. José María Alvarez, catedrático de instituciones de Justiniano en la real y pontificia universidad de Guatemala. Tomados los lugares mas importantes de los tomos I, II, III y IV que hacen la obra para el curso, de los discípulos del P.A. José Martínez, en cuya imprenta fue reimpreso a cargo de J.M.B., 1842. 168 pages.

(l) No. 206356: *Terminos de facilitar espedición para el deletreo y pronuncio.* Imprenta del P.A.J.M. a cargo de J.M.B., año de 1842. 8 pages. At the end, in Martínez's own handwriting, are some remarks entitled, "Primeros elementos de filosofía."

(m) No. 72997: Martínez, Antonio José (supposed author). *Historia consisa del cura de Taos Antonio José Martínez.* Taos, May 4, 1851. Imprenta de Vicente F. Romero. At the end, it is signed, "El Historiador." Very similar in style to his *Relación de Méritos . . .* 1838.

(3) Miscellaneous, Chronological Catalog: The following items have been copied from the chronological catalog of Americana in the Huntington Library (1493–1900). Some are specific to New Mexico while others are of general interest to scholars of the Mexican period:

(a) No. 202369: Printed circular (8 pages) entitled, *Noticia Al Público, I Por Disposición Del Exelentisimo SR. Gobernador y Comandante General Deste Departamento de Nuevo Mexico, sobre los resultados de la Campaña última al enemigo Nabajo. Manuel Armijo Gobernador y Comandante General del Departamento de Nuevo Mejico a sus Conciudadanos, Mis Amigos . . .* Includes the diary of operations of Mariano Chávez, Dec. 3, 1839, diary of the campaign against the Navajo, October 13, 1839, and diary of the campaign of Juan Andrés Archuleta, Dec. 13, 1839. [1839 Military Records in MANM include information on Archuleta's expedition. See Reel No.29, frames 1109ff.] These reports were printed in 1849.

(b) No. 256908: Mexico. Constitution, 1824. *Acta constitutiva de la Federación mexicana.* 8 pages.

(c) No. 256909: Mexico. Congreso Constituyente, 1824. *Decretos del congreso general constituyente de los Estados-Unidos Mexicanos.* 4 pages.

(d) No. 72884: Mexico. *Gaceta del gobierno supremo de la Federación Mexicana.* May 27, 1826.

(e) No number (not available): Mexico. Laws, statutes, etc. *Colección de los decretos y ordenes de la Cortes de España, que se reputan vigentes en la República de los Estados-Unidos Mexicanos.* 1829. 216 pages.

(f) No. R202368: Mexico. Laws, Statutes, etc. *Recopilación de leyes, decretos, bandos, reglamentos, circulares y providencias de los supremos poderes y otras autoridades de la República mexicana. Formada de orden del supremo gobierno por el Lic. Basilio José Arrillaga.* 1834–50.

(g) No. 49662: New Mexico *(Territorio) Jefe político y militar, 1835–37,* broadside dated June 26, 1835. This is a statement of Albino Pérez to New Mexicans.

(h) No number (not available): Mexico. *Ejército. Tarifa de los sueldos líquidos que disfrutan todas las clases del ejército.* 1838. 122 pages.

(i) No. R207066: New Mexico (Department) Gobernador, 1838–46 (Armijo). *El Gobernador constitucional y comandante principal del departamento de Nuevo Mejico a sus habitantes.* March 6, 1839.

(j) No. 49550: New Mexico (Department) Gobernador, 1838–46 (Armijo). *El gobernador y comandante general del departamento a Nuevo Mexico a sus habitantes.* 1841.

(k) No. 201803: Mexico. *Estado mayor del ejército . . . Noticia histórica de todos los cuerpos del ejército nacional, que desde 1821 han existido y existen actualmente.* 1845. 80 pages.

(4) Miscellaneous: A few manuscripts may be found in the *Guide to American Historical Manuscripts in the Huntington Library* (San Marino: Huntington Library, 1979). Since these are substantial collections ranging over many subjects, they may prove useful to scholars seeking a broader perspective on New Mexico.

   (a) Benjamin Davis Wilson Papers. 3,500 pieces deal principally with California but include information on the Santa Fe trade. The collection is described by John Walton Caughey in "Don Benito Wilson: An Average Southern Californian," *Huntington Library Quarterly* 2 (1938–39): 285–300.

   (b) California Historical Documents Collection. 162 pieces, 1812–1912, which concern, among other subjects, the activities of John Rowland in New Mexico and California (1835–65).

   (c) Dale Lowell Morgan Collection. Approximately 2,000 pieces (ca. 1809–57) dealing with the opening, exploration, and settlement of the West, Indians, and the Santa Fe trade. Many pieces are typewritten copies of newspaper items.

The Huntington Library also has a microfilm collection including select items from the Bancroft Library, the Department of State (consular despatches), the BLM, the *AGN,* and a complete set of the MANM. All of these collections have been described in Chapters I and II.

   C. THE SOUTHWEST MUSEUM RESEARCH LIBRARY. Specializing in Indian ethnology in the Western Hemisphere and Western Americana, the Southwest Museum contains limited source material on New Mexico in the Mexican period. The existing collections reflect the generosity of many donors, however, and it is not without possibility that additional New Mexicana will be acquired in the future.

   The Southwest Museum is located high on a hill in Highland Park, just off the Pasadena Freeway (Exit 143). Fittingly close to the home of Charles Fletcher Lummis, who contributed significantly to the building of the research collection, the Museum contains a variety of Southwest Americana. Unfortunately, no guide, calendar, or published finding aid exists for entry into the documents. In fact, the Southwest Museum is still in the process of organizing and cataloging its archival materials, and researchers will find that this state of affairs militates against free and open access to the collections. On the other hand, a determined investigation, very much like what is necessary in Mexican archives, may turn up a number of treasures. Preliminary efforts in this direction have produced the following:[16]

(1) Museum Archives

(a) MS No. 594: Wolfskill, William. Ledger, Taos, N.M. 1830–32. (Copied from the original account book by the courtesy of Mrs. Marcella Wolfskill Palethorpe, great-granddaughter of William Wolfskill.) The ledger mentions Ceran St. Vrain, Ewing Young, and others and discusses credits and debits regarding the purchase of goods used by fur traders in the Central Rockies.

(b) MS No. 204: Translations of Spanish language documents from the files of the U.S. Public Survey Office and the Historical Society of New Mexico were done by, and were a gift of, the Works Progress Administration. For the Mexican period, the collection contains 185 documents. Most are official in nature and therefore included in the MANM. In addition to the materials on Indians, this collection includes letters from the Bishop of Durango, correspondence dealing with mining in New Mexico, petitions for land, and rules and regulations regarding foreigners.

(c) MS No. 647: San Ildefonso, *Libro de Entierros* (1725–1840). This valuable record of deaths for the Pueblo of San Ildefonso lists not only the names of the dead but the priests in attendance, the race, age, and marital status of the deceased, and some interesting comments about why certain priests refused to provide the sacrament of extreme unction (*"Porque no havisaron,"* etc.).

(d) MS No. 648: *Confirmaciones celebradas en el Pueblo de San Lorenzo de Picurís por el Iltm͞o. S͞o͞r. D. José Antonio Laureano de Zubiría Dignissimo Obispo de la Diócesis hoy 29 [y 30] de Junio de 1833*. The name of each child confirmed is listed, along with his mother, father, padrino, and madrina.

(e) MS No. 649: Declaration of Intention to Wed, 1836, of Fernando Ortiz and Blas Medina at Santa Cruz de la Cañada.

(f) MS No. 650: Photocopy of a treaty between Mescalero and Gileño Apaches, August 30, 1832, Chihuahua, signed by Cayetano Justiniani and José Joaquín Calvo. The original is in the Bancroft Library. An English translation is provided.

(g) MS No. 651: Santiago Kirker. An article, "Don Santiago Kirker," *Santa Fe Republican*, November 20, 1847; and *Actas de la Sociedad de Guerra contra los Apaches* . . . Chihuahua, Imprenta del Gobierno, 1839. 4 pages.

D. CALIFORNIA STATE LIBRARY, SUTRO BRANCH. Mexican period research in California is not complete without a visit to the Sutro Branch of the California State Library in San Francisco. In 1889 Adolph Sutro bought an entire bookshop located in Mexico City. It contained most of the volumes from a seminary founded in the sixteenth century as well as very rare law books and theological works. Combined with the purchase of most Mexican pamphlets published between 1623 and 1888, these collected works came to be known as the Sutro Mexican Collection. Along with the University of Texas Latin American Collection, the Sutro Library has the largest holding of Mexican pamphlets.[17]

This pamphlet collection contains approximately 30,000 Mexican pamphlets, occupying nearly two-hundred linear feet of space. A card catalog, organized according to authors and various Mexican secretariats, directs researchers to titles dealing with politics, religion, government, statistics, and literature. For the Mexican period of New Mexico, there are various reports dealing with Apaches and other Indian problems along the northern frontier; instructions for implementing the Lancasterian System in Mexico's schools; expulsion of the Spaniards; *memorias* by public officials completing their terms in office; and several lengthy reports by José Agustín de Escudero, a lawyer whose writings about New Mexico form an important part of the literature available on the Mexican period in New Mexico.[18]

Through the efforts of Michael Mathes, the entire Mexican Pamphlet Collection has been microfilmed in cooperation with Lic. Juan López, *cronista* of the city of Guadalajara, Mexico. Positive copies of the film are available from Bay Microfilm, Inc. (737 Loma Verde Avenue, Palo Alto, California 94303).[19] About ninety-five percent of the collection titles are published in a chronological catalog with brief descriptions of each pamphlet.[20] Taken altogether, the Mexican Pamphlet Collection is a great source of information on Mexican points of view, including laws, *bandos,* decrees, broadsides, and private opinion. As a simple grouping of collected works, it is an outstanding source for Mexican research; as a source for the Mexican period, it will prove extremely valuable for putting New Mexico in national perspective.

2. ARIZONA:

A. Documentary Relations of the Southwest (DRSW). Although the DRSW has concentrated on Spanish colonial documents, the scope of this project eventually will encompass material from the Mexican period. Furthermore, the work being done by Dr. Charles W. Polzer, S.J., Associate Director[21] of the DRSW at the Arizona State Museum, and his staff is significant to Mexican period researchers because of information collected on translation problems, standards of measure, and other technical aspects of working with Spanish language documents that deal with Mexico's northern frontier.

The DRSW project was designed to publish select documents dealing with ethnohistory, cultural heritage, and humanities of the American Southwest.[22] Three volumes are planned: (1) Jesuit Relations of the Southwest; (2) Franciscan Relations of the Southwest; and (3) Civil-Military Relations of the Southwest. Additionally, the staff has completed two master indexes, DRSW I and II, which put in computer-readable form a reference tool of archival materials relating to the entire Southwest.[23] Master Indexes III and IV will not be worked on until funding improves, but the DRSW is continuing to develop the BIOFILE Southwest with money from the National Endowment for the Humanities.

An outgrowth of DRSW I and II, this project will be an historically focused encyclopedia of significant personages who lived during the colonial period of what is now the American Southwest.

Although the DRSW project has concentrated on Arizona and Sonora in the Spanish colonial period, neglecting New Mexico because it had been worked over most thoroughly in the past,[24] SANM II has already been filmed and the filming of Part I is presently under consideration. Other projects under way include a two-volume study of the presidial system in northern New Spain, a documentary study of Seri ethnohistory, and a three-volume set dealing with Jesuit missions in northwestern New Spain, 1744–45.

Most useful to those interested in the Mexican period of New Mexico is the first publication of the DRSW, *Northern New Spain, A Research Guide*. Combining their original plans to publish a "manual" and "source book" in one research guide,[25] this very informative volume contains a great deal of linguistic, bibliographic, and historical information applicable to the Mexican period. Individual chapters explain the nature of Spanish documents, paleography, documentary collections in the United States and Mexico, guides to these collections, the structure of colonial government, the nature of money, weights and measures, names of Indian tribes, and racial terminology. Maps, a glossary, and a bibliography divided by subjects make this an exceptionally useful researcher's tool. Even though many Hispanic institutions changed during the Mexican period, the essence of Borderlands communities, as well as the language of the people who inhabited this area, evolved very slowly after 1821. The authors of *Northern New Spain, A Research Guide* have taken an important first step in orienting contemporary scholars toward a better understanding of the documents pertaining to Hispano-Indian affairs in what is now the American Southwest.

B. MISCELLANEOUS. Mexican period scholars interested in Indian policy, Borderlands travelers, cooperative defense projects, and trader-trappers will want to look at the state archives of Sonora. The civil jurisdiction of the state extended to the Colorado and Gila rivers, thus embracing the southern portion of what is now Arizona. Records were kept at various places, including Arizpe and Hermosillo, but because of disturbances which followed independence, many were destroyed.[26] Nevertheless, Hermosillo became the permanent capital of Sonora in 1878, and it was here that the *Archivo Histórico del Estado de Sonora* was located.

The Sonora-New Mexico contact evolved on military and economic lines. Both areas struggled with Apaches and occasionally joined forces to restrict their activities. Meanwhile, Sonoran traders exchanged mules and silver in Santa Fe for dry goods brought in by North Americans, and Sinaloans carried salt, seafoods, and *panocha* (unrefined dark sugar) to Chihuahua and Durango.

Livestock were also taken to New Mexico along with livestock by-products: "hides, tallow, salted beer, finished leather goods, candles, and soap."[27] A few foreign merchants settled in Sonora and made yearly trips to New Mexico. The significance of this nexus has not been studied.

In 1966, the Arizona Historical Society in collaboration with the *Instituto Nacional de Antropología e Historia* microfilmed part of the "800,000 pages of official correspondence, reports, memoranda, executive decrees, minutes, and debates of the state legislature; judicial records; and other materials dating from the early years of the eighteenth century."[28] Fr. Kieran McCarty and Wisberto Jiménez Moreno went to the University of Sonora Library where the documents were housed in order to select those suitable for microfilming. The result was fifty-two reels of film. A master copy is located at the Arizona Heritage Center (Tucson), and a partial copy (Reels 5–46) is available at the Hayden Library, Arizona State University at Tempe.[29]

McCarty and Jiménez selected documents for filming related to the history of Arizona. Some of these materials deal tangentially with New Mexico. In addition to an unpublished sketch prepared by McCarty of the contents of the microfilm, a 3 x 5 card index of most of the state archive was compiled in Hermosillo and is available to researchers in the Arizona Heritage Center. It is this index which has the most promise for unearthing New Mexico material.

Two other publications may prove useful. Cynthia Radding de Murrieta and María Lourdes Torres Chávez compiled a catalog of some of the contents of the same state archive.[30] Their published work only scratches the surface of documentation available in the state archives. Another useful source is the second volume of McCarty's *Desert Documentary* covering the Mexican period. This collection of documents will be published by the Arizona Historical Society. It covers the years 1821 to 1846 and is based largely on the microfilm publication of the state archives of Sonora plus a few collections located in other archives.[31]

3. COLORADO:

A book recently published by the Museum of New Mexico entitled *A Dictionary of New Mexico and Southern Colorado Spanish* by Rubén Cobos makes it clear that the Mexican culture of the Rio Grande extended into what is now southern Colorado. The people who lived in Chimayó, Española, El Rito, Peñasco, Taos, Mora, and Chama had much in common with settlers in the Colorado communities of Antonito, Conejos, La Jara, Alamosa, Fort Garland, San Luis, Walsenburg, Trinidad, and La Junta.[32]

Unfortunately, Colorado has shown relatively little interest in its Hispanic roots. One crosses the border from New Mexico into Colorado and suddenly the Spanish language, culture, and traditions appear to be in conflict with the dominant Anglo-Saxon society. This is partly due to the role played by Hispanic people as urban and agricultural workers, but it is also a reflection of the isolation of Hispanic settlements in southern Colorado, far removed from the mainstream of developments along the Front Range. A few histories have evaluated the contributions of these *primeros pobladores* who came from New Mexico to live in Colorado.[33] But even though most of what is now southern Colorado, from the Arkansas River to the border with Mexico and along the Rio Grande in the San Luis Valley, was first settled by Spanish-speaking people,[34] the historical record of their activities remains poorly documented in Colorado archives. This is understandable, as Santa Fe was New Mexico's administrative capital during the Mexican period. Land grant records for Colorado between 1821 and 1846 will be found in the MANM, SANM I, and in other repositories controlled by the BLM and the state of New Mexico. (See Chapter I.) But archives and libraries in Colorado possessing copies of these materials are relatively few. The Mexican heritage has not been a matter of great interest to non-Hispanic Coloradans.

The Center of Southwest Studies at Fort Lewis College in Durango has made an attempt to address this problem. Although the bulk of its materials relating to the Southwest reflects a predominant interest in the American period, the Center has acquired a copy of both the SANM and the MANM microfilm. It also has some government documents on microfilm, some unpublished dissertations dealing with the Mexican Southwest, and an excellent collection on the Utes.

The Pioneers' Museum in Colorado Springs has the Francis Whittemore Cragin Collection. These materials include letters from George Bent, an 1844 drawing of Bent's Fort, and various other items from the Mexican period.[35]

At the Denver Public Library in the Western History Collection, researchers will find diaries, reports, and journals of fur traders, Santa Fe traders, and government explorers. Titles pertinent to this study will be found in Henry R. Wagner and Charles L. Camp, *The Plains and the Rockies. A Bibliography of Original Narratives of Travel and Adventure, 1800–1865*.[36] Volumes too fragile to extract from the vault, or non-existent in the holdings of the Western History Collection, can be viewed in the microfilm publication of the western history holdings of the Beinecke and Newberry libraries.[37]

In addition to the microfilm publications of the SANM and MANM, the Western History Collection at the Denver Public Library recently received the Harold H. Dunham Papers. These materials reflect the work of Professor Dunham on Spanish and Mexican land grants. Included in the seven boxes are his personal notes and clippings, Indian land claims, and biographical data on various figures in the Mexican period. An index and inventory have been prepared.

4. UTAH:

A. GENEALOGICAL SOCIETY OF UTAH.   Although the Genealogical

Society of Utah was founded in 1894 to provide church members with easier access to records, the filming of vital birth, death, and marriage documents did not begin until 1938. Since that time the society has created the largest archive of its kind in the world, with film crews that operate in forty countries and add forty thousand reels a year to the collection.[38] Mexican material alone amounts to 111,000 reels.[39]

Mexicans have cooperated eagerly with the society. Recognizing that many parish records and other church documents suffered from past neglect, the *Academia Mexicana de Genealogía y Heráldica* has assisted the society's film crews in gaining access to ecclesiastical records. A working partnership between the society and the *Academia* has proved beneficial to both countries. The society maintains a master copy of all film in its Granite Mountain Vault and loans out positive copies to 380 branch libraries throughout the world. In Mexico City, the *Academia* has established the *Archivo Microfílmeco de Genealogía* (known informally as the *Archivo de los Mormones*), which contains a copy of everything filmed in Mexico by the Genealogical Society of Utah.

Those using the microfilm either in Utah or in Mexico City will need to be familiar with the *Preliminary Survey to the Mexican Collection* and the *Supplement*.[40] Arranged alphabetically by state and territory, these two finding aids list the parish, record types, dates covered, number of reels, and a coding which tells researchers what the documents contain, i.e., confirmation records, marriage information, baptismal records by caste, death records, wills, church records, divorces, criminal cases, guardianship records, adoptions, and other items. The provenance of most records is either the parochial archive for church records or the state archive for civil records. Since some parish records remain unfilmed, the work of the Genealogical Society of Utah is incomplete.[41] Used in combination with other microfilm collections of ecclesiastical records of New Mexico, however, this source will prove invaluable to Mexican period research.

In 1956, the Genealogical Society contracted with Vance Golightly Microfilms to film the records of the Archdiocese of Santa Fe. This collection of several hundred reels (including registers not filmed in 1956) is accessible through microfiche available at branch libraries (LDS Stake churches). A microfilm card catalog (MCC) contains the most current information on the holdings of the society's main library in Salt Lake City. Searching for Mexican period data will be facilitated if researchers know the name of the church and the county in which it is located.

B. OTHER SOURCES IN UTAH.   Two universities in Utah have Mexican period holdings. The Microforms Department at the University of Utah Library contains the MANM collection plus some material filmed in the 1950s by the Benjamin Franklin Library in Mexico City from the *ramos Historia* (5 reels) and *Provincias Internas* (9 reels) of the *AGN*. Another collection cited as "New Mexico Archives, 1694–1843" (108 reels) represents the work of the Historical Records Survey of New Mexico during 1938–41. With material and equipment supplied by the University of New Mexico, Spanish and Mexican records, then housed at the Museum of New Mexico, were filmed for the first time. Photoprints of this film are located at the Bancroft and University of New Mexico libraries.[42]

In addition to the microfilm, two collections of papers contain materials relating to Indians and Indian-Mexican contact during the 1821–48 period. These are the S. Lyman Tyler and C. Gregory Crampton papers. Both are housed in the Special Collections department of the Marriott Library at the University of Utah. Many collections of papers dealing with the West are generated by the university's American West Center, but all of them are preserved and cataloged in the Special Collections Department of the main library.

A very important collection of Mexican period documents is awaiting final inventory at Brigham Young University. Purchased as part of the same Kenneth Sender collection discussed in Chapter I, these materials represent some of the lost records of Santa Cruz de la Cañada. A preliminary list prepared by the dealer who sold the documents to BYU reveals the following items:[43]

(1) 1822 November 22—*Facundo Melgares*. Original signed document, 3 pp., 8'' x 10'', Albuquerque. Colonel D. Facundo Melgares gives the charge as the provisional governor of New Mexico to Captain D. José Antonio Viscarra according to the order of October 12 from the General Commander. Files and papers are also put into his hands (papers are listed in the document).

(2) 1824 March 12—*Bartolomé Baca*. Original signed document, 2 pp., 8'' x 10'', Santa Fe. Instructions from the central government to the municipal government.

(3) 1824 March 28—*Mariano Chávez*. 2 pp., 8'' x 10'', Santa Cruz de la Cañada. A long dissertation concerning elections in Santa Cruz and verification of their elections to the various positions available.

(4) 1825 January 1—*Mariano Chávez*. 1 p., 8'' x 10'', Santa Cruz de la Cañada. By order of Don Mariano Chávez, mayor of the village, all elected officials are to assemble for the purpose of retiring and electing new members.

(5) 1826 January 7—*Antonio Narbona*. Original signed document, 2 pp., Santa Fe. A memorandum for instructions on directing tax collections and suggesting that Don Juan Ortiz be relieved of responsibilities of supervisor and collection of the same.

(6) 1826 February 11—*Antonio Narbona*. Original signed document, 2 pp., 8½'' x 10'', Santa Fe (Governor 1825–1827). A letter to the Constitutional Mayor of Cañada, Don Apolinario López, criticizing his lenience to Manuel Vigil and Antonio Bustos, and advising him to prosecute the same.

(7) 1827 May 2—*Antonio Narbona*. Broadside, 2 pp., 8½'' x 10'', Mexico City, March 16, 1827. Enactment by the President of the United States of Mexico concerning tariffs on cotton goods, etc. Signed and acknowledged in Santa Fe on May 2nd, 1827, by Antonio Narbona.

(8) 1827 March 24—*Antonio Narbona*. Broadside, 1 p., 8½'' x 10'', Mexico City, March 24, 1827. Announcement from the President of the United States of Mexico that the General Assembly has agreed to send if necessary as many as 3,000 men from the local militia to the state of Durango. Signed and acknowledged in Santa Fe, May 15th, 1827, by Antonio Narbona.

(9) 1827 August 13—*Manuel Armijo*. 2 pp., 8'' x 12'', Santa Fe. A short letter to the mayor of La Cañada for the apprehension of the criminal José Apestiequía and his companion whose nickname is "Cuchefeo."

(10) 1828 January 19—*Manuel Armijo*. 4 pp., 8'' x 10'', Santa Fe. A letter to the mayors of San Juan, Abiquiú, and Taos. He says that army deserters should first have a preliminary trial and then be sent back to their battalion with the results of the trial. This would save the expense of sending them to jail.

(11) 1828 August 28—*Joseph Pablo Martín*. 1 p., 8'' x 12'', Santa Cruz de la Cañada. Chief Mayor Joseph Pablo Martín officially informs the parish priest Don Manuel de Jesús Rada that he is to bury within the church the bodies of all persons who die from this time on.

(12) 1828 November 13—*Manuel de Jesús Rada*. Broadside, 2 pp., Chihuahua, Mexico. A long dissertation as a representative of New Mexico and the honor this affords him for the appointment.

(13) 1825 January 2—*Mariano Chávez*. 2 pp., 8½'' x 12'', Santa Cruz de la Cañada. This manuscript contains the results of the election taking place in Santa Cruz. It includes the candidates and persons elected, and the proceedings of the same.

(14) 1829 May 7—*(Padre) Antonio José Martínez*. 11 pp., 8½'' x 10'', signed will, San Fernando de Taos. Last will and testament of his mother. On first page is written: "Distribution of the testament of the late Doña María del Cosmel Santiestevan, who died in the year of 1829 as the firstborn of the same Don José Martínez.

"In San Geronimo de Taos, May 7, 1829, I Priest don Antonio José Martínez by verbal command of the late Doña María del Cosmel Santiestevan, I proceed to give destiny to her possessions subjected to her will. This was approved by the Bishop of Durango."

(15) 1830 March 21—*José Ignacio Ortiz*. 1 p., 8½'' x 10'', Santa Fe. A long dissertation on the counterfeiting of money and the filthiness of the public streets.

(16) 1830 June 11—*José Antonio Chávez*. 3 pp., 8'' x 12'', Santa Fe. A short letter to the second commander of the Villa de Cañada describing the difficulties of preparing a trial to prosecute a Mr. Diego Martín.

(17) 1831 January 26—*Anastasio Bustamante—Rafael Mangino*. Broadside, 3 pp., 8'' x 10'', Palace of the Federal Government, New Mexico, January 26. A long list of regulations pertaining to the administrative offices of the government and salaries, etc.

(18) 1833 January 21—*Santiago Abreú*. 2 pp., 8'' x 12'', Santa Fe (Governor 1831–33). Abreú explains that he has just received news that a new Mexican president, Don Manuel Gómez Pedraza, has been elected and agreements have been reached between Vice President Don Anastasio Bustamante and Don Antonio López de Santa Anna and tranquility has been secured.

(19) 1833 March 8—*(Padre) Antonio José Martínez*. 3 pp., 8 vo., original signed document, San Geronimo de Taos. *Hijuela* (Schedule of Partition) of Juan Pascual Martínez, 1833. Third portion of will of his father Don Severino Martínez. Signed and acknowledged by Carlos Beaubien.

(20) 1833 April 29—*Santiago Abreú*. 1 p., 4½'' x 8''. Payment of one gallon of brandy purchased by Manuel Alvarez from Thomas Massie.

(21) 1833 August 12—*R.H. Weightman*. 1 p., 8½'' x 8½''. Letter from Weightman authorizing Manuel Alvarez to pick up his mail.

(22) 1834 May 25—*Francisco Sarracino*. 2 pp., 8½'' x 8½'', Santa Fe. Short dissertation concerning the Reverend Corps and the difficulty of obtaining enlistments.

(23) 1835 January 3—*Francisco Sarracino*. Broadside, 1 p., 8'' x 12'', Santa Fe. The broadside discusses the friction arising between the municipal and central governments over nomination of D. Juan Estevan Pino for commission of brokers. It advises the municipalities to respect the authority of the government.

(24) 1835 January 13—*David V. Whiting*. 1 p., 7½'' x 10'', Santa Fe. The appointment of Manuel Alvarez as building commissioner.

(25) 1835 November 21—*Vallejo*. 1 p., 8½'' x 9'', Mexico. Concerns designation of ports open to coastal trade such as the ports of Tuxpan in the department of Pueblo, etc.

(26) 1837 December 21—*Juan Rafael Ortiz*. 1 p., 8'' x 12'', Santa Fe. A short note to the mayor of Santa Clara notifying him that he has received the act of elections performed in the city hall for the councilmen for the next year (1837).

(27) 1839 June 3—*Don Pablo Lucero*. 2 pp., 8 vo., San Geronimo de Taos. Don Pablo Lucero, first Justice of the Peace conducts and reviews a conflict of financial interest between Don José de Jesús Branchi and Don Blas Trujillo. Document signed by both parties and Stephen L. Lee.

(28) 1840 April 24—*Charles Bent*. 2 pp., 8'' x 9½'', Taos, New Mexico. A short note to Manuel Alvarez concerning shipments of buffalo robes to the United States and other matters.

(29) 1840 June 24—*José Valverde*. 3 pp., 6'' x 8½'', Santa Fe. A short note to Manuel Alvarez stating that he paid David Alexandro a sum of money owed to him.

(30) 1841 March 28—*Manuel Alvarez*. 1 p., 8'' x 10'', Santa Fe. An inventory of goods from the estate of David White.

(31) 1842 September 23—*William G. Doyden* [sic]. 3 pp., 8½'' x 10½'', Chihuahua, Mexico. Letter to the United States Consul in Santa Fe, Manuel Alvarez, that he had been shipwrecked on the coast of Texas and that Manuel Armijo had sent false information concerning the matter and that was the reason he was being held in jail in Mexico. He needs documentation as to what happened signed by Alvarez so he can be released.

(32) 1842 October 28—*Antonio Sena*. 1 p., 8½'' x 10''. Receipt of money received by Don Manuel Alvarez. Debt from Don Manuel Armijo.

(33) 1844 June 26—*Abott E. Stanley*. 3 pp., 8½'' x 9½'', Boonville, Texas. Letter to Manuel Alvarez stating that the murderers of Antonio José Cháves had been pardoned with the exception of W. Daniels.

(34) 1844 November 19—*Antonio Sena*. 1 p., 8'' x 12'', Santa Fe. To Don Manuel Alvarez. In a short letter he states that he took the oath of office for the prefect of that district.

(35) 1844 September 10—*Juan Bautista Vigil y Alarid*. 6 pp., 8½'' x 10'', Santa Fe. The Constitutional Assembly of the Department of New Mexico. Contains the laws and decrees passed by the assembly.

(36) 1845 March 9—*Charles Bent*. 1 p., 7½'' x 5'', Santa Fe. Bent asks Manuel Alvarez to pay three hundred dollars to the Leitensdorfer brothers.

(37) 1845 April 30—*Mariano Martínez de Lejarza*. Graduate General of the Mexican Army, Governor and General Commander of the Department of New Mexico. 2 pp., 8'' x 10'', Santa Fe. Short acknowledgment by Martínez that Captain Don Donaciano Vigil served in his company (Bado) for a period of eighteen months and his service was very commendable.

(38) 1845 May 10—*Francisco García Conde*. General in Chief of the Fifth Division of The Army. Broadside, 1 p., 8'' x 10'', Durango. To the inhabitants of the department of Durango, Chihuahua, and New Mexico. A long dissertation on the current difficulties of the times and the advantages of liberty to be gained by remaining united.

(39) 1845 July 21—*El Payo de Nuevo Mexico, Prospecto*. Broadside, 8'' x 10'', Santa Fe. Printing of the Government under Jesús María Baca. Announcement of a new newspaper to be published in the capital replacing the *Verdad*. A short dissertation of what the contents of the paper will be.

(40) 1846 November 29—*Joachim Zamorano*. Original signed documents, 2 pp., 8'' x 10''. Request by Joachim Zamorano of a small portion of land adjacent to two portions of property already owned. He begs that the small portion of land be donated to him.

At the bottom of the document it is stated that the title to the small parcel of land is registered in Book A, page 103; ''in my office which I certify with my signature and seal.

Santa Fe, March 29, 1846
Donaciano Vigil''
(41) 1846 July 16—*Manuel Armijo*. Torn document. 1 p., 8½'' x 10'', Santa Fe. States to give Mr. Nocolas [sic], 12 pesos for work done on the document not specified. Signed Bent and McKnight.
(42) 1847 September 4—*Leonardo Padilla, Als.* 2 pp., 8¼'' x 12¼''. He explains a letter sent to him by Santa Anna defining the disposition of articles obtained from enemy occupied territory.
(43) 1847 January 25—*Donaciano Vigil*. Broadside, 1 p., 4 vo., Santa Fe. A short dissertation on the gang of Pablo Montoya y Cortéz which has been terrorizing Taos and Mora. Mention is made of the apprehension of the conspirators in the future who will be duly punished for their crimes.

5. KANSAS:

The Kansas State Historical Society in Topeka has an excellent collection of library materials on the Santa Fe Trail. The society's library alone has approximately seven-hundred cataloged references on this subject.[44] The Manuscript Division contains private papers dealing with route surveys, reports of journeys to New Mexico, and opinions regarding the obstacles to commerce presented by Mexican taxes and Indian depredations. Some documents are newspaper articles or microfilmed copies from collections in other states. An unpublished guide to the major holdings of the society was prepared in 1977 by Patricia Ann Michaelis, Assistant Curator of the Manuscript Division. Combined with a representative sampling of contemporary printed sources, the society's manuscript materials constitute an important source for research on the Santa Fe-St. Louis nexus.

6. MISSOURI:

Two research institutions in Missouri also offer possibilities for productive research on the Santa Fe Trail: the Missouri Historical Society (St. Louis) and The State Historical Society of Missouri (Columbia). Manuscripts of The State Historical Society are housed in the Ellis Library of the University of Missouri along with the Western Historical Manuscript Collection.

Most published accounts of the Santa Fe Trail and trade during the Mexican period were collected by Jack D. Rittenhouse and published in *The Santa Fe Trail, A Historical Bibliography*.[45] Manuscript materials are scattered across the country from Harvard to the Bancroft Library. Because of the abundance of material, it is not possible to include a listing of the manuscripts available on this subject. Some contain a strong anti-Mexican, pro-Anglo bias, but penetrating comments from traders and travelers in New Mexico provide information on New Mexico and Mexicans involved in commerce with the United States.

A. MISSOURI HISTORICAL SOCIETY. Located in the Jefferson Memorial Building, the Missouri Historical Society is a private library for use by members and non-members who are qualified scholars. Although the staff is small, its professional attributes are outstanding. The manuscript collection is rich in Mexican period material. Even though no published guide to these holdings exists, various indexes assist the researcher in locating pertinent documentation. The following collections contain information on New Mexico in the Mexican period:

(1) Campbell Papers, 1831. Correspondence between W. L. Sublette and W. H. Ashley regarding trade and traders.

(2) Carson Family Papers, 1815–35. Receipts, bills, and memoranda dealing with business activities of William Carson.

(3) P. Chouteau Maffitt Collection, 1830–31. Communications from Ceran St. Vrain regarding New Mexico customs, business affairs, and problems of selling goods in Santa Fe. Much of the collection is indexed.

(4) Fur Trade Envelope, various dates. Deals with robberies and killings of North Americans engaged in the Santa Fe trade.

(5) Fur Trade Papers, 1824. William Parker gives an account of his trip to Santa Fe, discusses Indian trade and various problems encountered in dealing with New Mexicans.

(6) Indians Envelope, 1823–24. Some views from New Mexico regarding Indian difficulties as expressed by Bartolomé Baca and Antonio Vizcarra.

(7) Mexican War Papers, 1846–47. Correspondence, journals, etc., of the Missouri Volunteers reflecting their march from Fort Leavenworth to Santa Fe.

(8) Miller Papers, 1847. Views of John T. Hughes, writing from Chihuahua about the Battle of Sacramento and the possibility that ex-governor Armijo was imprisoned in Zacatecas.

(9) Parker-Russell Papers, 1828. Various reports of activities of Santa Fe traders in New Mexico.

(10) Santa Fe Papers, 1831, 1839. Correspondence from Ewing Young from Taos regarding trade in mules and his trip to the Gila River; also, inventory of trade goods belonging to Charles Bent.

(11) Sappington Papers, 1824–26. Correspondence of M. M. Marmaduke and others regarding 1824 trip to Santa Fe, including discussion of customs, description of another trip to Santa Fe in 1826, and opinions about the ''road'' to New Mexico.

(12) Sublette Papers, 1842, 1844. Includes correspondence of W. L. Sublette about Santa Fe, the fur trade, fears of a possible uprising, new wagon taxes, and the preference of New Mexicans for Manuel Armijo as governor.

(13) Turner Collection, 1823–46. Letters of Major Henry S. Turner to his wife with description of Santa Fe and several remarks on Manuel Armijo.

(14) Turley Papers, 1831–65. Letters and accounts of his business in Santa Fe.

(15) Waldo Papers, 1830s. Descriptions of various expeditions to Santa Fe. Published version in *Missouri Historical Society* V (April–June 1938): 59–64. The Waldo brothers did business in both Santa Fe and Chihuahua. A small collection of records also exists at the Jackson County, Missouri Historical Society in Independence, Missouri.

(16) Webb Papers, 1840s. One of the richest sources on the Santa Fe Trail, including extensive description of New Mexico. The basis for Ralph P. Bieber, ed., *Journal of a Santa Fe Trader,* Vol. I, Southwest Historical Series (Glendale: Arthur H. Clark Co., 1931). Since Dr. Bieber's death it is possible that the Webb Papers will be opened for investigation.[46]

B. THE STATE HISTORICAL SOCIETY OF MISSOURI. Located in Columbia, The State Historical Society of Missouri claims to be the largest of its kind in the United States. It also claims to have the largest and most complete collection of state newspapers in the nation. Since these papers contain reports from returning travelers and traders to Santa Fe, they are a good source of information on New Mexico and the people who entered into the Santa Fe trade.

Some newspapers are indexed. The Missouri *Intelligencer,* published variously in Franklin, Fayette, and Columbia, is indexed from April 1819 to December 1835. The St. Louis, Missouri, *Republican* is indexed for the years 1822 to 1828. Other newspapers have partial indexing, and all are on microfilm and available through Interlibrary Loan.

Manuscript collections are located at the University of Missouri. The emphasis of some forty Mexican period collections is the Mexican War. A guide to these holdings was prepared in 1949 with supplements added in 1952 and 1956.[47]

7. ILLINOIS:

Western Americana is concentrated at the Newberry Library in Chicago. Most material can be found in the Edward E. Ayer and Everett D. Graff collections. The Graff Collection is housed in the Ayer collection, and both form part of the publication, *Western Americana; Frontier History of the Trans-Mississippi West, 1550–1900,* mentioned earlier in this chapter. (See note 37.)

The Graff Collection comprises more than ten-thousand books, pamphlets, maps, broadsides, and manuscripts. Colton Storm's *Catalogue* of this collection arranges entries alphabetically and by collection number.[48] Since Graff left funds for the purchase of additional works which do not appear in Storm's *Catalogue,* researchers will have to consult the *First Supplement* (1970) and the *Second Supplement* (1980) to the *Dictionary Catalogue of the Edward E. Ayer Collection* for additions to the Graff Collection.[49] The following manuscript and contemporary printed items noted below are taken from Storm's

Catalogue and include his reference number.[50]

(1) No. 245: Bell, Josias F., [Manuscript] *Sketches of a Journey by Josias Fendall Bell. 1841–44.* 156-page diary relating the author's travels to Santa Fe, Chihuahua, and other points in Mexico. Samuel and James Magoffin joined Bell on the Santa Fe Trail.

(2) No. 2694: Martínez, Antonio José, *Esposición Que El Presbítero Antonio José Martínez Cura De Taos En Nuevo Mexico, Dirije Al Gobierno Del Exmo. Sor. General D. Antonio López De Santa-Anna. Proponiendo La Civilisación De Las Naciones Bárbaras Que Son Al Contorno Del Departamento De Nuevo-Mexico. . . .* J. M. Baca, 1843.

(3) No. 2770: Mexico. Laws. *Secretaría de Guerra y Marina, Sección 2.ª El Ecsmo. Sr. Presidente de Los Estados Unidos Mexicanos. . . .* Passed by the Mexican Congress on March 21, 1826, these laws provide for presidial companies and militia forces in the Eastern and Western Internal Provinces and the territory of New Mexico.

(4) No. 2989: New Mexico (Department). Gobernador (Manuel Armijo), [Broadside] *El Gobernador Constitucional y Comandante Principal Del Departamento De Nuevo Mejico, A Sus Habitantes. . . .* March 6, 1839. The governor calls on New Mexicans to save their country from attacks by the French.

(5) No. 2999: New Mexico Territory. Governor (Albino Pérez), [Broadside] *Hace algunas días que estaba por decidirme a . . .* August 3, 1835. This printed broadside was directed to the *Señores principales del Territorio,* asking them to meet at Santa Fe on August 15, 1835.

(6) No number. *Revista Oficial,* La. [Broadsheet] *Alcance Al Numero 31 De Revista Oficial. Extraordinario De Hoy Venido Del Nuevo Mexico, Sobre Invasión De Tejanos En El Mismo Departamento. . . .* Chihuahua, July 20, 1843. Announces the Snively invasion.

(7) No. 3675: Santa Fe, New Mexico, *Ayuntamiento,* [Broadside] *Lista De Los Ciudadanos Que Deberán Componer Los Jurados De Imprenta, Formada Por El Ayuntamiento De Esta Capital. . . .* August 14, 1834. Names certain citizens considered qualified and obligated to serve as jurors in lawsuits affecting the freedom of the press.

(8) No. 3733: Serrano y Aguirre, Francisco Pérez, *Exposición De La Provincia Del Nuevo Mexico. . . .* José María Ramos Palomera, 1822. This is an eloquent plea for social and political reforms in New Mexico. Among other suggestions, it argues for the importation of North American families.

(9) No. 4479: Vigil, Donaciano, *Breve Exposición Que Da Al Público El Ciudadano Donaciano Vigil, Capitán De La Compañía Del Bado, Como Vocal De La Exma. Asamblea, Manifestando Los Motivos Que Le Impelieron A Votar Por El Empréstito Forzozo Que A Pedimento Del Exmo . . . Sr. Gobernador Y Comandante General D. Mariano Martínez Decretó La Misma Honorable*

Asamblea En 14 De Febrero Del Corriente Año De 1845. Vigil gives his reasons why he supported a forced loan on New Mexicans.

Several collections of private papers not listed in Storm's *Catalogue* concern land tenure, church, and Indian affairs in Abiquiú in the eighteenth and nineteenth centuries. These are the William Greenlee Papers, the Pablo González Papers, the Joseph Chávez Papers, and the Espinosa-Quintana Collection.[51]

The Edward E. Ayer Collection, much more extensive than the Graff Collection because of its holdings on North American Indians, is useful for its rare imprints. Some manuscripts are included in the collection, but these are copies, facsimiles, microfilm, or other reproductions. For the Mexican period, the most significant works deal with overland journeys, Mexican history, Indian ethnology, cartography, and overland exploration of the trans-Mississippi West in the nineteenth century. The Newberry Library will make copies of select items, but everything in the collection is non-circulating.

8. WISCONSIN:

Located at the State Historical Society of Wisconsin in Madison are copies of several documents dealing with New Mexico Governor Manuel Armijo. Because these are the only Mexican period documents known to exist in Wisconsin, they are detailed below:

(1) From *Ministerio de Lo Interior,* Mexico, to Manuel Armijo, Alburquerque [sic], September 12, 1837, congratulating him for his role in the recent rebellion, naming him governor of New Mexico, and asking him to send information from time to time on the state of affairs while assuring him that the Supreme Government will do its best to send him the resources necessary to keep the peace.

(2) From *Ministerio de Guerra y Marina,* Mexico, to Manuel Armijo, Departamento de Nuevo Mexico, November 22, 1837, responding to Armijo's report that the rebellion has been crushed. The document also carries Armijo's appointment as Colonel in the active militia, and assures him that those who joined in putting down the rebellion will also be rewarded. Furthermore, the two-hundred rifles asked for by Armijo are to be delivered through Chihuahua.

(3) Award conferred upon Manuel Armijo by Antonio López de Santa Anna, *General de División y Presidente Interino de la República Mexicana,* June 24, 1839, appointing him *Coronel Suelto de Caballería.*

(4) Award conferred upon Manuel Armijo by Anastasio Bustamente, *General de División y Presidente de la República Mexicana,* appointing him *General de Brigada del Ejército Mexicano,* for his services in October 1837 and January 1839.

(5) Service Record of Manuel Armijo, March 28, 1842, in which are listed his years in grade, campaigns, and meritorious achievements through December 1841.

(6) From *Ministerio de Guerra y Marina,* Mexico, to Manuel Armijo, Nuevo Mexico, October 17, 1843, telling him that as a reward for his performance against the Texans, he will soon receive ten-thousand pesos monthly from the *aduana* in Mazatlán plus rifles and gunpowder for the troops. In addition, he will receive a medal for personal valor which will be inscribed, *"Salvó en Nuevo Mexico la integridad del Territorio Nacional."* Other awards are described for Armijo's supporters.

(7) From *Ministerio de Relaciones Exteriores, Gobernación y Policía,* Mexico, to Manuel Armijo, Nuevo Mejico, July 24, 1845, naming Armijo governor of New Mexico.

9. MASSACHUSETTS:

The few Mexican period sources at Harvard University would not be worth mentioning were it not for the fact that a number of New Mexico originals have disappeared since Adolph Bandelier extracted and transcribed fifteen volumes of manuscript material from original sources in Santa Fe. Compiled for the Hemenway Southwestern Expedition and later deposited in the Peabody Museum of Archaeology and Ethnology, these typescripts were inventoried by John P. Wilson at about the same time that the Peabody Museum archives were being organized.[52] The Bandelier transcripts are actually in the adjacent Tozzer Library along with some Surveyor General records (copies) and a collection of David J. Miller Papers which contain additional items from New Mexico in the Mexican period.

Of particular interest is the original manuscript of Adolph Bandelier entitled, "An Outline of the Documentary History of the Zuñi Tribe," partially published in 1892 as one of the Hemenway Expedition volumes: *A Journal of American Ethnology and Archaeology,* Vol. III, edited by J. Walter Fewkes. This manuscript in the Peabody Museum archives contains an unpublished Section 2 of Chapter III and an unpublished Chapter IV. Because of the extensive notes and references to eighteenth-century Zuñi life, this segment provides a useful background for research on the Zuñis under Mexican rule.

10. CONNECTICUT:

The Yale University Collection of Western Americana has long been a principal source of information for students of the American West. Enhanced by the William Robert Coe Collection in the 1940s and by the Texas Collection formed by Thomas W. Streeter, Yale's reputation as a center for rare books and manuscripts dealing with the American West has been justly earned. Partly responsible for the growth and accessibility of Yale's Western Americana was the curator, Archibald Hanna, who retired in 1981 after thirty years of service.

By the 1950s, Hanna was beginning to fill some gaps in the records of the Southwest. The Frederick W. and Carrie S. Beinecke Collection came to Yale with emphasis on the Spanish Southwest, California from earliest exploration through the Mexican War, and the subsequent gold rush to California. The collection contains manuscripts, printed books, broadsides, and pamphlets. A guide to the manuscripts was completed in 1965, supplementing the 1952 catalog which had been prepared earlier for the William Robertson Coe Collection.[53] Since the publication of these two catalogs, Yale University has made very few purchases in the area of Southwestern manuscripts,[54] but researchers will need to consult the *Catalogue of the Yale Collection of Western Americana* for additional citations. Although these volumes primarily emphasize rare books rather than the entire collection of Western Americana, they present a card-by-card catalog of most of the holdings (as of 1962), including a shelf list (Vol. 4) which arranges entries by geographic area.[55] Examples of Mexican period material noted in this shelf list are as follows:

(1) Broadside: Santa Fe, N.M. *Ayuntamiento. Lista de los ciudadanos que deberán componer los jurados de imprenta, formada por el Ayuntamiento de esta capital. . . . Santa Fe, Agosto 14 de 1834. Juan Gallegos precidente. Domingo Fernández, secretario.* Santa Fe, 1834.

(2) Imprint: *Memoria sobre las proporciones naturales de las provincias internas occidentales, causas de que han provenido sus atrasos, providencias tomadas con el fin de lograr su remedio, y las que por ahora se consideran oportunas para mejorar su estado, e ir proporcionando su futura felicidad. Formada por los diputados de dichas provincias que la subscriben.* Mexico, 1822.

(3) Broadside: Mexico. Laws, statutes, etc., 1823, July 24. *Francisco Molino del Campo, Gefe Superior Político interino de esta ciudad y su provincia. Por la primera Secretaría de Estado se me ha comunicado con fecha de 21 del actual el decreto que copio.* Provides for the creation of a bishopric in New Mexico and exemption from certain taxes. Mexico, 1823.

(4) Broadside: Chihuahua, Mexico. 1843–1845. *El gobernador y comandante general del departamento de Chihuahua a sus habitantes. Chihuahuenses: los Tejanos . . . que . . . hace algun tiempo tienen usurpada una parte de nuestro territorio . . . hoy por segunda vez pretenden invadir el Departamento de Nuevo Mexico hasta tomar su capital.* Chihuahua, 1843. (See Streeter No. 991.[56])

(5) Broadside: Chihuahua, Mexico, June 26, 1843. Governor Monterde announces that he is going to the aid of the New Mexicans and turning over his office to Colonel Mariano Martínez. Chihuahua, 1843.

(6) Imprint: Mexico. Laws, statutes, etc. March 31, 1844. *Se declaran abiertos al comercio estrangero las aduanas fronterizas de Taos en el Departamento de Nuevo-Mexico y las del Paso del Norte y Presidio del Norte en el de Chihuahua.* Mexico, 1844.

(7) Imprint: Mexico. Laws, statutes, etc. *Laws and decrees of the Republic of*

Mexico in relation to colonization and grants of land, more particularly in New Mexico and California from 1823 to 1846. New York: New York Printing Company, 1871.

(8) Broadside: New Mexico (Province) Governador, 1838–1844. Durango, Mexico (State) *Comandancia General. Por comunicación oficial que acaba de recibir el Sr. Comandante General de este Departamento, del Ecsmo. Sr. Gobernador y Comandante General del de Nuevo-Mexico se le participa la interesante noticia siguiente. . . .* Durango, 1841.

Manuscripts listed in *A Catalogue of the Frederick W. and Carrie S. Beinecke Collection of Western Americana* are mostly tangential to New Mexico in the Mexican period. Five entries are worth noting:

(1) No. 5: Baker, M. L. Three letters written to members of his family while he was in the army in Santa Fe and Fort Leavenworth. One of the letters, dated September 13, 1846, describes the city of Santa Fe and the life and customs of the New Mexicans.

(2) No.55: Coahuila and Texas (State) Gobernador, 1824–1826 (Gonzáles). Governor Rafael Gonzáles describes the individual areas of government under his supervision: militia, mail, health, charity, missions, industries, highways, agriculture, and Indians. Although this is not New Mexico, the comments of Governor Gonzáles reveal something of the nature of political responsibilities along the northern frontier.

(3) No. 138: Mayer, Brantz, 1809–1879. "Mexico in 1841 & 1842." This is a journal written by Brantz Mayer when he was secretary of the U.S. Legation in Mexico, 1841–42. References to the Texas question and the Mexican War as well as newspaper articles revealing the Mexican point of view make this an item of interest for the Mexican period.

(4) No. 165: Mexico. *Junta de Fomento de Californias.* These are drafts of two reports to the Junta on the implications for California of recent actions by the U.S. Congress in opening the Santa Fe Trail.

(5) No. 202: Prince, William E., d. 1892. Letter books from Fort Leavenworth and Santa Fe. The Fort Leavenworth letter book contains information on supplying the forces of General S. W. Kearny and Col. A. Doniphan. The Santa Fe letter book contains drafts of William Prince's official correspondence as Aide-de-Camp and Adjutant to Brigadier General Sterling Price from December 16, 1847, to January 3, 1848. Letters discuss civil and military affairs.

Not mentioned in the Beinecke *Catalogue* are the Armijo Papers. This is a collection of approximately twenty-five items spanning the years 1837 to 1878. The documents deal with the political and military career of Manuel Armijo. In addition to his *hoja de servicio* (military service record), the documents contain correspondence from the *Ministerio de Guerra y Marina* in which Armijo is notified of his military appointments, his award for patriotic defense of the nation during the uprising of 1837, and, finally, his discharge from the armed forces following the capture of Santa Fe in 1846 by General Kearny. Individual letters from Armijo comment on the strength of New Mexico's troops in 1841, his loyalty to the Mexican government, his desire to personally lead an attack against the Utes, and his need for assistance in the governor's office due to the excessive workload. Taken as a whole, these official communications provide an interesting glimpse of one of New Mexico's most controversial figures. (See chap. I, n. 51.)

11. TEXAS:

A. THE UNIVERSITY OF TEXAS AT AUSTIN; THE GENERAL LIBRARIES. According to calendars, indexes, and other finding aids, Mexican period material on New Mexico is sparse in the manuscript collections of The University of Texas at Austin. Some microfilm reproductions, transcripts, and photocopies of collections in Mexico and the United States will serve as an introduction to the Mexican period. The many archival collections have not been methodically screened for New Mexico material, however, and because of frequent contacts between Texas and New Mexico, particularly after 1836, additional documentation may very well be present in manuscript sources.

(1) The Eugene C. Barker Texas History Center:

Occupying Unit 2 of Sid Richardson Hall, the Barker History Center traces its beginning from the opening of the University of Texas in 1883. Growing steadily through succeeding decades, the Center consolidated its holdings under one roof in 1945. In 1971, it moved into the facilities it now shares with the Texas State Historical Association. The Center is divided into four units: Texas Collection Library; Archives and Manuscripts; Texas Newspaper and Non-Textual Records; and the Fleming University Writings Collections.

The Archives and Manuscripts Unit began in 1899 with the acquisition of the Béxar Archives followed by the papers of Moses and Stephen Austin. Its function is "to locate, acquire and preserve the papers, photographs, and records of persons, groups and organizations significant to Texas and Southwestern history; and to serve as the repository for the University's historically valuable official records."[57] The collection, which now measures more than 22,000 linear feet, continues to grow. Those selections noted below should be cited by name, including a reference to the Eugene C. Barker Texas History Center:

(a) Béxar Archives: Transferred to the University of Texas in 1899, these records of provincial Texas cover the years 1717–1836 and consist of more than 250,000 pages of manuscripts plus more than four-thousand pages of printed matter.[58] In 1902 the documents were arranged by subgroups as follows: (1) Coahuila and Texas Official Publications, 1825–35; (2) General Governmental Publications, 1730–1836; (3) Nongovernmental Publications, 1778, 1811–36; (4) Undated Documents and Undated

Fragments; and (5) General Manuscript Series, 1717–1836. A total of 81,000 calendar cards and an index had been prepared by the mid-1930s, when a full-time translator was employed.[59] In 1966, with grants from the National Historical Publications Commission, the University of Texas microfilmed the Béxar Archives. The third segment of the General Manuscript Series, 1822–1836, was reproduced on Reels 70–172.[60]

In addition to Indian relations, commerce with the United States, Anglo-American immigration, and plans to establish the Lancasterian school system, these documents contain correspondence from the Department of Texas, the governor of Coahuila-Texas, the commandant general at Chihuahua, and other officials who were concerned about affairs in New Mexico. Additional information may be found in civil and military reports, minutes of the provincial deputation, government ordinances, records of passports, military provisions, judicial proceedings, explorations, commerce, agriculture, and revolutions. As suggested by Malcolm D. McLean, professor of history and Spanish at the University of Texas at Arlington and editor of the Robertson Colony Collection, someone could make a great contribution by scanning the calendars at the beginning of each reel in order to summarize the frames that contain New Mexico material.[61]

Some of the Béxar Archives inadvertently found their way into the Nacogdoches Archives. This may have happened when the Department of Nacogdoches was created (1831) and the archives at San Antonio were divided.[62] In any event, when the Nacogdoches Archives were classified in 1903, one of the subgroups was designated "Béxar." It was comprised of "series (i) correspondence of the political chief at Béxar, October 1823–October 1835 (1,065 items); series (ii) miscellaneous material relating to the municipality of Béxar, 1825–35 (250 items) . . . and series (iii) correspondence of the principal commandant, 1825–35 (30 items)."[63] Following arrangement by the Archives Division of the Texas State Library, typed transcriptions were made for the years 1731 to 1836. These copies, constituting eighty-nine volumes, are located in the University of Texas Archives, the Stephen F. Austin State College Library in Nacogdoches, the North Texas State College Library in Denton, and the Newberry Library in Chicago.[64]

(b) Blake Collection: Robert Blake spent many years calendaring, indexing, transcribing, and translating the records in Nacogdoches relating to Spanish and Mexican Texas. Between 1942 and his death in 1955, he worked "on the Nacogdoches Archives and other materials in the Texas State Archives, the General Land Office records, and the University of Texas Archives." The Blake Collection in the University of Texas Archives includes ninety-three volumes covering the years 1744 to 1837. A calendar of the Blake Collection is in the University of Texas Archives.[65] Although it reveals an overriding emphasis on matters relating to Nacogdoches, given the confusion over the distribution of Béxar records it would be prudent for Mexican period scholars to check these materials for New Mexico references. Some caution should be exercised when using the

Blake materials. New translations are being prepared at the Texas State Archives.

(c) Reproductions from Mexico: Transcribing and photoduplicating archives in repositories in Mexico began in 1898. This work was continued by Herbert E. Bolton, Eugene C. Barker, William E. Dunn, Charles W. Hackett, Charles H. Cunningham, and others.[66] The Archives and Manuscript Unit has several of these collections which contain New Mexico material: (i) "Archivo General de Mexico, 1538–1849," which includes records from *Fomento, Colonización* (1821–1836), 17 vols.; *Guerra y Marina* (1827–1845), 45 vols.; *Relaciones Exteriores* (1806–1849), 20 vols.; *Guerra* (1706–1831), 6 vols.;[67] (ii) "Matamoros Archives, 1811–1859," which concerns "early movements in Texas and New Mexico,"[68] and records of *alcaldes* and *ayuntamientos* which contain information on Indians, trade with Americans, and lists of persons banished from the district.[69] The collection also includes a large number of copies of Mexico City newspapers for the years 1833 to 1849. A calendar was prepared by Carlos E. Castañeda for the entire collection. The sixty-seven volumes of transcriptions in the University of Texas Archives can also be found at the Catholic Archives of Texas and the Bancroft and Newberry libraries;[70] and (iii) "Saltillo Archives, 1688–1876" (50 vols.), and the proceedings of the Coahuila Congress, August 1824–May 1835, may also prove useful. Since Texas was associated with Coahuila as a state after 1824, these two sources treat frontier problems touching on New Mexico. The fifty volumes of the Saltillo Archives transcripts have been calendared.

(d) Manuscript Collections: Several manuscript collections described in Kielman's *The University of Texas Archives* list references to New Mexico: (i) Caryl Clyde Hill Papers, 1823 (1832–1916) deal with early phases of Texas history including the capture of the Texan Santa Fe expedition; (ii) George Wilkins Kendall Papers, 1846–1850, 1857, relate to Kendall's coverage of the Mexican War; (iii) New Mexico Archives, Records, 1532–1879, contain typescripts and photocopies of various records transcribed from the NMSRCA and the *AGN* dealing with Spanish and Mexican activities in New Mexico; (iv) Santa Fe Expedition, Order, 1841, is a typescript copy of an order book and commonplace book concerning Hugh McLeod's command of the Texan Santa Fe expedition; (v) Winfield Scott Papers, 1847–1850, are made up of two items treating the occupation of New Mexico by the state of Texas; (vi) Earl Vandale Papers, ca. 1819–ca. 1947, include Peter Gallagher's journal of the Texan Santa Fe expedition and his confinement in Perote Prison, etc.; (vii) Hugh Franklin Young's Narrative, 1843–44, is a typescript of Young's experience on the 1843 Snively Expedition into New Mexico.[71] Diligent research may also produce results in collections such as the Stephen F. Austin Papers, 1793–1836; the James Franklin Perry Papers, 1825–1874; the Robert Peebles Papers, 1832–1887; the Henry Austin Papers, 1806–1851; the Gail Borden Papers, 1830–1908; the Sam Houston Papers, 1814–1861;

the Anson Jones Papers, 1809–1910; the Collin McKinney Papers, 1809–1854; the T. J. Rusk Papers, 1824–1859; the Alexander Dienst Papers, 1765–1927; the David G. Burnett Papers, 1798–1899; and others.[72] Since the publication of Kielman's valuable guide to the University of Texas Archives, the Barker Texas History Center has accessioned a large quantity of additional manuscript material.

(2) The Nettie Lee Benson Latin American Collection:

The purchase of the Genaro García Library in 1921 was the first significant step taken by The University of Texas to build a Latin American Collection.[73] In addition to ten-thousand bound books, this collection included two-hundred-thousand manuscript folios containing documents dealing with Mexico's top civil and military leaders.[74] During the next fifty years, purchases, gifts, and special grants enabled The University of Texas to increase the size and scope of the Latin American Collection to include manuscripts and imprints from Central and South America.

In 1975, and in recognition of its former director, the collection was renamed the Nettie Lee Benson Latin American Collection. It is located in Unit 1 of Sid Richardson Hall, where it occupies all four levels with the exception of offices on the third floor which house the Institute of Latin American Studies. The collection has grown to include approximately 338,000 volumes, over two-million pages of manuscripts, about ten-thousand reels of microfilm, ten-thousand photographs, and fifteen-hundred maps.[75] The following collections contain material on New Mexico in the Mexican period:

(a) Presidential Papers: Papers of Vicente Guerrero (President, April–December 1829), Valentín Gómez Farías (Acting President, 1833–34), and Antonio López de Santa Anna (President and Commander of the Army that invaded Texas in 1836), as well as other collections, provide an official perspective on the northern frontier as viewed from Mexico City.

(b) William B. Stephens Collection: Acquired in 1938, this collection of twenty-thousand pages relating to the Spanish Southwest embraces the years 1488–1860.[76] Although the collection deals more with the colonial period, some manuscripts described in Castañeda and Dabbs' *Guide* concern the 1840s.

(c) Valentín Gómez Farías Collection: Correspondence, decrees, proclamations, and miscellaneous documents in this collection are cataloged in Pablo Max Ynsfran, *Catálogo de los manuscritos del archivo de don Valentín Gómez Farías; obrantes en la Universidad de Texas, Colección Latinoamericana*. Independent Mexico in Documents, Vol. 3 (Mexico: Editorial Jus, 1968). New Mexico items include several letters commenting on the general state of affairs in the northern provinces in 1837 and the rebellion in New Mexico; letters concerning the prolongation of civil war in Mexico and a new plan to save the country from the loss of California and New Mexico; a translation of Mirabeau B. Lamar's proclamation to the citizens of New Mexico, June 5, 1841; reports on the Warfield Expedition and the reaction in Santa Fe against the regime of Santa Anna; and material dealing with the conquest of New Mexico in 1846, including Mexican plans to reoccupy New Mexico.[77]

(d) Archives and Manuscripts on Microfilm: As of August 31, 1979, the Benson Latin American Collection contained over 6,300 reels of microfilm from national and foreign repositories.[78] Those which are most applicable to Mexican period research in New Mexico are: (i) Bustamante, Carlos María de, *Diary*, 1822–41, *Biblioteca Pública del Estado de Zacatecas* (25 reels); (ii) Ciudad Juárez, *Catedral, Archivo*, Selected documents, 1838–1917 (5 reels: 3–4, 9–11); (iii) Mexico, *AGN, Inventario de los fondos documentales del archivo llamado Casa Amarilla: Secretaría de Gobernación, Tramo* No. 1, 1611–1914 (1 reel); (iv) Mexico, *AGN, El Ramo de Gobernación*. Selected legislation from *Congreso General, Diputados*, and *Senadores* (1820s) (2 reels); (v) Mexico, *AGN, El Ramo de Historia—Operaciones de Guerra*, 1796–1826, Vols. 30–32, 794, 986, 987 (leaves 256–378) (3 reels); (vi) Mexico, *AGN, El Ramo de Justicia y Asuntos Eclesiásticos, Sección Instrucción Pública*, 1821–65, Vols. 1–51, 70–78, 80–81, 83–94 (56 reels); (vii) Mexico, *AGN, El Ramo de Provincias Internas*. 1617–1842, Vols. 1–265 (242 reels); (viii) Mexico, *AGN*, Selected documents relating to Guadalupe Victoria (1 reel); (ix) Mexico, *AGN*, Selected documents relating to Nicolas Bravo (1 reel); (x) Mexico, *Legación*, U.S., Notes from the Mexican legation in the U.S. to the Department of State, 1821–1906, NARS/M-54 (43 reels); (xi) NMSRCA, MANM (43 reels); (xii) U.S. Consulate, Chihuahua, Mexico, Despatches, 1826–1906, NARS/T-167, M-289 (5 reels); (xiii) U.S. Consulate, Santa Fe, Despatches, 1830–46, NARS/M-199 (1 reel); (xiv) U.S. Embassy, Mexico, Despatches from U.S. ministers to Mexico, 1823–1906, NARS/M-97 (179 reels).

B. TEXAS STATE ARCHIVES. Noting that the Texas State Archives were strong on substance and lamentably weak on "form" (finding aids), Seymour V. Connor prepared the first "horseback survey" of the manuscript material in the Archives of Texas, which was published in *The Southwestern Historical Quarterly* in 1956. In book form, this finding aid appeared as *A Preliminary Guide to the Archives of Texas*, published the same year by the Texas Library and Historical Commission.[79] In his introductory remarks, Connor traces the evolution of the Texas State Archives from their depository of "saddlebags" and "wallets" to the more ordered depository of the Archives Division of the Texas State Library.

Located today in the Lorenzo de Zavala State Archives and Library Building, these records contain a great deal of "unknown" material on New Mexico. As related to the author in a recent letter from the Archives' Director, several collections are possible repositories of material on New Mexico in the Mexican period.[80] The lesson is clear. Texas catalogers have not always concerned themselves with New Mexico in the Mexican period, and although finding aids are useful, they should not be considered the only measure of a collection's usefulness. Some already discovered New Mexico items will be found in:

(1) Lamar Papers, 1756–1859: Documents in this collection include references to New Mexico militia; plans to divert the Santa Fe trade into the valley of the Colorado River; communications from Mirabeau Lamar urging closer union between New Mexico and Texas; plans for, and Texas apathy toward, the Texan Santa Fe expedition; communications from Hugh McLeod regarding preparations for his march to New Mexico in 1841; and miscellaneous documents relating to volunteers, guides, and supplies for the Texan Santa Fe expedition.[81]

(2) Santa Fe Papers: This collection of papers pertains both to the Texan Santa Fe expedition and attempts to organize Santa Fe County after the Mexican War. The bulk of the expedition papers are typescripts of newspaper articles, requisitions for supplies, accounts, and receipts. Included are reports from New Mexico to the *Secretaría de Guerra y Marina* (October 1841) and other reports from Texans written from Chihuahua. These materials make up the first ninety folders of the Santa Fe Papers. The second section of sixty-nine folders contains some interesting points of view regarding Texan claims to New Mexico and a large number of volunteers offering their services to launch an expedition against the Mexicans in the 1850s.

(3) Miscellaneous: Because of his many social and commercial interests in New Mexico, James Wiley Magoffin is always a good subject for research in the Mexican period. The Texas State Archives has the James W. Magoffin Family Papers, 1836–1906. The A. J. Houston Papers, basically the files of father Samuel, should be combed for New Mexico references. The Journal of Peter Gallagher (typescript) and the papers of General Hugh McLeod (typescripts) as well as McLeod's 1841 Order Book (typescript and photostat) may be consulted for additional information on the Texan Santa Fe expedition. Originals are located at the Barker Texas History Center. The Texas State Archives also has a number of transcripts from the *AGN* as well as the Coahuila Archives, 1699–1824.

C. UNIVERSITY OF TEXAS AT EL PASO (UTEP).   In October 1967, the "Mexico on Microfilm" project was inaugurated "by a conference of forty-seven representatives from thirty institutions across the United States, held at Oyster Bay under the sponsorship of the State University System of New York."[82] The plan was to cooperate in the microfilming of Mexican archives to avoid duplication of effort as well as to share information on extant reproductions of Mexican archival sources. Texas institutions proceeded to form their own consortium composed of the Texas State Library and fifteen academic institutions. Calling themselves the "Texas Consortium for Microfilming Mexican Archival Resources," the members agreed to microfilm in certain

ıreas of Mexico.[83] For UTEP this meant concentrating on the resources of
Chihuahua and Durango. Results of UTEP's efforts include the following:

(1) *Archivo del ayuntamiento de la Ciudad Juárez*, 1690–1904 (91 reels).
(2) *Archivo del ayuntamiento de la Ciudad Chihuahua*, 1700–1940 (717 reels).
(3) *Archivo del Estado de Durango*, 1578–1848 (343 reels). Filming continues on this project.
(4) *Periódico Oficial del Estado de Chihuahua*, 1829–1971 (110 reels). Many
references to New Mexico in the Mexican period will be found here.
(5) *Boletín de la Sociedad de Estudios Históricos de Chihuahua*, Vols. 1–12
(6 reels).[84]

UTEP is also hoping to film the archives of the cathedrals of Durango
and Chihuahua, but a number of problems remain to be worked out. As indicated in Chapter IV, the UTEP microfilm collection also includes some ecclesiastical records, several newspaper collections of the Mexican period, the Béxar
Archives, and the MANM. Additional primary source materials are listed by
the Special Collection Department on a ''Microfilm Holding List,'' but the
incomplete nature of this compilation precludes citation at this point. Plans
are under way to compile a new list from a 3 x 5 card index.[85]

Manuscript holdings are equally difficult to describe. A *Guide* was
prepared by Mildred Torok in 1972, but she retired the following year. Subsequently, all the collection numbers were changed and the majority of manuscripts at UTEP were received after her departure. The Special Collections
Department has been ''thinking about putting the whole of our manuscript collections into a computer sometime in the near future.''[86]

D. MISCELLANEOUS. Suggestions for additional research in Texas must
be tempered with the warning that the harvest may not be worth the expenditure of time. Some sources appear to hold promise, however. Trinity University,
for example, has four-thousand reels of film from the archives of Nuevo León.
In addition to the fact that some of the governors of this state were quite active
in frontier affairs during the Mexican period, state records include documents
from the *Comandancia General* of the *Provincias Internas* and the *Provincias
Internas Oriental* for the years after 1800.[87]

Other sources of Mexican period documents are the General Land Office
(Texas) and the Laredo Archives. The former is something of an unknown
quantity because no finding aids are available. Since the boundary between
Texas and New Mexico was uncertain at the time of Mexican independence,
General Land Office records may include some interesting material.[88] The
Laredo Archives embrace the years 1768 to 1868. They include correspon-
dence between officials of Laredo and civil and military officials of Northern
Mexico, governmental decrees, local laws and ordinances, trade data, Indian
raids, and a host of documents dealing with local problems.[89] A number of
incomplete transcripts were made of these archives. A complete set of docu-

ments through 1847 was filmed in the 1950s for Texas Technological University. A positive copy of this microfilm (12 reels) is in the Colorado State Archives.[90]

Another Laredo source is Texas A & I University. As a result of Stanley Green's interests in the Mexican period, the university has a number of printed sources for the years 1822–33. Most are xerox copies of *memorias* from the *secretarías de Estado, Interior, Relaciones Exteriores, Hacienda, Justicia y Negocios Eclesiásticos,* and *Guerra y Marina.* Other *memorias, informes,* and *notas estadísticas* were copied from state sources for the following years: Chihuahua (1830, 1831, 1834); Nuevo Mexico (1834); Durango (1826, 1827); Coahuila-Texas (1827). The university collection also includes a number of bound materials on the Mexican period from Mexico and the United States.

Other possibilities abound in Texas, and researchers should view the above suggestions as little more than encouragement to pursue the search for documents in a state whose sense of history has remained strong for 150 years. Malcolm McLean has published some New Mexico items in his work on the *Papers Concerning Robertson's Colony in Texas.*[91] William C. Griggs has collected artifacts representing the material culture of New Mexico in the Mexican period at The Panhandle-Plains Historical Museum in Canyon, Texas.[92] The DeGolyer Library at Southern Methodist University has a number of manuscript collections covering the time period of this study which have not yet been fully processed and cataloged.[93] The quest is endless, but the Texas ground is fertile.

12. A SUMMARY OF THE MOST USEFUL DESCRIPTIVE REFERENCES AND FINDING AIDS EXCLUDING UNPUBLISHED INDEXES AND INVENTORIES:

(1) Barnes, Thomas C., Thomas H. Naylor, and Charles W. Polzer, *Northern New Spain, A Research Guide.* Tucson: The University of Arizona Press, 1981. This is a guide to materials gathered by the Documentary Relations of the Southwest (DRSW) project. In addition to types and classifications of documents, the *Guide* provides translation aids. Although it deals with the colonial period, the *Guide* presents an abundance of useful information for those working with Mexican period documents.

(2) Beers, Henry P., *Spanish and Mexican Records of the American Southwest.* Tucson: University of Arizona Press, 1979. Part II, "The Records of Texas," Part III, "The Records of California," and Part IV, "The Records of Arizona," are particularly important to this study.

(3) Butler, Ruth, comp., *A Check List of Manuscripts in the Edward E. Ayer Collection.* Chicago: The Newberry Library, 1937. This hard-to-find finding aid is available on microfilm through Interlibrary Loan. It is a very general listing of collections, arranged geographically to include North America (except Spanish settlements), Spanish America, the Philippines, and Hawaii. Two addi-

tional sections deal with Hawaiian and Indian languages.

(4) Castañeda, Carlos E., and Jack Aubrey Dabbs, *Guide to the Latin American Manuscripts in the University of Texas Library.* Cambridge: Harvard University Press, 1939. Organized geographically (California, Central America, Florida, Mexico, New Mexico, Philippines, South America, Spain and the Islands, and Texas), this guide describes collections which are now housed in the Rare Books and Manuscripts Unit, the Benson Latin American Collection, and the Barker Texas History Center. The majority of documents relate to the history of Mexico from the sixteenth to the nineteenth centuries.

(5) *Catalogue of Mexican Pamphlets in the Sutro Collection, 1623–1888,* prepared by the personnel of the WPA, A. Yedida, supervisor, and P. Radin, editor. Sponsored by the California State Library, San Francisco, 1939, and reprinted in New York by the Kraus Reprint Co., 1971. This catalog is arranged chronologically. It lists most of the Mexican pamphlets in the Sutro Collection.

(6) Connor, Seymour V., *A Preliminary Guide to the Archives of Texas.* Austin: Texas Library and Historical Commission, 1956. This slender volume represents the first attempt to list and describe collections in the Texas State Archives.

(7) Cottler, Susan M., Roger M. Haigh, and Shirley A. Weathers, *Preliminary Survey of the Mexican Collection.* Salt Lake City: University of Utah Press, 1978. See also Haigh, Roger M., and Shirley A. Weathers, *Supplement to the Preliminary Survey of The Mexican Collection.* Salt Lake City: University of Utah Press, 1979. Both volumes reference Mexican civil and ecclesiastical collections which were microfilmed by the Genealogical Society of Utah.

(8) *Dictionary Catalogue of the Edward E. Ayer Collection,* 16 vols., Boston: G. K. Hall, 1961. See also *First Supplement,* 3 vols. (1970) and *Second Supplement,* 4 vols. (1980). Entries in all volumes are alphabetically arranged entry cards of the original Ayer Collection and subsequent purchases.

(9) Garner, Jane, comp., *Archives and Manuscripts on Microfilm in the Nettie Lee Benson Latin American Collection. A Checklist.* Austin: The University of Texas Press, 1980. The large number of microfilm reproductions at the University of Texas makes this a particularly useful guide. There are 138 entries on Mexico alone.

(10) Goddard, Jeanne M., and Charles Kritzler, comps., *A Catalogue of the Frederick W. & Carrie S. Beinecke Collection of Western Americana.* New Haven and London: Yale University Press, 1965. This is a readable and well presented catalog of one of the major collections of Western Americana at Yale.

(11) *Guide to American Historical Manuscripts in the Huntington Library.* San Marino: Huntington Library, 1979. Although the *Guide* contains few references to New Mexico materials of the Mexican period, it is the major reference work for manuscript material at one of the most prestigious research institutions in the United States.

(12) "Guide to the Western Historical Manuscripts Collection," *Western Historical Manuscripts Collection Bulletin*, Nos. 5,6 (July 1, 1949, and November 8, 1952), and a *Supplement* to *Bulletin*, No. 6 (April 1, 1957). These three finding aids provide some assistance in reviewing manuscript collections at the University of Missouri, Columbia, Mo.

(13) Guillén, Irma, "Table of Contents to the *Boletín de la Sociedad Chihuahuense de Estudios Históricos.*" Typescript prepared at the University of Texas, El Paso, 1976.

(14) Kielman, Chester V., *Guide to the Microfilm Edition of the Béxar Archives, 1822–1836*, Vol. 3. Austin: University of Texas Archives, 1971. A reel-by-reel summary describes the contents of Reels 72–132 of the Béxar Archives.

(15) ————. *The University of Texas Archives. A Guide to the Historical Manuscripts Collection in the University of Texas Library.* Austin: The University of Texas Press, 1967. Although dated, this is a seminal work which is both well organized and reliable.

(16) Morgan, Dale L., and George P. Hammond, eds., *A Guide to the Manuscript Collections of the Bancroft Library*, 2 vols. Berkeley and Los Angeles: University of California Press, 1963. Volume I is arranged geographically and deals with California and the West. Volume II is arranged alphabetically by author and covers Central and South America.

(17) Radding de Murrieta, Cynthia, and María Lourdes Torres Chávez, *Catálogo del Archivo Histórico del Estado Sonora*, 2 vols. Hermosillo: Centro Regional Noroeste, 1974–75. These volumes are the beginning of a drawer-by-drawer project initiated by the Centro Regional Noroeste. The published catalogs represent a very small part of the total archive.

(18) Shaw, Dorothy P., "The Cragin Collection," *Colorado Magazine* 25 (1948), pp. 166–75. This collection, located in the Pioneers' Museum in Colorado Springs, is indexed by name and is useful for researching activities along the Upper Arkansas River during the Mexican period.

(19) Spell, Lota M., *Research Materials for the Study of Latin America at The University of Texas.* Austin: The University of Texas Press, 1954. In essay style, this work describes the origin and development of the University's Latin American Collection. Sources are grouped under themes: history, literature, geography, religion, philosophy, law, government, economics, education, and fine arts.

(20) Storm, Colton, comp., *A Catalogue of the Everett D. Graff Collection of Western Americana.* Chicago: The University of Chicago Press, 1968. The Graff Collection contains most, but not all, materials dealing with the West on deposit at the Newberry Library. Researchers will need to check the Edward E. Ayer Collection in order to complete a search for New Mexico items.

(21) Withington, Mary C., comp., *A Catalogue of Manuscripts in the Collection of Western Americana in the Yale University Library.* New Haven: Yale

University Press, 1952. This catalog was prepared for research in the William Robertson Coe Collection.

(22) Ynsfran, Pablo Max, *Catálogo de los manuscritos del archivo de don Valentín Gómez Farías; obrantes en la Universidad de Texas, Colección Latinoamericana*, Vol. 3 of Independent Mexico in Documents. Mexico: Editorial Jus, 1968. This is a calendar of approximately 4,700 documents, mostly correspondence from 1770 to 1892. It contains a number of items dealing with New Mexico.

NOTES

1. See Dale L. Morgan and George P. Hammond, eds., *A Guide to the Manuscript Collections of the Bancroft Library.* 2 vols. (Berkeley and Los Angeles: University of California Press, 1963).

2. Ibid., Vol. I, pp. vi–vii.

3. Fray Angélico Chávez, "Some Original New Mexico Documents in California Libraries," NMHR 25 (1950): 248.

4. "Key" to the Alphonse Louis Pinart Collection *(Colección de documentos sobre Nuevo Mexico,* 1681–1841), University of California, the Bancroft Library, p. 1.

5. Henry P. Beers, *Spanish and Mexican Records of the American Southwest* (Tucson: University of Arizona Press, 1979), p. 25 n.79.

6. Morgan and Hammond, *Manuscript Collections.* All but the last item are described in Vol. I.

7. Beers, *Spanish and Mexican Records,* p. 21.

8. Albert James Díaz, *Manuscripts and Records in the University of New Mexico Library* (Albuquerque: University of New Mexico Press, 1957), p. 73; Ralph Emerson Twitchell, *The Spanish Archives of New Mexico.* 2 vols. (Glendale, Calif.: The Arthur H. Clark Co., 1914).

9. The Bolton Papers were not included in Morgan and Hammond, *Manuscript Collections,* because they are classified with a California call number and consequently form part of Bolton's private archive. Letter from Vivian C. Fisher, Head, Microforms Division, the Bancroft Library, June 1, 1982.

10. Herbert Eugene Bolton, *Guide to Materials for the History of the United States in the Principal Archives of Mexico* (Washington, D.C.: Carnegie Institution, 1913), Kraus Reprint, 1965.

11. Rogélio López Espinoza, elaborador, *Catálogo del Ramo Expulsión de Españoles,* 2 vols., Serie Guías y Catálogos (26) (Mexico: Archivo General de la Nación, 1980). Also see Marc Simmons, "New Mexico's Spanish Exiles," NMHR 59(1984): 67–79.

12. Conversation with Marie Byrne, Head, Manuscript Division, the Bancroft Library, Berkeley, September 3, 1980.

13. Parts of this collection were published by F. A. Sampson, ed., in "M. M. Marmaduke's Journal," *Missouri Historical Review* 6 (October 1911): 1–10.

14. Letter from Donald Farren, Head, Special Collections Department, the University of New Mexico Library, May 3, 1982. Farren notes that the "present index to Ritch Papers at the Huntington is more complete" than the entries on film.

15. Letter from Virginia J. Renner, Huntington Library Reader Services Librarian, June 4, 1982.

16. The author wishes to express his gratitude to Ms. Glenna Schroeder, former archivist at the Southwest Museum, whose efforts uncovered several New Mexican items.

17. Richard E. Greenleaf and Michael C. Meyer, *Research in Mexican History: Topics, Methodology, Sources, and a Practical Guide to Field Research* (Lincoln: University of Nebraska Press, 1973), p. 148. A note in the *Western Historical Quarterly* says that the Sutro's Mexican pamphlet collection is the largest in the world. See Vol. 13 (April 1982): 231.

18. Antonio Barreiro, *Ojeada sobre Nuevo Mejico* in H. Bailey Carroll and J. Villasana Haggard, trans. and eds., *Three New Mexico Chronicles* (Albuquerque: The Quivira Society, 1942). In addition to Barreiro, the authors include D. José Agustín Escudero and D. Pedro Bautista Pino.

19. *Western Historical Quarterly* 13 (April 1982): 231. Researchers wishing to purchase specific Mexican pamphlets may also request microfilm copies by ordering directly from the Sutro Library.

20. *Catalogue of Mexican Pamphlets in the Sutro Collection, 1623–1888*, prepared by the personnel of the WPA, A. Yedidia, supervisor, and P. Radin, editor (sponsored by the California State Library, San Francisco, 1939, and reprinted in New York by the Kraus Reprint Co., 1971). The catalog does not include broadsides, government decrees, or any imprint over two-hundred pages. The original publication, completed between 1939 and 1941, is composed of ten parts plus a *Supplement*. The Sutro Library has three annotated copies.

21. The other associate directors are Thomas C. Barnes and Thomas H. Naylor. Correspondence should be directed to the DRSW, Arizona State Museum, University of Arizona, Tucson, AZ 85721.

22. An early description of the DRSW Project will be found in Charles W. Polzer, "The Documentary Relations of the Southwest," *Hispanic American Historical Review* 58 (1978): 460–65.

23. Letter from Bernard L. Fontana, The University of Arizona, June 24, 1980. See also Thomas C. Barnes, Thomas H. Naylor, and Charles W. Polzer, *Northern New Spain, A Research Guide* (Tucson: The University of Arizona Press, 1981), pp. 1–4. In a letter to the author, June 8, 1982, Polzer notes that

the DRSW work is being suspended due to a lack of funding.
24. Letter from Charles W. Polzer, Associate Director, DRSW, February 12, 1980.
25. Barnes, et al., *A Research Guide,* p. xi.
26. Beers, *Spanish and Mexican Records,* p. 313.
27. Stuart F. Voss, *On the Periphery of Nineteenth-Century Mexico: Sonora and Sinaloa, 1810–1877* (Tucson: The University of Arizona Press, 1982), pp. 38, 40, 44 n. 37. Voss cites Robert C. Stevens, "Mexico's Forgotten Frontier: A History of Sonora, 1821–1846" (Ph. D. diss., University of California at Berkeley, 1963), pp. 45, 47, and Rex Strickland, "The Birth and Death of a Legend: The Johnson 'Massacre' of 1837." *Arizona and the West* 18 (Autumn 1976), pp. 265–69.
28. Beers, *Spanish and Mexican Records,* pp. 316, 319. In "A Guide to the Hermosillo Microfilm at the Arizona Historical Society," 1982, Kieran R. McCarty notes that Reels 12–25 represent the richest source on the Apaches in southern Arizona during the Mexican period.
29. Ibid. The Hayden Library has Reels 5–46. Consuelo Boyd prepared a calendar of several reels (5, 6, 44), transcribing and translating some documents in this collection.
30. Cynthia Radding de Murrieta and María Lourdes Torres Chávez, *Catálogo del Archivo Histórico del Estado Sonora,* 4 vols. (Hermosillo: *Centro Regional del Noroeste,* 1974–75). The first volume (1974) includes *expedientes* 1–50 in *Archivero* 1–1. Volume II (1975) continues the sequence with *expedientes* 51–202. Volume III (1975) starts in *Archivero* 1–2 and lists the first 101 *expedientes.* The fourth volume (1977) lists 111 *fichas* from *gavetas* 3, 4, and 5 of the first *archivero.* All the *expedientes* are from the *Sección Ejecutiva* of the Sonora Archives.
31. Conversation with Fr. Kieran McCarty, O.F.M., July 28, 1982.
32. Rubén Cobos, *A Dictionary of New Mexico and Southern Colorado Spanish* (Santa Fe: Museum of New Mexico Press), p. vi. Inventories of Alamosa, San Luis, and Conejos county archives can be found in Historical Records Survey, *Inventory of the County Archives of Colorado and New Mexico* (Denver and Albuquerque, 1937–40).
33. Frances Leon Swadesh, *Los Primeros Pobladores; Hispanic Americans of the Ute Frontier* (Notre Dame: University of Notre Dame Press, 1974). See also José de Onís, ed., *The Hispanic Contribution to the State of Colorado: Four Centuries of History and Heritage* (Fort Collins: Centennial Publications, 1977). The most scholarly studies are by the late Morris F. Taylor: *Pioneers of the Picketwire* (Pueblo: O'Brien Printing, 1964); and *Trinidad, Colorado Territory* (Trinidad: Trinidad State Junior College, 1966). Taylor also contributed many articles in scholarly journals.
34. Mexican land grants in what is now the state of Colorado include the Vigil

and St. Vrain, Gervacio Nolan, Sangre de Cristo, Beaubien and Miranda, Conejos, and Tierra Amarilla. See Marianne L. Stoller, "Grants of Desperation, Lands of Speculation: Mexican Period Land Grants in Colorado," in John R. and Christine M. Van Ness, eds., *Spanish and Mexican Land Grants in New Mexico and Colorado* (Manhattan, Kans.: Sunflower University Press, 1980), originally published as part of the July 1980 issue of the *Journal of the West*.

35. This collection is described in Dorothy P. Shaw, "The Cragin Collection," *Colorado Magazine* 25 (1948): 166–75. It was used by Janet Lecompte in her research for *Pueblo, Hardscrabble and Greenhorn* (Norman: University of Oklahoma Press, 1978). Lecompte's excellent study of the Upper Arkansas region deals extensively with the Mexican period.

36. Henry R. Wagner and Charles L. Camp, *The Plains and the Rockies, A Bibliography of Original Narratives of Travel and Adventure, 1800–1865*, 3rd edition (Columbus, Ohio: Long's College Book Co., 1953). A revised version edited by Robert Becker and Michael Mathes was published by Grabhorn Press, San Francisco, 1981. See also *Western Americana: An Annotated Bibliography to the Microfiche Collection of 1012 Books and Documents of the 18th, 19th, and Early 20th Century* (Ann Arbor: University Microfilms International, 1976). References will be found to the works of Jacob Fowler, Lewis Garrard, Thomas James, James Ohio Pattie, George Ruxton, Rufus Sage, Adolphus Wislizenus, and others who sojourned in New Mexico in the Mexican period. See also the annotated bibliography in this book.

37. *Western Americana: Frontier History of the Trans-Mississippi West, 1550–1900*. 617 reels (Woodbridge, Conn.: Research Publications Inc. RPI, 1977). Most of the approximately seven-thousand titles were taken from the Everett D. Graff Collection at the Newberry Library and the William Robertson Coe Collection at the Yale University Library. Another useful publication by the same company is *Texas as Province and Republic, 1795–1845*, 125 reels (RPI, 1980). The majority of these titles were taken from Thomas W. Streeter, *Bibliography of Texas, 1975–1845*, 5 vols. (Cambridge: Harvard University Press, 1955–60).

38. Susan M. Cottler, Roger M. Haigh, and Shirley Weathers, *Preliminary Survey of the Mexican Collection*, Number 1 of Finding Aids to the Microfilmed Manuscript Collection of the Genealogical Society of Utah (Salt Lake City: University of Utah Press, 1978), p. xiii. Unless otherwise noted, remarks on "The Mexican Collection" were taken from this volume.

39. Estimate of Professor Norman Wright, genealogy specialist in the Department of History, Brigham Young University, as cited by Professor Ted J. Warner, Chairman, Department of History, Brigham Young University, in a letter to the author, September 16, 1980.

40. *Preliminary Survey to the Mexican Collection;* and *Supplement to the Preliminary Survey of the Mexican Collection*. The latter is by Roger M. Haigh

and Shirley A. Weathers (Salt Lake City: University of Utah Press, 1979).
41. For example, some of the church records of the cathedrals of Chihuahua and Durango await microfilming.
42. The filming of these documents is described in an article by George P. Hammond, "The Use of Microphotography in Manuscript Work in New Mexico," in A. F. Kuhlman, ed. *Archives and Libraries*. Papers presented at the 1939 Conference of the American Library Association (Chicago: The American Library Association, 1939), pp. 99–102.
43. This list has been copied with minor editing from the preliminary inventory prepared for the author by Dennis Rowley, Curator of Archives and Manuscripts, Harold B. Lee Library, Brigham Young University. In a letter dated September 2, 1982, Rowley notes that a final inventory should be completed by early 1983. In subsequent discussions, he indicated that the collection consists of several thousand documents preserved in approximately a dozen document cases.
44. Letter from Larry Jochims, Research Historian, Kansas State Historical Society, July 21, 1982.
45. Jack D. Rittenhouse, *The Santa Fe Trail, A Historical Bibliography* (Albuquerque: University of New Mexico Press, 1971).
46. In a letter to the author, Frances H. Stadler, Archivist of the Missouri Historical Society, September 4, 1969, says, "the collection is closed pending Dr. Bieber's possible wish to make further use of it." Dr. Bieber's son (William P. Bieber) is presently (1983) soliciting assistance in editing his late father's papers.
47. Citations as follows: "Guide to the Western Historical Manuscripts Collection," *Western Historical Manuscripts Collection Bulletin* No. 5 (July 1, 1949), No. 6 (November 8, 1956), and *Supplement* to *Bulletin* No. 6 (April 1, 1957).
48. Colton Storm, comp., *A Catalogue of the Everett D. Graff Collection of Western Americana* (Chicago: The University of Chicago Press, 1968). A guide to the map collection of more than six-hundred maps of the nineteenth-century West was prepared by Robert W. Karrow, Jr., ed., and Brenda Berkman, comp., *Index to Maps in the Catalogue of the Everett D. Graff Collection of Western Americana* (Chicago: Newberry Library, 1972).
49. *First Supplement to the Dictionary Catalogue of the Edward E. Ayer Collection,* 3 vols. (Boston: G. K. Hall, 1970) and *Second Supplement . . .,* 4 vols. (Boston: G. K. Hall, 1980).
50. In addition to items listed here, both the Graff and Ayer collections include many printed books by North American authors whose sojourns in New Mexico for commercial or military purposes resulted in government reports or published memoirs. Some of these items are included in a bibliography of contemporary printed works at the end of this book, since they are not necessarily

unique to the Newberry Library.

51. For a good bibliography on the Abiquiú area, see John L. Kessell, "Sources for the History of a New Mexico Community: Abiquiú," NMHR 54 (October 1979): 249–85.

52. Letter from John P. Wilson, Las Cruces, New Mexico, July 6, 1980. Wilson's inventory of sixty-seven pages was sent to the Peabody Museum.

53. Jeanne M. Goddard and Charles Kritzler, comps., *A Catalogue of the Frederick W. & Carrie S. Beinecke Collection of Western Americana* (New Haven and London: Yale University Press, 1965). See also Mary C. Withington, comp., *A Catalogue of Manuscripts in the Collection of Western Americana in the Yale University Library* (New Haven: Yale University Press, 1952).

54. Letter from Archibald Hanna, Curator, Western Americana Collection, Yale University Library, August 7, 1980. Hanna is now retired.

55. Yale University Library, *Catalogue of the Yale Collection of Western Americana*, 4 vols. (Boston: G. K. Hall and Co., 1962).

56. This is a reference to the Thomas W. Streeter Collection, which also contains a great deal of information on the Texan Santa Fe expedition. See Thomas Winthrop Streeter, *The Celebrated Collection of Americana Formed by the Late Thomas Winthrop Streeter*, 4 vols. (New York: Parke-Bernet, 1967–68).

57. Brochure (November 1980) of the Eugene C. Barker Texas History Center.

58. Beers, *Spanish and Mexican Records*, p. 104.

59. Ibid., p. 105. Beers notes that by 1970, translations had been completed for the years 1717–79 and 1804–08. According to William H. Richter, Assistant Archivist, Barker Texas History Center, this work has been advanced to 1789 and 1803–12. Letter, July 21, 1982.

60. A published guide describes the general content of each reel. See Chester V. Kielman, *Guide to the Microfilm Edition of the Béxar Archives, 1822–1836,* vol. 3 (Austin: University of Texas Archives, 1971).

61. Letter from Malcolm D. McLean, Arlington, Texas, July 17, 1980.

62. Beers, *Spanish and Mexican Records*, p. 107.

63. Ibid., pp. 107–08.

64. Ibid., p. 109.

65. Ibid., pp. 109–10, and p. 109 n. 23.

66. Ibid., pp. 113–14.

67. Chester V. Kielman, comp. and ed., *The University of Texas Archives. A Guide to the Historical Manuscripts Collections in the University of Texas Library* (Austin: The University of Texas Press, 1967), pp. 10–11. Kielman notes that these manuscripts are by no means representative of all the material in the *AGN*, but they are "quite comprehensive for the historical development of the Texas region and to a lesser extent for the rest of the American Southwest." Letter to the author, September 11, 1969.

68. Carlos E. Castañeda and Jack Aubrey Dabbs, *Guide to the Latin Ameri-*

can Manuscripts in the University of Texas Library (Cambridge: Harvard University Press, 1939), p. 180.

69. Herbert E. Bolton, *Guide to the Materials for the History of the United States in the Principal Archives of Mexico* (Washington, D.C.: Carnegie Institution, 1913), Kraus Reprint, 1965, p. 448.

70. Beers, *Spanish and Mexican Records,* p. 115. A one-volume "key" in the Bancroft Library indicates that photoprints of this collection were made between 1928 and 1930. The "key" is made up of all calendars bound together. Although most documents reflect mundane affairs of the Matamoros *ayuntamiento,* information is also available on Comanche and Apache activities, the expulsion of Spaniards, medicines used in the 1840s, José Luís Berlandier, and other matters of tangential interest to New Mexico.

71. See items numbered 1023, 1169, 1574, 1889, 1910, 2226, and 2422 in Kielman, *The University of Texas Archives.*

72. For brief descriptions of these collections, see Beers, *Spanish and Mexican Records,* pp. 126–40.

73. Castañeda and Dabbs, *Guide to Latin American Manuscripts,* p. vii.

74. Lota M. Spell, *Research Material for the Study of Latin America at the University of Texas* (Austin: The University of Texas Press, 1954), pp. 3–4.

75. Brochure (May 1977) of the Nettie Lee Benson Latin American Collection, The General Libraries, The University of Texas at Austin. Beers notes that the Genaro García Library contains 350,000 pages of manuscripts for the years 1325–1921. See *Spanish and Mexican Records,* p. 134.

76. Beers, *Spanish and Mexican Records,* p. 135; Spell, *Research Materials,* p. 5.

77. See items numbered 461, 465, 472, 702, 825, 966, 1105, 1326, 1397, 1540, 1767, 1770, 2407 in Ynsfran's *Catálogo.*

78. Jane Garner, comp., *Archives and Manuscripts on Microfilm in the Nettie Lee Benson Latin American Collection. A Checklist* (Austin: The University of Texas Press, 1980).

79. Seymour V. Connor, *A Preliminary Guide to the Archives of Texas* (Austin: Texas Library and Historical Commission, 1956), pp. 5, 11.

80. Letter from David B. Gracy II, Director, Texas State Archives, July 6, 1982. Gracy also noted, "Indeed, as we were drafting this letter, we thought of the A. J. Houston materials and we found three items right off the bat." A 3 x 5 card index consisting of over six-thousand entries is mostly from the 1836–45 period. New Mexico items deal with the Santa Fe trade and Indian problems in the area between New Mexico and Texas.

81. See documents numbered 21, 61, 64–65, 1049, 1198–99, 1773, 1850, 1972, 1980, 1984, 1990, 1992, 2007, 2010, 2013, 2033, 2036, 2038, 2040, 2049, 2053, 2063, 2070, 2077, 2126, 2163, 3102. A revised and expanded calendar to the Lamar Papers was completed in the fall of 1982.

82. Beers, *Spanish and Mexican Records,* p. 117.

83. Ibid., p. 80.

84. Irma Guillén extracted all the tables of contents from most of the *Boletines* from Vol. I, No. 1 (May 15, 1930) through Vol. XII, No. 6 (July–August 1970). Prepared in 1976 for the University of Texas at El Paso, this 118-page typescript lists titles of articles dealing with Indians, governors of Chihuahua, lost archives, newspapers of the state, and other matters of interest to New Mexico. Vol. I, No. 12, and Vol. II, No. 12, are indexes of previous issues. Guillén's work does not circulate.

85. Letter from Simeon B. Newman, Special Collections, UTEP Library, July 5, 1982.

86. Ibid.

87. Some samples are listed in Bolton, *Guide,* p. 414. In an interview with Francisco R. Almada, May 15, 1980, the author was told several times to look for lost New Mexico materials in the collections of *Provincias Internas* documents both in the *AGN* and in the frontier states of New Mexico.

88. The GLO in Texas has always been a state agency. Once part of the State Archives, it was transferred to a new building in 1974. Spanish language documents deal mostly with empresario grants and land conveyances in east Texas. Correspondence between political chiefs and laws relating to land ownership are also included in this collection. In her book entitled *The Spanish Archives of the General Land Office of Texas* (Austin: The Lone Star Press, 1955), Virginia H. Taylor notes that most of the land grants are from the Mexican period in Texas (1824–35). In a telephone conversation with the author (August 25, 1982), she mentioned the historical value of several collections of papers not exclusively land documents. The entire collection of Spanish language records has been microfilmed on thirty-four reels, but these are not yet available to the public.

89. Beers, *Spanish and Mexican Records,* pp. 167–68.

90. Ibid., p. 168.

91. Malcolm D. McLean, comp. and ed., *Papers Concerning Robertson's Colony in Texas,* Vols. I–VI (Fort Worth: Texas Technological University Press, 1974–79). As of July 1980, six volumes had been published. Although they contain relatively few references to New Mexico, the bibliographies for the Mexican period are helpful.

92. Letter from William C. Griggs, Director, The Panhandle-Plains Historical Museum, Canyon, Texas, July 23, 1980.

93. Letter from Dawn Letson, Curator of Manuscripts, Degolyer Library, Southern Methodist University, June 30, 1982.

Circular from the Secretaria de Guerra y Marina, *Mexico, to the* Comandante Principal *of New Mexico, announcing Vicente Guerrero as the second president of the Mexican Republic, April 1, 1829.* (Mexican Archives of New Mexico, *Comandante Principal Papers, Communications Received from Mexico. New Mexico State Records Center and Archives.) Photograph by Daniel Martinez.*

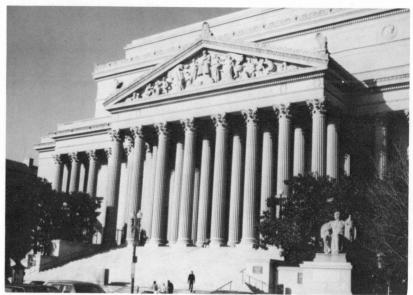

National Archives and Records Service, Washington, D.C. Photograph by Cindy Gross.

CHAPTER III
RECORDS IN THE FEDERAL ARCHIVES OF THE U.S.A.

1. NATIONAL ARCHIVES AND RECORDS SERVICE, WASHINGTON, D.C.:

L ocated across the mall from the Smithsonian Institution on 8th Street and Pennsylvania Avenue (Metro stop Smithsonian), the National Archives and Records Service (NARS) maintains records "created or formerly maintained by Federal agencies in the Washington area that are not in current use and need to be preserved indefinitely because of their value for research or other purposes."[1] Researchers enter from Pennsylvania Avenue, sign in at the register, and proceed to the second floor to apply for an identification card. Consultants and finding aids (preliminary inventories, special lists, reference information papers, microfilm publications pamphlets) are available in the same room (200B).

The organization of the National Archives is based on a system of more than four-hundred record groups that are controlled by branches. The record group is a unit of entry into the archives. It is a "body of organizationally and functionally related records established with particular regard for the administrative history, complexity, and volume of the records and archives of an agency."[2]

The most efficient use of the National Archives results when prior notification of the research topic and time of arrival in Washington are shared with the staff. Upon arrival, the researcher and a branch specialist will consult further before permission is granted to request documents in the main reading room.

Microfilm publications are available by mail order. *National Archives Microfilm Publications* (Washington: National Archives and Records Service [NARS], 1974) is the standard guide to filmed materials. Reprinted in 1979, this 184-page reference guide is the most recent listing of those records which have been filmed. The price of a roll of film is $13.00; order forms are included at the end of the guide. Checks should be made out to the National Archives Trust Fund and sent to: Cashier, National Archives Trust Fund Board, Washington, D.C. 20408. Expect a wait of from four to eight weeks.

The following discussion of specific record groups containing material on the Mexican period begins with RG 59 and RG 84. These two categories appear to have the greatest amount of relevant material, but researchers should bear in mind that other record groups may contain unexpected surprises and should not be overlooked.

RECORD GROUPS.
(1) RG 59. General Records of the Department of State

(a)   Diplomatic Correspondence (1785–1906): For the 1791–1833 period, volumes are "arranged chronologically without regard to country."[3] After 1833, volumes are continued for individual countries (Mexico) or groups of countries (American States).The most useful microfilm publication is M77 (175 reels), "Diplomatic Instructions of the Department of State, 1801–1896," which includes communications to Mexico from May 29, 1833, to April 6, 1854 (Reels 111, 112).[4]

Also included in this group of records are the diplomatic despatches which are complementary to the above-mentioned correspondence. Despatches are incoming letters received by the Department of State from diplomatic representatives together with enclosures, "such as copies of notes received from ministers of foreign states or printed or manuscript material bearing on foreign conditions."[5]

"Despatches from United States Ministers to Mexico, 1823–1906" (M97, 179 reels) is the microfilm publication. Reel 1 is a register. Reels 2–13 cover the period from March 15, 1823, to January 26, 1847.[6] These despatches emanate from Mexico City and not from consular posts in Northern Mexico, but researchers may expect to find copies of notes exchanged with other officials and printed matter relating to the state of affairs in New Mexico.

"Notes from the Mexican Legation in the United States to the Department of State, 1821–1906" (M54, 39 reels) is also useful. These records consist of notes from the Mexican Embassy in Washington registering complaints against U.S. officials and citizens. They include pamphlets, newspapers, and other printed matter. The first two reels of this series contain notes and enclosures transmitted between November 30, 1821, and June 28, 1848.[7] "Notes to Foreign Legations in the United States From the Department of State, 1834–1906" (M99, 99 reels) is the reciprocal side of "Notes From . . ." These notes comment on frontier disorders, Indian raids, extradition of fugitives, and an interesting exchange revealing the Mexican complaint that North Americans were obstructing Mexican efforts to persuade their people to return home under the terms of the Treaty of Guadalupe Hidalgo.[8]

A final series of diplomatic correspondence of interest to the Mexican period researcher includes records "relating to the appointment of special agents, missions, and commissions employed by the President and the Secretary of State for such functions as the negotiation and ratification of treaties, the collection of information on political conditions and public opinion and investigations of various kinds."[9] Here one can find instructions given to Anthony Butler and Joel R. Poinsett regarding the purchase from Mexico of territory in Northern Mexico. Also included are instructions to Henry E. Lawrence to obtain the release of Franklin Coombs and other Americans taken prisoner with members of the Santa Fe expedition from Texas.[10]

(b) Consular Correspondence (1789–1906): Consular posts were established in many Mexican communities to protect the rights of U.S. citizens and to oversee matters of commercial interest between the two countries. Consular records germane to New Mexico in the Mexican period are available for Santa Fe, Chihuahua, and Mexico City.

   i. Santa Fe: Consuls at Santa Fe were appointed in 1825, 1830, 1834, and 1839, but the consulate was never officially recognized by the Mexican government. Manuel Alvarez, a Spanish immigrant who moved to Santa Fe from St. Louis in 1824, served as de facto consul and commercial agent after 1839, however. His letters and communications to the State Department are mostly concerned with claims of discrimination presented by Santa Fe traders and merchants. M199 (1 reel), "Despatches from United States Consuls in Santa Fe, New Mexico, 1830–46" contains these communications.[11]

   ii. Chihuahua: Joshua Pilcher declined the first consular commission of March 7, 1825. Charles W. Webber, appointed two years later on March 3, 1827, followed suit. The first man to accept the post was John Ward, who arrived in Chihuahua on November 27, 1830. The State Department received only two despatches from Ward. For the entire period between 1825 and 1848, only six communications exist. Since a fire destroyed the early records in 1922, the only extant communications will be found in M289 (3 reels), "Despatches from United States Consuls in Chihuahua, Mexico, 1830–1906."[12]

   iii. Mexico City: M296 (15 reels), "Despatches from United States Consuls in Mexico City, Mexico, 1822–1906," contains the records of the Consulate General in Mexico City. Because of the consular traffic between Mexico City and Chihuahua, these documents include communications on trade, passports, Indians, and the Mexican War.[13] Unexplained gaps in the record occur between April 10, 1825, and March 25, 1832, and also between April 26, 1847, and December

8, 1848. During the latter period, John Black was consul. Organized chronologically, the first five reels cover the years 1822–59. Information about the Mexican economy, customs policies, international trade, a history of coinage, anti-American feelings, and other subjects provide useful data which help explain policies and problems of tangential interest to New Mexico.

Communications to consular posts "are arranged chronologically without regard to post, except that for the years 1835–74 they are arranged geographically and thereunder chronologically."[14] Some of these communiqués are filmed in M78 (7 reels), "Consular Instructions of the Department of State, 1801–34."[15] Materials from 1835–74 are not filmed.

iv. Miscellaneous Correspondence: State Department correspondence with people in foreign countries, who were not diplomatic or consular officers, bears investigating. "Domestic Letters (Sent) of the Department of State, 1784–1906" (M40,171 reels) consists of letters to persons dealing with foreign policy matters as well as the domestic duties of the State Department such as census taking.[16] For example, one letter to the district attorney at St. Louis, November 4, 1843, alerted Missouri to the plan of Colonel Charles A. Warfield to rob the Santa Fe caravans.[17] Domestic letters (received) include the opinions of Charles Bent and other U.S. citizens resident in Mexico regarding a variety of subjects. These letters, comprising 1,533 volumes and loose papers, include registers for the 1817–1906 period which are useful for locating correspondence of U.S. citizens in New Mexico. The NARS microfilm publication is M179 (1,310 reels), "Miscellaneous Letters at the Department of State, 1789–1906."[18]

Some demographic, topographical, and land ownership problems will be resolved by reference to "Cartographic Records, 1844–1967."[19] Maps of Mexico dated in the 1840s and 1850s contain information reflecting boundaries and population centers in the Mexican period. See the *NARS Guide* (1974) for other record groups with cartographic holdings.

(2) *RG 84. Records of the Foreign Service Posts of the Department of State*
The duties of diplomatic and consular officers were different. Diplomatic officials concerned themselves more with policies of state, while the latter addressed themselves to the rights and obligations of Americans in foreign countries, passport problems, and commercial matters. Many of the records kept by consular posts are incomplete, destroyed by fires and floods, or nonexistent due to poor record-keeping practices. Some officers, upon leaving their posts, regarded their correspondence as private property and took it with them. Fortunately, the instructions received from the Department of State and the copies of despatches to the department are duplicated by records main-

tained in RG 59. RG 84 has not been microfilmed. "Records of Diplomatic Posts, 1788–1945," includes the records of the U.S. Embassy in Mexico City, 1825–1940.[20] Of value to the researcher interested in New Mexico are passport records; correspondence between posts; marriages, births, and deaths of American citizens; and records concerning the disposal of property. Also included are copies of despatches prepared by U.S. diplomatic officers in Mexico and sent to the State Department, along with notes to and from the Mexican Minister of Foreign Relations, some of which concern the invasion of New Mexico by Texans in 1841 and 1843. Since Cerán St. Vrain represented the interests of the United States in Santa Fe from 1834 to 1838, his activities are revealed in "Records of Mexico City Consulate General, Letters Sent (Series C8.1), Letterbook!"[21]

On March 2, 1833, the State Department tried to formalize the matter of records preservation in consular posts. Instructions were issued providing for the care and retention of post records and the type of records that should be kept. Some officials continued to view these documents as private property, however; these have disappeared from the public archives. The post records of Chihuahua and Santa Fe would be particularly useful if they could be found. To find the names of consular officers and their dates of tenure, consult M587 (21 reels), "Lists of United States Consular Officers, 1789–1939."[22]

(3) *RG 76. Records of Boundary and Claims Commissions and Arbitrations*
Four sections of this record group (none of which is microfilmed) contain some information of interest to New Mexico: "Records Relating to International Boundaries. 1783–1952"; "Records Relating to Claims. 1794–1941"; "Records Relating to International Arbitrations. 1866–1945"; and "Cartographic and Audio-Visual Records. 1794–1952." Boundary dispute records include the journals, maps, progress reports, and field records of several boundary commissions. Claims commission records consist of U.S.-Mexican disputes from 1825 to 1938. Located at the General Archives Division in Suitland, Maryland, these records include among others Claim No. 66 of Manuel Alvarez, David Waldo, and other U.S. merchants in Santa Fe for damages incurred as a result of the 1837 uprising in New Mexico (Area V, R31:42. Box 7, Envelope 19). The claim was rejected on February 18, 1842.[23] Other claims which went before the 1849–51 commission are cases against Mexico based on incidents arising before the signing of the Treaty of Guadalupe Hidalgo. The 1868 Claims Commission heard Claim No. 379 submitted by the father of Trinidad and Irinea Baca, grandchildren of Manuel Armijo, in the amount of $7199.56. The plaintiffs alleged that this amount represented the unpaid salary owed to Armijo while he was governor of New Mexico. It was rejected in 1870, but the documents presented in this case include wills, marriage and baptismal certificates, business dealings, and many other papers which were originally created in the Mexican period.[24] Claims presented by Mariano Armijo (No.

386), Diego Archuleta (No. 711), and Donaciano Vigil (No. 945) provide similar kinds of information on other important New Mexicans.

(4) *RG 107. Records of the Office of the Secretary of War*

Some correspondence between Army officers and U.S. government officials is located in this record group. Records relating to Indian affairs are located in RG 75, but "Letters Received and Sent 1791–1889" contains correspondence relating to other kinds of military affairs for the 1818–1847 period. Mexican War correspondence can be found in the "Military Books" for the 1800–1870 period. Included in this section are nine letters to Stephen Watts Kearny written between May 1, 1845, and October 7, 1846.[25] Microfilm publications include "Letters Sent by the Secretary of War, 1800–1809" (M6, 110 reels), "Registers of Letters Received by the Office of the Secretary of War, Main Series, 1800–1870" (M22, 134 reels), and "Letters Received by the Secretary of War, Registered Series, 1801–1870" (M221, 317 reels).

(5) *RG 94. Records of the Adjutant General's Office, 1780–1917*

Record Groups 94, 107, and 393 are in the custody of the Navy and Old Army Branch of the National Archives. The Adjutant General's Office (AGO) was organized in the 1790s, and in 1821 it was separated from the Inspector General's Department. Reports of military engagements which had been filed previously with the Office of the Secretary of War went to the AGO after 1821. The majority of correspondence between Army officers and the United States government for the Mexican period will be found in RG 94 because the Adjutant General was the principal record keeper for the War Department.

The AGO was "charged with matters relating to command, discipline, and administration of the Military Establishment, and has had the duties of recording, authenticating, and communicating the Secretary's orders, instructions, and regulations to troops and individuals in the Army."[26] Among the "General Records, 1784–1917" can be found several interesting collections of documents:[27]

(a) "Letters Received" (Book Period, 1805–1889). The file of Brig. Gen. Stephen Watts Kearny describes the entry of the Army of the West into New Mexico and its advance down the Rio Grande. These documents include Col. Sterling Price's report on the Taos Rebellion, Col. Alexander William Doniphan's expedition against Navajos and Utes, and other materials concerning Indian depredations on the Santa Fe Trail.

(b) "Compiled Records of Service and Related Indexes Pertaining to Volunteers from New Mexico Who Served in the Indian Wars, 1849, 1854 and 1855" (7E2, R29:14B–D. Woodruff File Holders 50753–50762). These records are important for age and mustering-in points of New Mexican citizens.

(c) "Muster Rolls of Volunteer Organizations: Civil War." Boxes 2538–2543, 2538–2544, and 2538–2548 show when and where men enlisted and their ages.[28]

(d) "Compiled Records of Service and Related Indexes Pertaining to Volunteer Union Soldiers from Arizona, California, New Mexico, and Texas: 1861–66." These are "carded records" containing all the information available on soldiers from these areas, i.e., muster rolls, returns, morning reports, hospital and prison records, etc. Some original documents are filed with the "card." For New Mexico, see boxes 1094–1101.

Pertinent microfilm publications include:

(a) M242 (4 reels) 16 mm. "Index to Compiled Service Records of Volunteer Soldiers Who Served in Organizations From the Territory of New Mexico."
(b) M427 (46 reels) 16 mm. "Compiled Service Records of Volunteer Union Soldiers Who Served in Organizations From the Territory of New Mexico."
(c) M565 (63 reels). "Letters Sent by the Office of the Adjutant General (Main Series), 1800–1890."
(d) M711 (85 reels). "Registers of Letters Received, Office of the Adjutant General, 1812–1889."
(e) M567 (636 reels). "Letters Received by the Office of the Adjutant General (Main Series, 1822–1860.)"[29]

(6) RG 393. Records of U.S. Army Continental Commands, 1821–1920
   A War Department General Order of May 17, 1821, divided the United States into Eastern and Western departments and subsequently into military divisions which were further subdivided.[30] Within the record group is a section entitled "Other Records of Military Installation. 1835–1920," which contains the records of the 9th Military Department and the Department of New Mexico. Among morning reports, personal papers, and post letter books will be found correspondence with citizens of New Mexico at the time when Americans assumed control. The National Archives has microfilmed "Letters Sent by the 9th Military Department, the Department of New Mexico, and the District of New Mexico, 1849–1890" (M1072, 7 reels) and is currently preparing to film the letters received by the 9th Military Department and the Department of New Mexico.[31] Maps and plans compiled by forces invading New Mexico will be found in "Cartographic Records. 1837–1920."

(7) RG49. Records of the Bureau of Land Management (BLM)
   The BLM was created in 1946 when the General Land Office (GLO) and Grazing Service were merged. Charged with the responsibility of classifying, managing, and disposing of the public lands and their resources, the BLM became the depository of certain records created by the long struggle to clear title to Mexican land grants. Before working with BLM records, researchers should understand how this agency has functioned historically as a record-keeping institution.

Soon after the signing of the Treaty of Guadalupe Hidalgo, Congress provided for the appointment of a Surveyor General in New Mexico. William Pelham, the first appointee, opened this office in Santa Fe in January 1855. His principal responsibility was to investigate private land claims "and report thereon to the Secretary of the Interior, who was to report to Congress."[32] For the next six months, two clerks, who were familiar with Spanish, worked on separating land records from the mass of papers (two wagonloads) inherited by the United States as a result of the conquest of New Mexico. "From 168 packages containing 168,000 papers, 1,715 grants, conveyances of land, and other documents referring to grants of land were selected for retension. . . . Altogether 1,014 land grants were found, of which 197 were private grants."[33] These documents reveal the extent of land-grant activity in both the Spanish colonial and Mexican periods.

The records remained in the hands of the office of the Surveyor General until 1925 when that office was abolished, "and its duties and records were transferred to the district cadastral engineer in charge of the Public Survey Office in Santa Fe."[34] After 1946, this office came to be known as the Bureau of Land Management State Office.[35] In 1934–35, the Civil Works Administration prepared transcriptions and translations of these records which were microfilmed from 1955 to 1957 by the University of New Mexico library.[36] When the BLM office received a positive copy of the sixty-six reels of microfilm, it retired the original records from active use. In 1972 these records were transferred to the New Mexico State Records Center and Archives (NMSRCA).

In addition to this body of records, survey notes with plats, maps, and correspondence can be found in the BLM district offices at Santa Fe and Denver. Other records of the Surveyor General of New Mexico are located in the Denver and Forth Worth federal records centers. These sources are discussed in more detail at the end of this chapter.

The most important papers in RG 49 are the docket papers accumulated and maintained by the Private Land Claims Division (Division "D") of the GLO. These records, located at the General Archives Division at Suitland, Maryland (Area IV. R18:50) are arranged alphabetically by state and then numerically documented by claim. Thirty-nine boxes (dockets 1-215) relate to Colorado and New Mexico claims. Documents include legal papers used to substantiate a tract of land, petitions, plats, depositions, deeds, abstracts of title, appeals, court decisions, and correspondence.[37] Other items of importance include an index of field notes of New Mexico surveys, an incomplete set of tract books for New Mexico, a docket of private land claims in New Mexico, Spanish documents with English translations filed with the Surveyor General, a list of confirmed private land claims surveyed in Colorado and New Mexico, and miscellaneous records further documenting the history of Mexican land titles. Contracts for the survey of private land grants and the legal limits of pueblos and town sites are also included in this collection. Letters received from surveyors general provide interesting reading on the history of archival record keeping as well as comments on the difficulties associated with getting land documents from local residents.

Another source of information in RG 49 is the section entitled "Cartographic Records Branch." Maps, survey notes, and protraction diagrams (plats) provide more data on land grants (and private land claims) in addition to other forms of land concessions. Eight volumes for New Mexico and one for Colorado "show the name of the grantee; the boundaries of the grant; its relationship to public land surveys; courses for the survey; topographic features; name of the deputy surveyor [who made the original field notes]; date and number of the surveying contract; certificates from the Surveyor General and Court of Private Land Claims approving the survey; date and record of patent; houses, ranches, or ruins of the same and other structures; cultivated lands; and information as to lot, township, range, and number of acres."[38]

The only microfilm publications from this record group pertaining to the Mexican period are "Miscellaneous Letters Sent by the General Land Office, 1796–1889" (M25, 228 reels) and "Letters Sent by the General Land Office to the Surveyor General, 1796–1901" (M27, 31 reels).[39] Copies of letters sent to the Surveyor General for New Mexico appear in separate volumes for the period 1854–1891 and are not microfilmed.

(8) *RG 49. Records of the Secretary of the Interior*

Two potential sources of information exist in this record group and both are located in the "Records of the Division of Appointments 1849–1908." The first is the *Annual Reports* of the surveyors general, which comment on a variety of land problems. The second relates to the appointments of individuals who were recommended for federal positions in New Mexico, of whom fifty had Spanish surnames. Letters of recommendation and applications for appointment provide information on Mariano Armijo, Francisco Chávez, and others. See the microfilm publication entitled "Interior Department Appointment Papers: Territory of New Mexico, 1850–1907" (M750, 18 reels).[40]

(9) *RG 29. Records of the Bureau of the Census*

The Seventh Census of the United States (1850) was the first to list all household members. Schedules contain information on age, sex, country of birth, value of real estate owned, and occupation of each household member. The existing counties in New Mexico (Bernalillo, Rio Arriba, Santa Fe. Santa Ana, San Miguel, Taos, and Valencia) are included as part of the microfilm publication, "Seventh Census of the United States, 1850" (M432, 1009 reels).[41]

(10) *RG 11. General Records of the United States Government*

These records contain both ratified and unperfected treaties and international agreements. Of particular interest to students of the Mexican period are the Treaty of Limits, January 12, 1828, and April 5, 1831; the Treaty Regarding

Claims, April 11, 1839; and the Treaty of Guadalupe Hidalgo, February 2, 1848.

(11) *RG 46. Records of the United States Senate*

Among the many reports, memorials, minutes, and petitions in this record group are the "Territorial Papers of the United States Senate, 1789–1873" (M200, 20 reels).[42] These include select papers of the U.S. Senate relating to the affairs of the territories. For New Mexico, the inclusive dates on Reel 14 are 1840–1854. Other records in RG 46 are: (a) the report of commissioners Thomas Mather, Benjamin Reeves, and George S. Sibley informing the Secretary of War of the completion of their survey of a road from Missouri to New Mexico in 1827;[43] (b) a report from the Secretary of War including a handwritten report from Lt. William H. Emory describing Kearny's march; and (c) Private Land Claims records relating to the confirmation of land grants.

(12) *RG 267. Records of the Supreme Court of the United States*

Cases appealed from lower courts include some which involve private land claims. In the "Final Report of the U.S. Attorney for the Court of Private Land Claims" (printed in the *Report of the Attorney General*, 1904, pp. 95–109) is a list of fifty-seven claims dating from titles authorized by Spanish and Mexican authorities. A card index to case files, 1792–1909, constitutes part of this record group. The appellate jurisdiction records, 1792–1972, sometimes contain a copy of the transcript proceedings from the lower court including petitions, maps, deeds, depositions, and other documents presented to the court. An index in case files gives names of the parties involved.[44] Microfilm publications include "Dockets of the Supreme Court of the United States, 1791–1950" (M216, 27 reels) and "Index to Appellate Case Files of the United States Supreme Court, 1792–1909" (M408, 20 reels).[45]

(13) *RG 75. Records of the Bureau of Indian Affairs*

These records are at best tangential to New Mexico under Mexican sovereignty. Indians who were affected by the movement of people along the Santa Fe Trail and by the search for buffalo and beaver hides in Mexican territory were of concern to both U.S. and Mexican governments, but Mexican sources are richer. "Letters Received by the Office of Indian Affairs 1824–1880" (M234, 962 reels)[46] contains some information. The Central Superintendency, for example, established in 1851 as successor to the Missouri and St. Louis superintendencies, accumulated a few letters from its predecessors whose jurisdiction included the Platte River. (See M234, Reels 747–756.) Likewise, Thomas Fitzpatrick, first agent of the Upper Platte Agency, established in 1846, wrote a number of letters regarding New Mexico and the Santa Fe Trail from his base at Bent's Fort.[47] Thorough research should include a glance at "Records of the New Mexico Superintendency of Indian Affairs, 1849–1880" (T21, 30 reels) and the "Register of Letters Received by the Office of Indian Affairs, 1824–1880" (M18, 126 reels).

(14) *RG 56. General Records of the Treasury*

As the main port of entry for the Santa Fe trade, St. Louis was an important entrepôt for New Mexicans involved in this commerce. Records of the Customs Service relating to all phases of customs administration include "Letters Sent by the Secretary of the Treasury to Collectors of Customs at all Ports (1789–1847) and at Small Ports (1847–78)" (M175, 43 reels). Reels 2–9 cover the years of the Mexican period and contain appeals from importers concerning value appraisals and assessment of duties, applications for the return of excess duties, and the enforcement of laws. In July 1846, for example, the Surveyor of Customs at St. Louis was authorized to permit goods purchased at Pittsburg before the declaration of war and destined for Santa Fe to be exported through Independence, Missouri.[48] Related publications are: (a) "Correspondence of the Secretary of the Treasury with Collectors of Customs, 1789–1833" (M178, 39 reels). This collection duplicates letters filmed in M175 but arranges them by customs district and includes copies of letters received by the Secretary from the collectors; and (b) "Letters Received by the Secretary of the Treasury from Collectors of Customs, 1833–1869" (M174, 226 reels).

2. REGIONAL BRANCHES OF THE NATIONAL ARCHIVES (FEDERAL ARCHIVES AND RECORDS CENTERS):

The National Archives and Records Service operates a nationwide system of depositories, all of which have some microfilm publications useful for research on the Mexican period. These regional branches of the National Archives were originally developed for the purpose of responding to the torrent of paper created by the federal bureaucracy. During their early years, they were principally concerned with problems related to the management of records created by Washington and subordinate federal agencies. Now, however, they are able to offer assistance and research facilities for researchers. Since they are constantly receiving publications (microfilm) from the NARS, they should be consulted prior to a long and expensive trip to Washington. Microfilm holdings can be borrowed through Interlibrary Loan.

Each of these regional archives also stores "operational records of limited current use which belong to the federal agencies in their respective regions."[49] In other words, in addition to the NARS microfilm holdings common to all of the regional branches, each has document collections of particular importance to the surrounding area. New Mexico-related materials are located in Denver, even though the Fort Worth region now has jurisdiction over New Mexico.[50] Mexican period documents will be found in the following collections:

(1) *Records of the Bureau of Land Management*

These records include correspondence created by the Surveyor General of New Mexico relating to land grants. Handwritten copies of letters sent, surveys, plats, conflicts in claims, field notes, annual reports, and other materials provide data on grants made during the Mexican period. This body of documents was created by the Santa Fe office of the Surveyor General's office and was accessioned in Denver over a twenty-year period until the entire collection was available for archival use in 1972.[51]

(2) *New Mexico District Court Records*

One of the most common and valuable collections of documents in all of the Federal Records Centers is the records of the district courts of the United States. Those for New Mexico contain a few items on the 1847 murder of Charles Bent as well as photostat copies of Mexican period land deals. An unpublished inventory is available.[52]

Regional branches of the National Archives are located in Boston, New York, Philadelphia, Atlanta, Chicago, Kansas City, Fort Worth, Denver, San Francisco, Los Angeles, and Seattle. All have copies of the following NARS microfilm publications, most of which are discussed earlier in this chapter.[53]

(a) "Diplomatic Instructions of the Department of State, 1801–1906" (M77, 175 reels).

(b) "Consular Instructions of the Department of State, 1801–1834" (M78, 7 reels).

(c) Diplomatic Despatches: "Mexico, 1823–1906" (M97, 179 reels).

(d) Consular Despatches: "Mexico, 1821–1906" (M54, 39 reels).

(e) "Correspondence of the Secretary of the Treasury with Collectors of Customs, 1789–1833" (M178, 39 reels).

(f) "Letters Received by the Secretary of the Treasury from Collectors of Customs, 1833–1869" (M174, 226 reels).

(g) "Letters Sent by the Secretary of the Treasury to Collectors of Customs at All Ports (1789–1847) and at Small Ports (1847–1878)" (M175, 43 reels).

(h) "Seventh Census of the United States, 1850" (M432, 1009 reels).

Because the regional branches are constantly accumulating additional microfilm holdings, researchers should contact the nearest one for inventory updating. The search for original documents, however, has revealed the paucity of materials in all but the Denver archive. No Mexican period documents dealing with New Mexico will be found at Fort Worth.[54]

An article by Gerald K. Haines in the March 1977 *Newsletter* of the Society for Historians of American Foreign Relations suggests that today's citations of State Department material often contain false or insufficient information. What Haines suggests for the citation of diplomatic records should serve as a guide for all NARS record groups.

Haines emphasizes the importance of citing the correct record group, without which researchers and archivists are frequently unable to locate a particular document. In addition, footnotes must show the exact location of the document in the National Archives, the Washington National Records Center, Suitland, Maryland, or one of eleven federal records centers located throughout the country. For microfilm publications, Haines suggests using the full citation of the record group followed by the microfilm publication number, reel number, and frame number. He encourages writers to use complete information for the first citation followed by accepted abbreviations, i.e., RG (Record Group), NA (National Archives), WNRC (Washington National Records Center, Suitland, MD), FRC plus a city (Federal Records Centers), and M or T to identify microfilmed records. Because accurate footnoting is a responsibility scholars owe to their readers, it should be viewed as a chore of significance and consequence not to be taken lightly.

3. THE LIBRARY OF CONGRESS:

The Library of Congress is located on Capitol Hill (Metro stop Capitol South). Manuscripts are located on the third floor behind the main Library of Congress and may be consulted by anyone engaged in serious research who presents proper identification, completes the Manuscript Division's registration form, and agrees to adhere to the Library's rules for the use of rare materials.

Since the various Hispanic collections were being surveyed during the preparation of this chapter, they were not consulted in detail. The staff presently is preparing a guide which will replace the outdated "Draft to a Reference Guide to Hispanic Manuscript Collections in the Library of Congress." Researchers are also referred to a calendar prepared by Vicente Cortés Alonzo entitled "Latin American Miscellany." Compiled in 1960–62 and revised in 1964, the calendar lists a variety of materials relevant to the Southwest.

Unfortunately, the holdings on New Mexico in the Mexican period are sparse. Some scientific data can be obtained from the Luis Berlandier Papers. They deal primarily with explorations in upper Mexico and what is now Texas, but they also include journals of his travels and various Mexican War experiences. Berlandier manuscripts can also be found at Harvard, Yale, the University of Michigan, and the Thomas Gilcrease Institute of American History Library in Tulsa, Oklahoma.[55]

Several other collections hold some promise for Mexican period material. Military orders and correspondence regarding protection of the Santa Fe caravan of 1839 can be found in two folders that also include correspondence between a certain General Arbuckle and John and Josiah Gregg. Further information on the war in New Mexico can be found in "Mexican War: Polk Documents." These materials contain statistics, casualties, engineers' reports, and battle plans.

Some maps of interest to Mexican period historians will be found in the Woodbury Lowery Collection. This collection was originally comprised of 300 original and facsimile maps relating to former Spanish possessions within the United States. Lowery's notes on 750 additional maps plus reproductions purchased by the Library of Congress have made this a significant cartographic source for study of the Spanish Borderlands.[56]

Library of Congress microfilm holdings include a few collections related to the Mexican period. In addition to the Spanish and Mexican Archives of New Mexico (SANM, MANM), one can find the papers of John Russell Bartlett dealing with the Mexican Boundary Commission, 1850–77, and records of the 1850 Census. Early State Records *(Records of the States of the United States of America)* filmed in cooperation with the University of North Carolina contain some significant information on New Mexico. Reel 1, 1822 to 1852, has the Journal of the Santa Fe legislature, April 22, 1822, to March 12, 1824; March 31, 1824, to January 29, 1828; February 1, 1828, to February 15, 1837; January 1, 1845, to December 31, 1845; January 1, 1846, to August 10, 1846. Other documents of the Mexican period can be found in this reel, some of which are duplicates of those filmed in the MANM.[57]

Some Mexico City newspapers can be found at the Library of Congress: *El Sol* (1821–1828); *El Observador* (1827–1830); and others. Researchers should consult *Latin American Newspapers in United States Libraries. A Union List,* compiled in the Serial Division, Library of Congress, by Steven M. Charno and published by the University of Texas Press, 1968. Also useful is *Newspapers in Microfilm: Foreign Countries, 1948–1972,* published by the Library of Congress in 1973. For thoroughness in Mexican period newspaper research, however, one must review the holdings in the *hemerotecas* in Mexico City.[58]

4. A SUMMARY OF THE MOST USEFUL DESCRIPTIVE REFERENCES AND NARS FINDING AIDS:

A. REFERENCES.

(1) Beers, Henry Putney. *Spanish and Mexican Records of the Southwest.* Tucson: University of Arizona Press, 1979. Largely a compilation of public records, this extremely valuable resource also gives a vast amount of information on the history of archives and their collections. Arranged geographically (New Mexico, Texas, California, Arizona), the book's scope is from 1600 to the mid-nineteenth century. An extensive classified bibliography is included.

(2) *Catalog of National Archives Microfilm Publications.* Washington: NARS, 1974. Lists the microfilm publications available in all Record Groups along with some brief descriptions of the nature of holdings for major sections of individual Record Groups. Explains the significance of "M" and "T" prefixes and provides order forms.

(3) *Guide to the National Archives of the United States.* Washington: NARS, 1974. Supersedes the 1948 *Guide to the Records in the National Archives.* This volume describes records accessioned as of June 30, 1970, and includes a *very valuable* list of references to published documents, indexes, and other sources at the end of each record group section. A completely revised edition

was to appear in 1983.

(4) Lounsbury, Ralph G. "Materials in the National Archives for the History of New Mexico Before 1948." *New Mexico Historical Review* 21 (1946): 247–56. Although dated, this article provides valuable information on NARS holdings. References to "C" numbers are explained in footnote 21 of this chapter.

(5) Ulibarri, George S., and John P. Harrison. *Guide to Materials on Latin America in the National Archives of the United States*. Washington: NARS, 1974. Supersedes the 1961 edition. This is a specialized supplement to the *Guide to the National Archives of the United States*, but it contains very little information relevant to New Mexico.

(6) ————. "Guide to Materials in the National Archives Relating to Hispanic People in the Southwest." Compiled in 1977 and awaiting NARS publication, this is a very useful study of almost five-hundred typewritten pages which provides many suggestions for research into the heritage of Hispanic people in the Southwest.

B. NARS FINDING AIDS.

For a quick reference to NARS record groups, NARS publications, and specialized finding aids such as preliminary inventories (PI), special lists (SL), and reference information papers, see the *Select List of Publications of the National Archives and Records Service*. General Information Leaflet, Number 3. Washington: NARS, 1977. For record groups cited in this chapter, the following finding aids will be useful.

RG 59:   General Records of the Department of State (PI157 and SL7 and SL37).

RG 84:   Foreign Service Posts of the Department of State (PI60 and SL9).

RG 76:   Boundary and Claims Commissions and Arbitrations (PI135, PI136, PI143, PI170, and PI177 and SL26).

RG 94:   Adjutant General's Office (PI17 and SL33).

RG 49:   Bureau of Land Management (PI33 and SL19, SL23, SL27, and SL29).

RG 48:   Office of the Secretary of the Interior (PI81 and SL18).

RG 29:   Bureau of the Census (PI103 and PI161 and SL24 and SL34).

RG 11:   General Records of the U.S. Government (PI159).

RG 46:   United States Senate (PI12, PI23, PI42, PI48, PI59, PI61–63, and PI75 and SL20, and SL23, and SL32).

RG 267:   Supreme Court of the United States (PI139 and SL21).

RG 75:   Bureau of Indian Affairs (PI163 and SL6, SL13, and SL23).

RG 56:   Department of the Treasury (PI187).

If they are not out of print, these pamphlets may be obtained free of charge by writing Publications Sales Branch, National Archives, General Services Administration, Washington, D.C. 20408. Microfilm publications pamphlets are also available at this address without charge. See the *Catalog of National Archives Microfilm* for a list of "M" series pamphlets.

NOTES

1. Philip M. Haines, ed., *A Guide to Archives and Manuscripts in the United States* (New Haven: Yale University Press, 1961), p. 126.
2. *Guide to the National Archives of the United States* (Washington: NARS, 1974), p. 6. (Hereinafter cited as *NARS Guide.*) A newer edition was to be published in 1983.
3. Ibid., p. 131.
4. *Catalog of National Archives Microfilm Publications* (Washington: NARS, 1974), pp. 12, 13. (Hereinafter cited as *NARS Microfilm Catalog.*) An explanation of "M" and "T" prefixes on microfilm publications can be found in the first two pages.
5. *NARS Guide*, p. 132.
6. *NARS Microfilm Catalog*, p. 20.
7. Ibid., p. 59.
8. George S. Ulibarri, "Guide to Materials in the National Archives Relating to Hispanic People in the Southwest." This is an unedited manuscript prepared in 1977 and awaiting publication by NARS. (Hereinafter cited as "Guide.")
9. *NARS Guide*, p. 132.
10. Natalia Summers, comp., *List of Documents Relating to Special Agents of the Department of State, 1789–1906*. SL7 (Washington: NARS, 1951).
11. *NARS Microfilm Catalog*, p. 50.
12. Ibid., p. 31.
13. Ibid., p. 42.
14. *NARS Guide*, p. 132.
15. *NARS Microfilm Catalog*, p. 13.
16. Ibid., p. 85.
17. Ulibarri, "Guide" ms. No pagination.
18. *NARS Microfilm Catalog*, pp. 86–92.
19. *NARS Guide*, pp. 137–38.
20. Diplomatic posts include embassies and legations. Consular posts include consulates general, consulates, and commercial and consular agencies. See Mark G. Eckhoff and Alexander P. Mavro, comps., *List of Foreign Service Post Records in the National Archives*. SL9 (Washington: NARS, 1958), revised 1967, p. 1.
21. Ralph G. Lounsbury, "Materials in the National Archives for the History of New Mexico Before 1848," *New Mexico Historical Review* (NMHR) 21

(1946): 251. "C" numbers were used as an inventory system for diplomatic and consular post records included in what is now RG 84. A State Department circular to diplomatic and consular posts of January 8, 1931 (Decimal File 124.02/265a), "gives a detailed breakdown of the classifications. The 'C' numbers no longer reflect the arrangement of the post records, but provide helpful guides for locating them." Letter from Ronald E. Swerczek, Diplomatic Branch, Civil Archives Division, NARS, July 23, 1980.

22. *NARS Microfilm Catalog*, p. 92.

23. Ulibarri, "Guide" ms., and George S. Ulibarri, comp., *Records of the United States and Mexican Claims Commission*. PI136 (Washington: NARS, 1962), Entry 7; Lounsbury, "Materials in the National Archives," p. 253n.22 says that "Records of the Claims Commission, 1849–51" consist of *Awards*, 2 vols., *Opinions*, 3 vols., and *Letter Books*, 3 vols.

24. See Ulibarri's "Guide" ms. for the following reference: Suitland, NNG, Area V, R31:42, Box 46 Envelope 60; see also Entry 41 in Preliminary Inventory (PI)136.

25. Ulibarri, "Guide" ms.

26. *NARS Guide*, p. 231.

27. Ulibarri, "Guide" ms.

28. Use box numbers with caution since the records are often reboxed, rendering the numbers meaningless.

29. *NARS Microfilm Catalog*, pp. 102, 104–5.

30. *NARS Guide*, p. 273. See also Elaine C. Everly et al., comps., *Preliminary Inventory of the Records of United States Army Continental Commands, 1821–1920*. Record Group 393. Vol. IV, Military Installations, 1821–81 (Washington: NARS, 1973).

31. Letter from Elaine C. Everly, Assistant Chief, Navy and Old Army Branch, National Archives, Washington, April 7, 1981.

32. Henry Putney Beers, *Spanish and Mexican Records of the Southwest* (Tucson: University of Arizona Press, 1979), p. 46.

33. Ibid., p. 47.

34. Ibid., p. 49.

35. Ibid., p. 49n.28.

36. Albert James Díaz, *A Guide to the Microfilm of Papers Relating to New Mexico Land Grants* (Albuquerque: University of New Mexico Press, 1960).

37. See Harry P. Yoshpe and Philip P. Browner, comps., *Land-Entry Papers of the General Land Office*. PI22 (Washington: NARS, 1949).

38. Beers, *Spanish and Mexican Records*, p. 56. See also Laura E. Kelsay, comp., *List of Cartographic Records of the General Land Office*. Special List (SL)19 (Washington: NARS, 1964).

39. *NARS Microfilm Catalog*, p. 116.

40. Ibid., p. 115.

41. Ibid., p. 120.

42. Ibid., p. 10.

43. See also Buford Roland, ed., "Report of the Commissioners on the Road from Missouri to New Mexico, October, 1827," NMHR 14 (1939): 215–29. Roland describes the records in the files of the U.S. Senate.

44. Ulibarri, "Guide" ms.

45. *NARS Microfilm Catalog*, p. 11.

46. Ibid., p. 116.

47. See Edward E. Hill, comp., *Records of the Bureau of Indian Affairs*, Vol. II, PI163 (Washington: NARS, 1965); and pamphlet accompanying M234. *Letters Received by the Office of Indian Affairs, 1824–1880* (Washington: NARS, 1966).

48. See Lounsbury, "Materials in the National Archives," p. 255n.33; and *NARS Guide*, p. 169. An explanation of the functioning of the Customs Service and its historic role in the Treasury Department is included in the NARS pamphlet accompanying M175.

49. Gerald T. White, "Government Archives Afield: The Federal Records Centers and the Historian," *The Journal of American History* 55 (1969): 833.

50. Fort Worth (Region 7) collects records created by federal agencies in Arkansas, Louisiana, Texas, Oklahoma, and New Mexico. Denver (Region 8) serves Colorado, Montana, North Dakota, South Dakota, Utah, and Wyoming. New Mexico belonged to Denver until 1972, but the District Court and Bureau of Land Management Records were not transferred to Fort Worth when the change of jurisdiction was made. Denver continues to receive records created by these federal agencies in New Mexico.

51. According to archivist Joel Barker, some of the Surveyor General's records were sent to Washington. In most cases, however, copies are available in this collection. No inventory has been prepared, but a series title listing serves to identify the title and date of specific items. Interview with the author, January 7, 1981. For a more detailed discussion of the Surveyor General's records, see Beers, *Spanish and Mexican Records*, pp. 51–57.

52. Thomas Wiltsey, "Preliminary Inventory of Records of the United States District Court of New Mexico" (Denver Archives and Records Center, 1981).

53. See Charles South, comp., *List of National Archives Microfilm Publications in the Regional Archives Branches* (Washington: NARS, 1975).

54. Letter from Kent Carter, Chief Archives Branch, Fort Worth Archives and Records Center, July 21, 1980.

55. Beers, *Spanish and Mexican Records*; see also Smithsonian Institution, *Catalogue of the Berlandier Manuscripts Deposited in the Smithsonian Institution, Washington, D.C.* (New York: Folger and Turner, Printer, 1853).

56. See U.S. Library of Congress, Division of Maps. *The Lowery Collection: A Descriptive List of Maps of the Spanish Possessions within the Present Lim-*

its of the United States, 1502–1820. Prep. by Woodbury Lowery; ed. by Philip Lee Phillips (Washington: Government Printing Office, 1912).

57. U.S. Library of Congress, *A Guide to the Microfilm Collection of Early State Records* (Washington: Library of Congress, 1950), p. 153.

58. See Chapter V. What used to be known as the *Hemeroteca* is now part of the *Instituto de Investigaciones Bibliográficas* located at the Universidad Nacional Autónoma de México. Another *hemeroteca* functions as part of the *AGN.* Both have significant collections.

Chihuahua Cathedral, which houses the Archivo de la Catedral, *Chihuahua, Mexico. Photograph by W.H. Jackson, ca. 1883, Courtesy Museum of New Mexico.*

CHAPTER IV

RECORDS IN NORTHERN MEXICO
(CHIHUAHUA AND DURANGO)

1. RESEARCH IN NORTHERN MEXICO; GENERAL CONSIDERATIONS:

In 1949 Antonio Pompa y Pompa, Director of the Biblioteca de la Escuela Nacional de Antropología e Historia, sent a questionnaire to regional and state archives asking for information on the organization and present condition of official documents. Although his conclusions were incomplete, the reports he received indicated that with the exception of Coahuila (Saltillo) the condition of state and local archives in the north was deplorable. "Archives," Pompa y Pompa concluded, "are little more than warehouses where insects and humidity accelerate the destruction of the national patrimony."[1]

For today's scholars, archival conditions in Northern Mexico have improved substantially. More funds are available for the preservation and indexing of existing records, cooperative microfilming ventures with U.S. institutions have promoted research in collections heretofore inaccessible, and the *Archivo General de la Nación (AGN)* has launched an ambitious program to save other repositories from destruction. Research in Northern Mexico is still difficult, however.

Some materials are not where finding aids say they should be. Others are chronologically disorganized or combined with records created by several agencies. Since the nineteenth century was one of instability, revolutions and uprisings affected record keeping, and as one violent incident followed another, the actual destruction or disappearance of records became common. In addition,

121

the many changes in jurisdictional authority resulting from the birth pangs of the young Mexican Republic contributed to the loss of public records.[2] Some archives were ransacked by U.S. and French soldiers (Chihuahua and Durango). Others were broken into by Mexicans who appropriated documents for sale to foreigners.[3] Progress is being made in the organization of both civil and ecclesiastical archives, but much remains to be done. Researchers in Northern Mexico should guard against too much optimism and too little patience.

Research facilities also vary in quality. Physical comforts found in most archives in the United States are not normally available in Mexico. Hours of service reflect limited staffing, involvement of archivists in other jobs, budgetary limitations, and daily work schedules which coincide with the demands of local business. Copying facilities, microfilm readers, and other research paraphernalia are scarce, but the virtues of patience, tact, and a more leisurely pace of life can make research in Northern Mexico both profitable and enjoyable. What often appears to be confusion is also a sign that the archival content is relatively unknown and may embody untold historical treasures.

Access to collections need not be difficult if researchers first present themselves to the local historical society, the *cronista* of the city, or a respected historian. Seeing the "right" people first is the most efficient way to gain the confidence of those charged with the care and maintenance of public records. Mexicans are courteous and gracious. They also believe that scholars should be gentlemen, and they expect all researchers to be *gente culta*. They will show genuine enthusiasm for foreigners willing to respect their hours, their customs, and their modus operandi.

Knowledge of the political environment is equally important. State and local politicians respond to pressures of the national political scene. Although the PRI (Partido Revolucionario Institucional) will probably dominate Mexican politics for years to come, local party officials have sufficient authority to set local policies. An outgoing alcalde or governor might close an archive to foreigners if he fears a critical review of his record or if he considers a research topic politically sensitive. Consequently, researchers should be aware of political circumstances which might affect their work. Research in Mexico is not a democratic right, even for Mexicans, and those of us who have grown accustomed to a more open system must accept the limitations imposed by a different cultural environment. It is safe to say, however, that if foreigners manifest a sensitivity and understanding of the cultural milieu, their hosts will be generous to a fault. In sum, it is best to maintain formality in professional dealings, contact the best local professionals in your field, know the political environment, be patient, and be cognizant of the needs and limitations of your hosts.

This advice is equally applicable to research in ecclesiastical records, although one additional factor bears mentioning. Factions may exist that tend to divide the scholarly community against itself. Reflecting the long struggle in Mexico between church and state, the situation can best be described as a subtle undercurrent of possessiveness. In Chihuahua, for example, the control of cathedral archives rests in the hands of the *Comisión General de Conservación de Monumentos,* whose functions include the administration of a museum, religious shrines, and the historical documents of the archdiocese. The archbishop, his staff, and the priests do not set policy for the use of archival materials, but they work closely with the commission and its several committees. Durango, also the center of an archdiocese, does not have a similar commission, but the cathedral archives are closed to some historians, which suggests the continuation of local jealousies. One simply must recognize the continuum of history and be alert for what amounts to minor inconveniences. In Chihuahua, for example, the historical society and historians who use state and municipal records pursue their own investigations while the church concentrates on programs to preserve and restore what it refers to as *"artes sacros."*[4] In Durango, the separation of research-related projects and responsibilities echoes the situation in Chihuahua.

The records of Juárez, Chihuahua, Parral, and Durango have been chosen for inclusion in this guide for several reasons. First, these communities lie astride the route of the old Santa Fe-Chihuahua Trail, which extended even farther south to San Juan de los Lagos. Many New Mexicans and North Americans participated in this commerce during the 1821–1846 period. Along the way they built homes, made friends, married, got in trouble with the law, and sometimes died. Clues to their past are to be found in local archives. Second, Chihuahua was the seat of the *Comandancia General* for New Mexico from 1821 to 1839. Military decisions affecting Indians, fur trappers, scalp hunters, and the movement of people and commerce along the "Royal Road"[5] were made in Chihuahua. Chihuahua and New Mexico also maintained close economic ties. Third, the secular clergy in New Mexico was under the control of a bishop in Durango who corresponded with civil and military authorities, maintained vital records, and kept *diezmos* (accounts of tithing). Fourth, in the case of El Paso (Ciudad Juárez), even though the city was part of the state of Chihuahua for most of the Mexican period, its proximity to New Mexico and its important location on the road to Chihuahua are reasons to give high priority to its records. In sum, New Mexico was tied to Chihuahua and Durango by political, economic, military, and religious arrangements which had been in existence prior to the creation of the Mexican Republic in 1824. These ties resulted in the production of records, some of which can still be found in the same area where they were created.

2. MICROFILM PROJECTS:

Due to the high cost of travel and the uncertainty of doing research in provincial Mexican archives, scholars should be aware of microfilm repositories and ongoing projects which make historical data available at a lower cost. The following is a thumbnail sketch of certain developments relating specifically to Mexican period microfilm:

(1) University of Texas at El Paso (UTEP). Both as repository and funding institution, UTEP has been a leader in microfilming records of the Mexican borderlands. Collections mentioned in this chapter are available on Interlibrary Loan (ILL) and are partially indexed.

(2) Genealogical Society of Utah. Given its intention to gather records on everyone who has ever lived, it is not surprising that the society has the largest collection of filmed manuscripts in the world. Most, but by no means all, of the documents are parish and civil registers. The rolls are stored in the Granite Mountain Records Vault east of Salt Lake City, but researchers may use the film either at the Genealogical Library in Salt Lake City or by request through a stake church. Although filming is not yet complete for Chihuahua and Durango, some records are available. Researchers should consult the *Preliminary Survey of the Mexican Collection* (Salt Lake City; University of Utah Press, 1978) and the *Supplement to the Preliminary Survey of the Mexican Collection* (Salt Lake City: University of Utah Press, 1979).

(3) *Archivo Microfílmeco de Genealogía.* Researchers in Mexico City will find this archive particularly useful. Located near the Taxqueña exit of the metro at Cero de Jesús 67 and known informally as the *Archivo de los Mormones,* this repository of microfilm contains many of the same films relating to New Mexico which are preserved in Salt Lake City. The reason for this is that in 1953 the Genealogical Society of Utah began to microfilm records in Mexico. Access to collections was made possible by the influence of the *Academia Mexicana de Genealogía y Heráldica.* In return for this favor, the society agreed to provide the *Academia* with a copy of the film. Thus the archive was created. Permission to use it should be sought from the Secretary General of the *Academia.*

(4) Other projects.

   (a) Cooperative projects in the United States. Since 1966 various plans have been discussed to coordinate the research interests of universities and other institutions interested in Mexico. More than forty representatives met in Oyster Bay, New York, in 1967, and since then meetings in other cities have indicated the ongoing need for some sort of pooling of information. Researchers would be well advised to check the holdings of institutions with strong Mexican research interests. The many Texas colleges and universities, for example, have microfilm collections resulting from specific contracts with sister institutions across the border.

   (b) *Departamento de Registro Nacional.* As one of the several agencies of the *AGN,* the function of the *Departamento* is to provide aid to states and municipalities who have expressed the need for assistance in preserving their archival materials. In addition to providing organizational skills and publishing inventories, the *Departamento de Registro* plans to do as much microfilming as its budget will permit. See Chapter V for additional information.

3. THE ARCHIVES OF CHIHUAHUA:

A. CIUDAD JUAREZ.

(1) *Archivo de Ayuntamiento de Juárez* (Municipal Archive). Located in the Palacio Municipal in Juárez, this archive has a collection consisting of "more than 100,000 items in 365 volumes."[6] Bolton knew practically nothing of these materials. Their value to the Mexican period of New Mexico has become apparent as a result of the microfilming done by UTEP. The "bulk of the collection concerns purely local matters and is strong on civil and criminal cases, although much official correspondence between Santa Fe, Chihuahua, and El Paso is also included."[7]

Thirty-one of the ninety-one reels of the Juárez municipal archives pertain to the Mexican period. Because the filming was done in 1962 under difficult circumstances, twenty percent of the collection is illegible, and all frames are lacking reference numbers. Fortunately for the researcher, these deficiencies are being addressed in the preparation of an entirely new microfilm edition to be available for borrowing on Interlibrary Loan by 1983.[8] According to Professor Wilbert H. Timmons, who has worked with the microfilm edition of the Juárez archives quite thoroughly, the primary orientation of the documents is toward Chihuahua since El Paso del Norte had become part of the state of Chihuahua as a result of the constitution of October 4, 1824. The *ayuntamiento* had been founded the year before. Some of the earlier records which came into its possession date back to 1690, but the Mexican period documents have singular importance because of the burning of the state archives in the city of Chihuahua in 1941.[9]

(2) *Archivo de la Iglesia Parroquial de Guadalupe*. Church records are located at the bishop's house in Ciudad Juárez, but the Catedral de Ciudad Juárez is a good place to make inquiries. These records contain vital statistics which reveal something of the social intercourse between families of New Mexico and the region of El Paso del Norte. They include baptisms (1820–25; 1820–34; 1834–39; 1845–48); marriages (1815–45); burials (1812–26; 1826–35; 1835–42; 1842–48); circulars and orders from the Bishop of Durango; pre-marriage investigations *(diligencias matrimoniales);* confirmations; and miscellaneous correspondence.[10] Documents are from the Church of Guadalupe as well as the surrounding missions.

The Genealogical Society of Utah microfilmed the records of the Parroquia de Nuestra Señora de Guadalupe for the years 1671 to 1918.[11] A copy of this film accompanied by some mission records is on deposit at the UTEP library.

B. CIUDAD CHIHUAHUA.

(1) *Archivo del Ayuntamiento de Chihuahua.* The Palacio Municipal *(ayuntamiento)* is the home of several hundred bundles *(legajos)* of documents arranged chronologically.[12] Located on the Plaza de Constitución, directly opposite the cathedral, the *ayuntamiento* continues to be the center of activity for all municipal matters. Records are kept in the basement of the building under the control of the alcalde of Chihuahua, but permission to do research should be initiated through the local historical society *(Sociedad Chihuahuense de Estudios Históricos)* at the Museo de Benito Juárez, Calle Juárez 321. The president of the society or the *cronista* of the city will provide researchers with assistance.

The more than 600,000 pieces which make up the *ayuntamiento* archive date from 1709, when the city was founded, to 1940. Microfilming these records was completed in 1973, and 717 reels are now available from UTEP through Interlibrary Loan. Similar to other municipal archives, the Chihuahua records contain abundant information on problems relating to city governance, communications between state and local authorities, and citizen involvement in legal and economic affairs. References can be found in these documents to New Mexicans whose business affairs are detailed in petitions, appeals, special ordinances, and legal summons. This is a rich source for the Mexican period.

(2) *Archivo del Tribunal Supremo de Justicia.* Combined with the *Registro Público de Propiedad* at Calle Allende 901, this archive is arranged chronologically. Documents are organized in packages containing *"causas* held before the *subdelegados* and *corregidores* of Chihuahua in the later eighteenth and nineteenth centuries."[13] These sources should be used in conjunction with the *ayuntamiento* archives in search for New Mexicans involved in legal proceedings. The *Registro* is equally well organized, and because it contains information on landholdings, houses, and other forms of personal property, it, too, can be used to trace the activities of New Mexicans in Chihuahua.

(3) *Archivo de Carrizal.* Now located at the Casa de Gobierno and awaiting a permanent home, these documents constitute part of the municipal records of Carrizal, an important bastion of defense in the colonial period and a checkpoint for travelers and traders on the Camino Real during the Mexican period. Correspondence between Carrizal authorities and other civil and military figures points to the fact that this little town became an important gateway to Mexico in the Mexican period. Problems with North Americans and Indians and challenges to economic survival suggest that these forty boxes of chronologically organized documents will prove extremely valuable when used in conjunction with the municipal records of other communities in the region.[14] The Carrizal Archives are available at UTEP on twenty-three reels of microfilm.

(4) *Archivo General del Estado.* This archive was destroyed by fire on June 21, 1941. It is mentioned here because there seems to be some confusion about

its contents, and because copies of many of its documents may be available in other respositories.

The Palacio del Gobierno, Plaza Hidalgo, was a secure archive until fire broke out one afternoon when few people were in the building. It spread from room to room, destroying various government offices. When the firemen finally arrived, they were unable to extinguish the blaze because of the lamentable condition of their hoses and problems encountered with the hydrants. Dynamite was used to snuff out the flames; what was not destroyed by fire and water was blown apart by these blasts.[15]

What Bolton described as the *Archivo de la Secretaría de Gobierno* was totally lost. This included the *"Papeles Viejos,"* or records of the *Comandancia General;* correspondence of the departmental (state) governors with the federal government, other state governors, military authorities, and local officials; reports concerning Indian affairs; papers from El Paso del Norte concerning the 1837 revolution in New Mexico; and minutes of the departmental juntas.[16] Also lost were the "Regular Files," in which Bolton had located correspondence with other governors; records dealing with Apache and Comanche depredations; information on the Texan Santa Fe expedition and the Texas invasion of 1843; and miscellaneous correspondence concerning the activities of foreigners.[17] The loss of this archive is a blow to research on the Mexican period in New Mexico.

The *Archivo de la Tesorería General* disappeared at the same time.[18] It contained records of the state treasury dating back to 1821. Among these were "the records of the *Administración General de Rentas de Chihuahua* whose jurisdiction included New Mexico."[19] The *Archivo del Congreso del Estado* was also lost. This is particularly tragic because of the loss of secret correspondence, laws, and decrees dating back to 1823.[20]

What happened to the *Archivo del Poder Ejecutivo* is anyone's guess. Bolton does not mention it, but Carrera Stampa believes that seventy-five percent of it was saved after the fire.[21] Another view is that most of the records were destroyed by the Americans in 1847, and what remained was removed by the French in 1865.[22] Most recently, it has been suggested that this archive might exist as part of the material included in the *Archivo del Tribunal Supremo de Justicia.*[23]

Another archive, that of the *Comandancia de las Provincias Internas,* might also have disappeared in the 1941 fire.[24] The lost records are supposed to be uniquely from the colonial period, but certain clues suggest that the military authorities at Durango and Chihuahua added to this collection in the Mexican period. Furthermore, some doubt exists about the whereabouts of the archive at the time when fire raged through the Palacio del Gobierno in 1941.

According to Bolton, the last known mention of this archive appears in 1827 when it was in the hands of the *Comisario General* in Chihuahua. Some scraps may have been sent to Saltillo, but Bolton was sure that the archive was never sent to the *AGN* in Mexico City.[25] In 1938, Francisco R. Almada, Chihuahua's leading historian, wrote that some loose documents from this archive existed in the *Archivo General del Estado* (Chihuahua), while other remnants eventually were found in the *Archivo del Tribunal Supremo de Justicia* and the *Archivo del Ayuntamiento*.[26] Taken altogether, however, the total scarcely equaled the twenty-eight boxes of records sent from Durango to Chihuahua by the Mariscal de Campo, D. Alejo García Conde, *Comandante General de las Provincias Internas,* during the last decade of the eighteenth century.[27] So where did this archive go?

One possibility, suggested by Vito Alessio Robles, is that the "lost" archive might have been sent to the *Secretaría de Hacienda,* since *Hacienda* was, in fact, the parent federal agency of the state *comisarios*.[28] In view of the enormous amount of uncataloged material in the *Hacienda* archive today, Alessio Robles' suggestion is definitely worth pursuing.

(5) *Archivo de la Catedral.* As an archdiocese, Chihuahua is the administrative center for that state's ecclesiastical records. An understanding of the relationship between the cathedral, the office of the archbishop, and the *Comisión General de Conservación de Monumentos* is necessary for successful research.

In addition to being an historical landmark, the cathedral in Chihuahua has long been the repository of church records for the city of Chihuahua and some of the outlying missions. These records, presently located in the south tower of the cathedral, are composed of approximately 275 books of two-hundred pages each. They were organized for microfilming by Dr. Clara Bargellini of the Museo de Antropología in Mexico City and are presently off limits to researchers.[29]

Some of the records have already been filmed by the Genealogical Society of Utah. The *Preliminary Survey of the Mexican Collection* lists filmed records of the Misión de Encinillas (1757–1884), the Parroquia del Sagrario (1709–1956), the Parroquia de San Juan Bautista (1776–1839), and the Archivo del Catedral, Registro Misional (1733–1903).[30] Bargellini estimates that the society filmed approximately fifty percent of the recorded burials, five percent of the marriages, and all baptisms. Appended to her 1979 report to the *AGN* are photocopies of the society's file cards showing the extent to which Mexican period material was included in this initial filming.[31]

Two final suggestions might prove useful for researchers in Chihuahua. First, the *Periódico Oficial del Estado de Chihuahua,* begun by Cayetano Ramos in 1828 and published under a variety of names into the twentieth century, appeared almost weekly during most of the Mexican period. It has not been systematically mined for New Mexico material, and even a superficial review of some of the volumes reveals the immense value of this source. In the city of Chihuahua, a complete run of this newspaper can be found under lock and key on the third floor of the Palacio del Gobierno. It can be used with permission of the *Secretario de Gobierno*. A microfilm copy consisting of 108 reels is available for borrowing from UTEP on Interlibrary Loan, and a list of the tables of contents was prepared at UTEP by Irma Guillen.[32]

A second suggestion concerns the use of private libraries. The *Periódico Oficial* in the Palacio del Gobierno was donated by Francisco R. Almada. His collection of books, manuscripts, and journals was later purchased by the state government in the summer of 1980 and was then organized for research purposes in an institute established in his honor. Equally important is the private collection of Lic. Manuel E. Roussek, *Secretario de Gobierno* of Chihuahua until the summer of 1980. His library, located at Avenida Juárez and V. Carranza, contains 25,000 volumes, many of which are hard-to-find law books containing Mexican period legislation. Lic. Roussek has an office in the same building as his library and is particularly generous to visiting scholars.

C. PARRAL.

(1) *Archivo Municipal*. Most frequently referred to as *the* Parral Archives, this collection of documents includes the records of the *jefatura política* and the *ayuntamiento*. Materials are in boxes located at the Benjamin Franklin Library on the main plaza. They have been there since the early 1960s when an Arizona-based team microfilmed records dealing with the colonial period, 1631–1821.[33] The Parral Archives have thus become more widely known as an excellent source of information on Nueva Vizcaya. Parral was also frequented by New Mexicans engaged in trade during the Mexican period, and the unfilmed portion of the Parral Archives contains useful data for research on the years 1821–1848.

Records for both the colonial and Mexican periods of the Parral Archives are divided into six sections: Section I, *Causas Administrativas y de Guerra*, includes military reports dealing with Indian activities and matters pertaining to administration at the national level; Section II, *Minas Solares y Terrenos*, has to do with the purchase and sale of lands including mining properties; Section III, *Protocolos*, contains the *residencias* of government officials; Section IV, *Causas Civiles*, deals with suits regarding personal property disputes and money matters; Section V, *Causas Criminales*, is a good source for social history, since the records include accusations, trials, and punishments for every conceivable kind of criminal offense, all of which are often expressed in very salty language; *Papeles Varios* contains unidentified documents, and parts thereof, that could not be classified accurately.

Among these categories, researchers will find orders from the governor of Chihuahua, census records, acts of congress, and military reports dealing with issues related to New Mexico. A criminal *expediente* for the North American trader Juan Anderson, income and expenses of the *Administración de Rentas*, and extensive information on the Apaches are specific examples of how the

Parral Archives can be used for research on New Mexico.

The unfilmed documents are mostly loose except for those already bound in *cuadernos*. Boxes containing the loose documents are stored in the rear of the Benjamin Franklin Library, along with janitorial supplies, where their condition deteriorates with the passage of time. They need to be reorganized and filmed.[34]

(2) *Archivo de la Parroquia.* Located on the first floor of the parochial church just off the Plaza Principal, these well-guarded records are wrapped in plastic and sealed behind glass. Because Parral (Hidalgo del Parral) formed part of the same diocese as Santa Fe, Chihuahua, Juárez, and Durango, correspondence from the bishop and vital statistics on traveling New Mexicans may be found among the marriage, death, confirmation, and baptism records. In the 1930s, José G. Rocha was preparing a catalog of this archive, but it was not completed. The only other finding aid is a guide being prepared by the *Departamento de Registro* of the *AGN*.[35]

A microfilm edition of the parochial records was made by the Genealogical Society of Utah. It consists of forty reels of the records of the Parroquia de San José for the years 1632 to 1958.

4. THE ARCHIVES OF DURANGO:

A. DURANGO.

(1) *Archivo de la Catedral.* To understand what constitutes the records of the Durango cathedral, it should be remembered that Durango was the ecclesiastical see for New Mexico during the Mexican period. Contact between the two provinces was limited to official correspondence until December 19, 1833, when the New Mexico missions were secularized.[36] In that same year, the new Bishop of Durango, José Antonio Laureano López de Zubiría, made the first of three visits to New Mexico prior to the invasion of that province by the United States. These were the first visitations of a bishop to New Mexico since the arrival of Bishop Pedro Tamarón in 1760.

Although New Mexico's ecclesiastical records were also created by Franciscans before 1833,[37] communication between Durango and Santa Fe concerned business affairs which were outside the purview of the regular clergy. It is for this reason that the cathedral records are important for New Mexico history.

Located a short distance from the Plaza Cuarto Centenario, the cathedral is entered from Calle Negrete. Both the archives and the archbishop's office are located on the second floor. Successful access to the documents depends on the inclinations of the archbishop, whose proprietary attitude toward ecclesiastical records is both a result of his concern for their protection and his fear that they will be misquoted by those wishing to damage the image of the church. Of particular value is the *Archivo de la Haceduría de Diezmos,* whose contents are chronologically arranged and may be entered by use of indexes prepared by Francisco Atuñez for the 1630–1847 period.[38] These tithing records will contribute to a better understanding of social and economic life in New Mexico by revealing the productive capacity of various segments of the population.

The *Actas Capitulares* contain the business affairs of the cathedral. Dating from 1735 to the present and filmed by the Genealogical Society of Utah,[39] they are often confused with the vast amount of unfilmed material which includes the previously mentioned records of the *diezmero* and *papeles varios*. The latter are stored in a separate room awaiting microfilming.[40]

Adjacent to the archive is a modest museum containing a great many religious artifacts of the nineteenth century: books of instruction, vestments, robes, altar paraphernalia, etc. In another room the archbishop has stored portraits of the bishops and archbishops of Durango. For the ecclesiastical historian, these items of material culture will prove to be as valuable as the documents.

(2) *Archivo General del Gobierno del Estado*. The state archive of Durango is easily found in the Palacio de Gobierno, which itself dominates the Plaza Cuarto Centenario at 5 Febrero and Bruno Martínez. Located on the ground floor in the center of the building, the archive appears to be in a total state of disarray and susceptible to losses from theft, fire, and rodents. A project sponsored by UTEP has managed to extract a large volume of documents for microfilming, however, along with an index which clearly shows the value of this collection to New Mexico history.

Durango was the base for military operations in the *Provincias Internas* from 1813 to 1820. In 1821, the headquarters returned to Chihuahua. During the Mexican period, Chihuahua served as the *Comandancia General* with control over New Mexico's military affairs, but records in the state archives of Durango indicate that each state shared information with the other, because Chihuahua and Durango had so many problems in common. Some examples taken from the index will illustrate this point:[41]

Exped. No.	Rollo No.	Exped. No.	Fojas No.	Contenido
2325	119	85	120	Correspondencia del Sr. Gobernador Intendente de Durango, etc. 1822–1828.
3046	180	86	107	Ordenes de los Hacedores de Diezmos y dispensas de cargos de Jurisprudencia, etc. 1826.
3058	181	98	79	Leyes y Ordenes sobre pasaportes de extranjeros, etc. 1826.
3103	184	133	107	Documentos de los extranjeros

Exped. No.	Rollo No.	Exped. No.	Fojas No.	Contenido
				que se presentan al Gobierno, en solicitud de pasaportes, etc. 1828.
2443	129	103	43	Nota de los Efectos guiados en esta Administración General de Durango, para la Aduana Nacional de la Misma, 1831.
2445	129	105	70	Camara de Diputados, Correspondencia con las Diputaciones permanentes de los Estados, en el primer período del Tercer Congreso Constitucional del Estado, 1831.
2472	131	12	42	Expediente sobre contrabandos de diez cargas de armas, 1832.
3241	197	11	33	Circulares sobre la incomunicación de esta Capital y los Estados Unidos, sobre los tratados de amistad, Limites, comercio, y otros, 1832–1833.
3277	200	47	37	Decretos y otra correspondencia de varios gobiernos del país, y del gobierno eclesiástico de Durango, 1833.
2515	134	55	29	Documentos de los Obispos, Gobernadores, de la Mitra y Religiosos, 1834.
2558	137	98	32	Tornaguías y correspondencia, que se recibe en el Departamento de Alcabalas, 1836.
2953	138	13	76	Facturas y guías de Efectos, enviados y recibidos, 1837–1838.
2617	141	37	104	Documentos de correspondencia de las Administraciones Foráneas y Aduanas de otros Departamentos, 1837–1839.

Exped. No.	Rollo No.	Exped. No.	Fojas No.	Contenido
3591	228	121	44	Guías de la Administración Principal de Rentas del Dpto. de Chihuahua, de Parras, y otros lugares. Y ejemplos de los efectos de Nuevo Mexico, 1838–1841.
3548	223	78	76	Documentos que amparan las Cartas de seguridad de los Extranjeros, circulares y otros documentos, 1842.
2863	164	43	97	Correspondencia de varios asuntos de diferentes Gobernadores, 1843.
3794	244	134	22	Oficos, Correspondencia de la Compañía Lancasteriana de Durango, 1843.
2929	171	109	107	Padrones y correspondencia de los extranjeros que viven en Durango, 1844.
4007	263	17	29	Correspondencia de los Gobiernos de Queretaro, Mexico, Nuevo Mexico, Michoacán, Nuevo León y Coahuila con el Gob. de Dgo. 1844.
111	272	121	46	Ordenes . . . Sobre la invasión de los indios barbaros, 1845.
261	286	11	38	Correspondencia de la Comandancia Principal de Durango [con] la Quinta División Militar.

The above examples show that Durango was involved in many of New Mexico's affairs (trade, tithes, education, Indians, etc.) and that a careful perusal of these documents will produce important information which would have been available in the state archive of Chihuahua had it not burned.

5. A SUMMARY OF DESCRIPTIVE REFERENCES AND FINDING AIDS:

(1) Alessio Robles, Vito. *Bosquejos Históricos*. México: Editorial Polis, 1938. Very general information is included on the archives of Durango and Parral,

among others, and in a chapter entitled *"Un valioso archivo perdido,"* Alessio Robles gives his views on the fate of the archive of the *Comandancia General de las Provincias Internas.*

(2) Anderson, Robert R. "A Note on the Archivo de Hidalgo del Parral," *Arizona and the West* 4 (Winter 1962): 381–85. Anderson describes the filmed Parral papers, 1631–1821. His article is useful for reviewing the kind of material collected in this municipal archive, but it leaves the false impression that the so-called Parral archive contains nothing after 1821.

(3) Beers, Henry Putney. *Spanish and Mexican Records of the American Southwest.* Tucson: The University of Arizona Press, 1979. Beers is an archivist and historian who has produced in one volume a scholarly reference work on New Mexico, Texas, California, and Arizona. Little is said about specific collections south of the border, but the descriptions of record-keeping by Spanish and Mexican authorities is valuable in facilitating research in civil and ecclesiastical archives in the United States.

(4) Bolton, Herbert Eugene. *Guide to Materials for the History of the United States in the Principal Archives of Mexico.* Washington: Carnegie Institution, 1913 (Kraus Reprint, 1965). This classic, lauded by Mexican and North American historians alike, is still useful. Bolton searched in 1907–08 for documents relevant to U.S. history. Since then some collections have been moved or lost, but this volume still has worth if it is used in conjunction with that of Manuel Carrera Stampa.

(5) Carrera Stampa, Manuel. *Archivalia Mexicana,* Núm. 27, Publicaciones del Instituto de Historia. Mexico: Universidad Nacional Autónoma del Mexico, 1952. This is the best guide to the archives of Northern Mexico. Although scholars will find that the titles and location of certain collections will not agree with Bolton's *Guide,* the volume is essential as an introductory manual.

(6) Gallegos C., José Ignacio. "Durango: La Historia y Sus Instrumentos." *Historia Mexicana* XI (1961): 314–20. Gallegos is Durango's *cronista de la ciudad* and, for all intents and purposes, the city's only historian. This article is a very general view of what is contained in Durango's church and state archives.

(7) Gómez Canedo, Lino. "Some Franciscan Sources in the Archives and Libraries of America." *The Americas* 13 (1956): 141–74. The author suggests where to find records of Franciscan missions of the northern provinces of Mexico, but also notes that "acts of violence against religious institutions . . . facilitated . . . dispersion of archives, as they afforded favorable opportunities to collectors" (p. 149).

(8) Greenleaf, Richard E., and Michael C. Meyer. *Research in Mexican History.* Lincoln: University of Nebraska Press, 1973. Dealing with a broad spectrum of topics, methodology, and sources, this work is a practical guide to field research. Chapter 10 is entitled "Research on Nineteenth-Century Topics."

(9) Millares Carlo, Agustín. *Los archivos municipales de Latinoamérica; libros de actas y colecciones documentales*. Maracaibo, Venezuela: Universidad de Zulia, 1961. This is an anthology of works which discuss archives in Mexico City and the Mexican states. It is useful for reviewing works by Mexican authors.
(10) Porras Muñoz, Guillermo. "Los Archivos de Durango." *Divulgación Histórica* VI (1943): 164–66. The author refers to changes effected in the archives of the *ayuntamiento*, the cathedral, and the *Secretaría de Gobierno*.
(11) Weber, David J. "The Municipal Archive of Ciudad Juárez." NMHR 42 (1967): 26. The author comments briefly on the UTEP microfilm project and notes that thirty-one reels of the Juárez materials pertain to the Mexican period and include official correspondence among Santa Fe, Chihuahua, and El Paso.
(12) West, Robert C. "The Municipal Archive of Parral, Chihuahua, Mexico." *Handbook of Latin American Studies*. Washington, D.C., 1940: 523–39. West describes the archive before it was arranged for microfilming. This article is useful as an introduction to the organization and documentation available in this archive for the colonial period. Although a similar description could be made for the Mexican period, West's article ends in 1821.

NOTES

1. Antonio Pompa y Pompa, "Contribución del Instituto Nacional de Antropología e Historia para la conservación de los Archivos Mexicanos fuera de la capital," *Memoria del Primer Congreso de Historiadores de Mexico y los Estados Unidos, celebrado en la ciudad de Monterrey, Nuevo León, Mexico, del 4 a 9 de septiembre de 1949* (Mexico: Editorial Cultura, 1950), pp. 71–81.
2. The missing archive of the *Comandancia General de las Provincias Internas* is the best example. See Francisco R. Almada, "Archivos Perdidos," *Boletín de la Sociedad Chihuahuense de Estudios Históricos* II (1939): 235–40.
3. The discovery and subsequent sale of the Carrizal archives to the University of Texas at El Paso is a good example of ongoing difficulties. See Daniel Tyler, "The Carrizal Archives: A Source for the Mexican Period," NMHR 57 (July 1982): 257–67.
4. These would include documents, artifacts, and church monuments over which a *Secretario General* of the commission presides.
5. Max L. Moorhead, *New Mexico's Royal Road* (Norman: University of Oklahoma Press, 1958).
6. Beers, *Spanish and Mexican Records*, p. 35.
7. David J. Weber, "The Municipal Archive of Ciudad Juárez," NMHR 42 (1967): 26.

8. In addition to being blurred and lacking frame numbers, the 1962 edition only goes to 1904. The new edition was begun with the filming of the 1895–1940 period (Part I) and will continue with the years 1762–1895 (Part II). As of July 1982, fifty reels had been filmed: ten are on the colonial period since 1750; the rest are from the 1895–1940 period.

9. Wilbert H. Timmons, interview with the author, May 13, 1980.

10. Bolton, *Guide,* pp. 462–63; Beers, *Spanish and Mexican Records,* pp. 184–85.

11. See Roger M. Haigh and Shirley A. Weathers, *Supplement to the Preliminary Survey of the Mexican Collection* (Salt Lake City: University of Utah Press, 1979), p. 11. The authors cite eleven reels of marriage and church records.

12. The following organization of Mexican period *legajos* is based on an inventory made by the *Departamento de Registro Nacional (AGN),* which includes a report of Dr. Stella María González, October 22, 1980.

Municipal de Chihuahua: Doc. Histórica

Legajo No.	Year	Legajo No.	Year
181	1821	198	1832
182	1822	199	1833
183	1823	200	1833
184	1824	201	1834
185	1825	202	1834
186	1826	203	1835
187	1826	204	1835
188	1827	205	1836
189	1827	206	1837
190	1828	207	1838
191	1829	208	1839
192	1830	209	1840
193	1830	210	1841
194	1831	211	1842
195	1831	212	1843
196	1831	213	1843
197	1832	214	1844

Municipal de Chihuahua: Doc. Leyes y Decretos

Legajo No.	Year
215	1825–1833; 1836
216	1845
217	1846
218	1847
219	1848

Municipal de Chihuahua: Fondo Histórico

Legajo	Year
Registro de Minas	1789–1824

Reg. de Salidas Presos	1827
Demandas	1842, 1845
Acuerdos	1844
Actas	1846
Juicios de Conciliación	1840
Juicios Verbales	1845

13. Bolton, *Guide*, p. 459.
14. See Tyler, "Carrizal Archives."
15. Guillermo Porras, "La destrucción de un archivo," *Divulgación Histórica* II (1941): 517–18. Unless otherwise noted, facts on the fire are taken from this article. See also Salvador Rasuva, "Incendio del Palacio del Gobierno," *Boletín de la Sociedad Chihuahuense de Estudios Históricos* III (1941): 149–51.
16. Bolton, *Guide*, pp. 452–54.
17. Ibid., 454–58.
18. See Porras, "La destrucción," p. 517. A conflicting view is expressed by Manuel Carrera Stampa, *Archivalia Mexicana*, Núm. 27, Publicaciones del Instituto de Historia (Mexico: Universidad Nacional Autónoma de Mexico, 1952), p. 132.
19. Bolton, *Guide*, p. 460.
20. Ibid.
21. *Archivalia Mexicana*, p. 130.
22. Francisco Almada, "El Archivo de la Comandancia General de las Provincias Internas," *Boletín de la Sociedad Chihuahuense de Estudios Históricos* I (1938): 73.
23. Alfonso Escarcega, *cronista* of Ciudad Chihuahua, to the author, in an interview, May 20, 1980.
24. This is Carrera Stampa's opinion as noted in *Archivalia Mexicana*, p. 129.
25. Bolton, *Guide*, p. 460.
26. Almada, "Archivo," p. 72.
27. Ibid.
28. Vito Alessio Robles, *Bosquejos Históricos* (México: Editorial Polis, 1938).
29. Mexican period records for the Chihuahua cathedral were noted by Bargellini as follows:

Baptisms. Cajón 2: Book No. 5 (Sept. 25, 1821–June 27, 1827); Book No. 6 (July 26, 1827–June 18, 1832); Book No. 7 (June 14, 1832–Nov. 21, 1834); Book No. 8 (Nov. 22, 1934–April 24, 1836); Book No. 9 (April 24, 1836–June 27, 1839); Book No. 10 (June 27, 1839–Jan. 18, 1843); Book No. 11 (Jan. 18, 1843–April 18, 1845); Book No. 12 (April 15, 1845–June 24, 1849). See also a loose-leaf notebook with assorted baptismal entries dating from the nineteenth century.

Confirmations. Cájon 2: An unnumbered book which includes the years 1833 to 1845, and a notebook for the years 1845 and 1846.

Burials. Cájon 3: Located in twenty *Libros de Entierros* dating from 1711

to 1873. A notebook of loose records and a book of burials for the *Hospital Militar* (Jan. 7, 1797, to July 20, 1835) are also included in this *cájon.*
Marriages. Cájon 4: Two unnumbered books for the years 1814 to 1828 are followed by Book No.3 (1828–1848) and Book No.4 (1848–1857), which both also contain marriage records for the years 1794 to 1823. *Cájon* 6: Includes additional matrimonial records for the years 1834 to 1898. *Cájon* 9: Contains additional matrimonial records for the years 1794 to 1833.

The report which comprises this information was presented to the *Departamento de Registro, AGN,* in September 1979. The *Comisión General de Monumentos,* Chihuahua, Mexico, retains a copy.

30. Susan M. Cottler, Roger M. Haigh, and Shirley A. Weathers, *Preliminary Survey of the Mexican Collection.* No. 1 of Finding Aids to the Microfilmed Manuscript Collection of the Genealogical Society of Utah (Salt Lake City: University of Utah Press, 1978), pp. XXI, 14.

31. *Parroquia de Sagrario, Registro parroquial, 1709–1956.*

Baptisms:	Film No.	162,665 (1800–1827)
		162,666 (1827–1836)
		162,668 (1843–1852)
Marriages:	Film No.	162,690 (1792–1857)
		162,692 (1814–1870)
Deaths:	Film No.	162,699 (1780–1839)
		162,700 (1833–1856)

32. Irma Guillen, "Table of Contents to the *Boletín de la Sociedad Chihuahuense Histórico.*" Typescript prepared at the University of Texas, El Paso, 1976.

33. Organization of these records dates from the early 1930s when the director of *El Correo de Parral,* José G. Rocha, began cataloging correspondence of the government of Nueva Vizcaya, whose administrative center was Parral from 1633 to 1739. Rocha prepared indexes to the seventeenth and early eighteenth centuries. His work was continued by Charles Di Peso, Director of the Amerind Foundation, whose interest in finding references to Casas Grandes prompted a trip to Parral in July 1959 with George Chambers of *Arizona Silhouettes.* Chambers and Di Peso formed a team which filmed almost 500,000 manuscript pages on 333 reels and prepared an index that preserved and elaborated on the system developed by Rocha. The following information is found on the title page of the index: *"Index to el Archivo de Hidalgo del Parral, 1631–1821,* Copyright, 1961, *Arizona Silhouettes,* printed by Xerox process in the United States of America."

34. Boxes have years on them, but the organization only approximates a sequential chronology. The present order is as follows: 1(1835), 2(1841), 3(1836), 4(1841), 5(1829), 6(1842), 7(1841), 8 (1827), 9(1837), 10(1838), 11(1828), 12(1825), 13(1843), 14(1843), 15(1842), 16(1842), 17(1837), 18(1831–32), 19(1828), 20(1839), 21(1834–45), 22 (1845), 23(1843), 24(1844), 25(1822–23,

1824), 26(1846), 27(1847), 28(1848), 44(1826), 49(1830), 77(1840), 78(1833).
35. Separate references to the Rocha catalog can be found in Robert C. West, "The Municipal Archive of Parral, Chihuahua, Mexico," *Handbook of Latin American Studies*, Washington, D.C., 1940, pp. 523–39; and in Carrera Stampa, *Archivalia Mexicana*, p.131,n.43. Rubén Rocha Chávez, son of José G. Rocha, is editor of *El Correo de Parral* and might have further information on his father's cataloging endeavors.
36. Arnold L. Rodríguez, O.F.M., "New Mexico in Transition," NMHR XXIV (1956): 288.
37. Fray Angélico Chávez organized the extant Franciscan records of New Mexico in his Archives of the Archdiocese of Santa Fe, 1678–1900 (Washington: Academy of American Franciscan History, 1957). It is not certain where missing documents will be found, however. The Museo de Antropología in Mexico City has some records. Others are located in the old Biblioteca Nacional, where researchers may consult Ignacio Del Río's *Guía del Archivo Franciscano de la Biblioteca Nacional de Mexico*, Vol. I (Mexico: Universidad Autónoma de Mexico, Instituto de Investigaciones Bibliográficas, 1975) and Fray Lino Gómez Canedo, *Indice de Documentos Franciscanos existentes en la Sección de Manuscritos*, 2 vols. (Washington: The Academy of American Franciscan History, n.d.). Chávez believes that New Mexico's Franciscans sent copies of documents to the Province of the Holy Gospel in Mexico City and that these records were dispersed by repeated revolutions.
38. See Bolton, *Guide*, p. 408, and Carrera Stampa, *Archivalia Mexicana*, pp. 133–34, n.44.
39. *Actas Capitulares* consists of twenty reels of microfilm and is also available at UTEP through Interlibrary Loan along with a typed index. The Genealogical Society of Utah has also filmed the records of the Parroquia del Sagrario Metropolitano, 65 reels (1604–1903); the Parroquia de San Juan Bautista de Analco, 30 reels (1646–1901); the Parroquia del Santuario de Nuestra Señora de Guadalupe, 13 reels (1792–1902); and the *Protocolos del Arquidiócesis* of Durango, 8 reels (1622–1859), which contain notarial records. See *Preliminary Survey*, pp. xxxii, 21.
40. The Rio Grande Historical Collections at New Mexico State University plans to microfilm the *papeles varios* if the money can be raised.
41. Documents were selected for filming by José Ignacio Gallegos, *cronista* for the city of Durango. Gallegos also holds the titles *Jefe del Archivo Histórico de Gobierno* and *Director de la Biblioteca Pública*. Preparation of the index was done by Sra. María de la Luz Valtierra Sifuentes. Three hundred and forty-three reels of microfilm have been processed to date, covering the years 1578 to 1848. Negative copies are retained by the state of Durango, while UTEP keeps a positive copy for distribution through Interlibrary Loan. The goal of this cooperative project is to film records of the nineteenth century at the approximate rate of five-hundred documents a day.

Archivo General de la Nación, *Mexico City*. *Photograph by Daniel Tyler*.

Escudo *(logo) of the* Archivo General de la Nación, *Mexico City*.

CHAPTER V

RECORDS IN MEXICO CITY

1. THE ARCHIVAL REVOLUTION; GENERAL OBSERVATIONS:

Chaos has reigned for a long time in the national archives of Mexico City. The good will of Mexican historians and the persistence of archivists searching for historical data have not overcome the years of neglect and sometimes violent history of this national patrimony. Finding aids were scarce and untrustworthy; inadequate staffing prevented organization and classification of holdings; and storage facilities proved inadequate. Added to this was a particular lack of interest in the Mexican period. Though understandable from the standpoint of Mexican national pride, the tendency of historians to ignore the second quarter of the nineteenth century is unfortunate. It has been reflected in most archives, where materials dealing with territory lost to the United States were ignored or overlooked as researchers showed their preference for the less controversial colonial period.[1]

Fortunately, the situation is improving. After the 1976 presidential election, the government spent more money than ever before on the organization and preservation of documentary resources. Due to President José López Portillo's scholarly inclinations and the new petroleum largess, a transformation occurred in one *sexenio* that was little short of revolutionary.

As this volume goes to press, workers have finished moving vast quantities of sorted and unsorted materials from the old *Edificio de Telecomunicaciones* (Tacuba 8) to the new home of the *Archivo General de la Nación (AGN)* in the remodeled Lecumberri prison. Two blocks from a metro stop and practically

141

adjacent to the new *Palacio Legislativo*,[2] the *AGN* is conveniently located for research. Two audiovisual presentations are available to researchers and visitors interested in the history of Lecumberri and the holdings of the *AGN*.

One person is particularly responsible for these accomplishments. Dr. Alejandra Moreno Toscano was appointed as Director of the *AGN* by President López Portillo while she was on the faculty of the Colegio de Mexico. Aware that the Tacuba facilities were temporary, she soon began looking for a structure that would allow the archive to offer full service to the public with enough additional space to increase its holdings for at least a generation. Lecumberri prison caught her eye. Designed during the Porfiriato, the prison was completed after eighteen years and was opened for inmates in 1900.[3] It was built with seven *crujías* (wings) and with a panoptic dome overseeing all. Dr. Moreno learned that the government was planning to tear down the old structure, but she saw in the seven *crujías* and panoptic design a chance to organize the seven existing *unidades*[4] of the *AGN* in separate but centrally related areas with work space for researchers and a large reception hall under the dome which could also be used for displays, conferences, and public receptions. The president supported her plan. Instead of tearing down the structure, it was remodeled into a singularly attractive and utilitarian national archive.

The government's plans for the *Biblioteca Nacional* and the *Hemeroteca Nacional* have been equally imaginative. Both were located in congested parts of downtown Mexico City in older buildings which had begun to give up the fight against earth tremors, the subway, and torrential annual rains. Like the cathedral on the Zócalo, the *Biblioteca Nacional* had begun to lean dizzily, opening cracks in the walls and ceiling that threatened precious books and manuscripts with inundation every time it rained. A new facility was needed combining the function of both institutions. The result was a new building and a move to the campus of the national university.

Other archives, public and private, have moved, changed directors, added staff, and upgraded finding aids to their collections. What was once an accurate guide, *Research in Mexican History* by Richard E. Greenleaf and Michael C. Meyer, must now be used with caution.[5] Six years of improved funding has had a positive effect on Mexican archives. At the same time, the city has become more congested, and public transportation at certain hours and during inclement weather is overloaded. Parking is difficult in most places, and the best advice for anyone doing research in the Distrito Federal is to estimate the maximum time needed for accomplishing project objectives—then double it!

2. INSTITUTO DE INVESTIGACIONES BIBLIOGRAFICAS:

Combining the *Hemeroteca Nacional* and the *Biblioteca Nacional* in one building has created problems as well as new opportunities for research. Located in a modern building just off Insurgentes Sur between the main university campus and the Periférico, the *Instituto de Investigaciones Bibliográficas* is now under the control of the Universidad Nacional Autónoma de Mexico. Researchers expecting to use the *Hemeroteca* will find that all printed material which had been previously stored in the old church of San Pedro y San Pablo is now available in its new location. This includes facsimiles, newspapers (official and private), pamphlets, and broadsides. Author-title catalogs are supplemented by card files listing newspapers by different regions. All entries provide information on the publisher, years and frequency of publication, and size of printed sheets. Because so many important documents for the Mexican period have been lost or misplaced, official newspapers have become an essential tool for historical research. The following publications are available at the *Hemeroteca* for research on the Mexican period:

Gacetas de México (1784–1831); *Aguila Mexicana* (1823–1827); *El Sol* (1823–1832); *Gaceta Diaria de México* (1825–1826); *Gaceta del Gobierno Supremo de la Federación* (1826); *El Amigo del Pueblo* (1827–1828); *Correo Semanario de México* (1826–1827); *El Observador de la República Mexicana* (1827); *Varios Papeles* (1827–1828); *El Correo de la Federación Mexicana* (1828); *El Gladiador* (1830–1831); *Registro Oficial de Los Estados-Unidos Mexicanos* (1830–1832); *Registro Oficial Extraordinario* (1830); *Voz de la Patria* (1830–1831); *Los Amigos del Pueblo* (1831); *La Egida de la Ley* (1831); *El Federalista Mexicano* (1831); *El Fenix de la Libertad* (1831–1834); *El Tribuno del Pueblo Mexicano* (1831); *Boletín de Noticias* (1832); *El Duendo* (1832); *El Genio* (1832); *La Antorcha* (1833); *Boletines Varios* (1833); *La Columna de la Constitución Federal de la República Mexicana* (1833); *El Democrata* (1833); *El Democrata. Federación o Muerte* (1833); *El Indicador de la Federación Mexicana* (1833–1834); *La Lima de Vulcano* (1833–1836); *El Telégrafo* (1833–1834); *El Telégrafo. Periódico Oficial del Gobierno de los Estados Unidos Mexicanos* (1833); *La Verdad Desnuda* (1833); *El Mosquito Mexicano* (1834–1835); *La Oposición. Federación y Unión* (1834); *Revista Mexicana* (1835); *El Cosmopolita* (1836); *Municipal Mexicano* (1837); *El Diorama* (1837); *El Independiente* (1837); *El Mono* (1833); *Suplemento al Diario del Gobierno de la República Mexicana* (1837–1838); *El Observador Judicial y de la Legislación* (1842–1843); *El Mexicano* (1838); *El Mosáico Mexicano* (1838); *El Termómetro* (1838); *Boletín de la Sociedad Mexicana de Geografía y Estadistica* (1839–1852); *Voto Nacional* (1839); *Almacén Universal* (1840); *Boletín del Gobierno* (1840); *El Apuntador* (1841); *Boletín Oficial* (1841); *La Bruja* (1841–1842); *El Clamor de la Nación* (1841); *El Cosmopolita* (1841); *Semanario de la Industria Mexicana* (1841–1842); *El Siglo Diez y Nueve* (1841–1845; 1848–1858); *Un Periódico Más* (1841); *El Eco de la Nación* (1842); *El Registro Oficial. Periódico del Gobierno del Departamento de Durango* (1842–1848); *El Vocero del Cooperativismo* (1842); *Album Mejicano* (1843); *El Ateneo Mexicano* (1844); *Boletín de Noticias* (1844–1845); *El Defensor de las Leyes* (1845); *El Patriota Mexicano* (1845); *La Voz del Pueblo* (1845); *Boletín Extraordinario. Victoria de Durango* (1846);*

El Católico (1845–1847); *Diario del Gobierno* (1846); *El Republicano* (1846–1847); *El Sonorense. Periódico Oficial del Gobierno de Sonora* (1846); *The American Star* (1847–1848); *Diario del Gobierno de la República Mexicana* (1847).

Curiously, the new facilities of the *Biblioteca Nacional* do not include manuscripts and rare books. These will remain in the old building, which will be turned into a museum and converted into a library service center with tapes and special materials for the blind.

3. BIBLIOTECA NACIONAL (OLD LOCATION):

Located on the corner of Isabela Católica and Rep. El Salvador, the *Biblioteca San Agustín,* as it is now named, contains some collections useful to students of the Mexican period:

A. LA FRAGUA COLLECTION. Approximately 1,580 volumes compiled by the political liberal José María La Fragua (1813–1875), first director of the *Biblioteca Nacional,* came to the library at the time of his death. Composed primarily of books and manuscripts dealing with the 1821–1853 period, the collection was indexed by Lucina Moreno Valle and published in her *Catálogo de la Colección La Fragua de la Biblioteca Nacional de Mexico, 1821–1853* (Mexico: Universidad Autónoma de Mexico, Instituto de Investigaciones Bibliográficas, 1975). A card catalog also provides access to the collection with both alphabetical and chronological entries. Materials relating to New Mexico include congressional decrees, newspaper reports, various government manifestos, and some correspondence.[6]

B. ARCHIVO FRANCISCANO. Records of the Franciscans are scattered between New Mexico and the Distrito Federal. The *Biblioteca Nacional* may have additional uncataloged records. Ignacio Del Río's *Guía del Archivo Franciscano de la Biblioteca Nacional de Mexico* (Mexico: Universidad Nacional Autónoma de Mexico, Instituto de Investigaciones Bibliográficas, 1975) lists only one document relevant to New Mexico in the Mexican period.[7] Likewise, the *Indice de Documentos Franciscanos existentes en la Sección de Manuscritos de la Biblioteca Nacional* (Washington: The Academy of American Franciscan History, n.d.) includes only this same reference.[8] Although one might conclude that Mexican period materials are concentrated in some other archive, researchers should not rule out the possibility of turning up additional information in some unexpected corner of the old *Biblioteca Nacional.*[9]

C. IMPRESOS. Among several sections in the card catalog describing printed materials is a heading entitled, *Memorias.* Most of these are recollections, or final reports, submitted by politicians to state or national assemblies in which the authors discuss conditions, problems, and accomplishments related to their terms of government service. The reports are quite lengthy, sometimes self-serving, and invariably informative. Many are authored by state governors from Northern Mexico; others are by secretaries of War, Treasury, Foreign Relations, and Justice, all of whom had some responsibility for affairs in New Mexico. The *Memorias* are an excellent source for Mexican period research.

4. ARCHIVO GENERAL DE LA NACION (AGN):

Before entering into research on the Mexican period in the *AGN*, it is helpful to understand the relationship between the existing *unidades* and *ramos* and the evolution of the bureaucratic agencies of the government since 1821. Familiarity with contemporary government agencies and their relationships to each other will assist students of the Mexican period in making intelligent guesses regarding the possible repositories of uncataloged materials.[10]

The chart on page 167 will show that four ministries dominated in the Mexican period: *Hacienda, Justicia y Negocios Eclesiásticos, Relaciones Exteriores e Interiores,* and *Guerra y Marina*. Between independence and the presidency of Benito Juárez, these ministries experienced few structural changes. Variations in function were more a factor of individual leadership than a result of internal bureaucratic modifications. Daily administrative duties, the circulation of official reports, and the development of communication channels with other departments of state and the federal government remain something of a mystery due to the characteristic *personalismo* in Mexican politics. But armed with the *Ley Orgánico, Manual de Organización del Gobierno Federal,* and an accurate list of the *gabinetes* (ministers of state) for the Mexican period,[11] researchers should be able to identify channels of communication and archival depositories where historically significant materials were created and/or archived. Thus prepared, the researcher will be able to research the records of the Mexican period *unidades* with a better understanding of their probable contents.

A. GOBERNACION.   As noted in the structural chart, *Gobernación* emerged from the *Ministerio de Relaciones Exteriores e Interiores* in 1843. By 1853 it had become a separate ministry. Because of the existence of several finding aids,[12] *Gobernación* has become the most accessible and frequently used *unidad* for research on the Mexican period of New Mexico. It is composed of correspondence between the central government and the states (departments) or territories. Within the various *ramos* (branches) of this *unidad,* information is available on municipal budgets, declarations of local office holders, requests for licenses to leave the country, reports on income received from *aduana* receipts, statistics on migration, lists of nominees for political office, reports on rebellious activities, invasion of public lands, local elections, health epidemics, the disposition of paper currency, congressional debates, etc.[13]

More specifically New Mexican, the following examples serve to illustrate some of the many kinds of documents in this *unidad:*

(1) *Legajo* 166. Correspondence between Governor D. Mariano Martínez and the *Secretaría de Guerra y Marina* concerning a request that Martínez make an appearance in Mexico City. When Martínez died unexpectedly, he was replaced by D. José Chávez. The remainder of the *legajo* is composed of correspondence leading to the appointment of Manuel Armijo as governor on November 16, 1845.

(2) *Legajo* 173. This, too, is a series of letters dealing with the process of selecting New Mexico's governor. In this case Governor Albino Pérez criticized the *terna* of candidates drawn up by the local assembly to replace him in office. He suggested another list. The remainder of the *legajo* includes various comments on the Revolution of 1837 in New Mexico along with a copy of a letter from the Bishop of Durango to the *Ministerio de Interior* offering his influence to help put down the rebellion.

(3) *Legajo* 177. In this somewhat comical exchange, the Governor of New Mexico, Manuel Armijo, was engaged in a feud with Father Francisco Leyva, *primer vocal* of the New Mexico Assembly in 1841. Armijo was accused of despotism, mismanagement of public funds, and abandonment of the presidial company of Santa Fe. Armijo responded by saying that Leyva's private behavior did not conform to accepted moral standards and that his anger was rooted in the inability of the government to pay him for his services.

(4) *Legajo* 208. Governor Armijo wrote to the *Ministro de Relaciones* in December 1843 asking to be relieved of his post as *Comandante General* because the very severe cold aggravated a wound he had received in 1835. Armijo recommended D. Mariano Chávez y Castillo as his replacement.

(5) *Legajo* 1636. This lengthy exchange in 1845 is between New Mexico's treasurer, Ambrosio Armijo, and the General in Chief of the 5th Division of the Mexican Army, General D. Francisco García Conde. The correspondence reveals not only a dispute between Chihuahua and New Mexico over money, but raises the question of war with the United States.

    B. HACIENDA. *Unidad Hacienda* contains an abundance of information on New Mexico's economic life in general and the Santa Fe trade in particular. Since the primary functions of this ministry were to collect revenue for the federal government, supervise customs operations, and formulate monetary policy, the fiscal affairs of each state and territory were central to this branch of the bureaucracy. Even the titles of many of *Hacienda's ramos* suggest the existence of economic information on New Mexico: *Administración de Rentas; Aduanas; Comisarias—Correos; Papel Sellado; Tribunal de Cuentas,* etc.[14] Until recently, the records have not been available for research.

    Many *Hacienda* documents are unbound, uncataloged, unorganized, and, for all practical purposes, unknown. With consummate patience, *Hacienda* archivists have worked at identifying the loose papers, placing them in *cajas* (boxes), and recording their contents in a *libreta* (ledger). Working through the 1970s, they have managed to organize more than 2,500 boxes of documents, but a third of this archive is still without any kind of order or classification.[15]

Finding aids tend to be confusing. The first guide to *Hacienda*, *Guía del Archivo Histórico de Hacienda* (2 vols.), was published in 1940. It is a select list of documents of historical value located in the old *Archivo de Real Hacienda*. The publication was actually a series of *Boletines*, edited by Agustín Hernandez, who was commissioned by *Hacienda* for this task. According to the 1978 *Inventario de Ramos*, the guide covers approximately half of the material in the *ramo*, *Archivo Histórico de Hacienda*.[16] Another work completed by Esperanza Rodríguez, *Indice Analítico De La Guía Del Archivo Histórico De Hacienda*, was completed in 1975. It is a thematic and alphabetical aid to the same material indexed in the 1940 publication.[17]

The *fichero* (card catalog) will also prove useful. Eleven drawers contain file cards from which information was taken for the first two-volume guide to *Hacienda*. The top drawers are organized by *ramo* and then alphabetically by geographical region. Bottom drawers contain the same material organized geographically, including the entries filed by the archivist from 1970 to 1982. These new entries correspond to the ledger entries in the previously mentioned *libreta*.

The following citations are a sampling of the kind of material found in the principal finding aids of this *unidad:*

(1) *Guía del Archivo Histórico de Hacienda*, Vol. I.

Year	Subject	Reference
1834–35	*Aduana de Nuevo Mexico*	*Legajos*, 117–1, 176–1 to 176–4.
no date	Establishment of *aduanas* in Taos, San Miguel del Vado, Presidio de San Carlos, Presidio del Norte del departamento de Nuevo Mexico, etc.	
1821–48	*Libros y Folletos del Archivo Histórico de la Secretaría de Hacienda.* These publications pertain to customs legislation, *alcabala* and *consumo* taxes, *papel sellado*, organization of cavalry, infantry, and militia, decrees regarding resistance against U.S. forces, etc.	*Legajo*, 117–1 33A1 to 35D3.30.

(2) *Guía del Archivo Histórico de Hacienda*, Vol. II. *Cartas de Seguridad* (Passports and travel permits): The following alphabetical list for the years

1842–43 has been copied in full from the *Guía:*[18]

Name	Year	Legajo
Ackerly, Royal C.	1843	476–362
Aldrich, Silvano	1842	475–478
Atocha, Alejandro Jose	1843	476–479
Baker, Carlos	1842	475–382
Baker, George	1842	475–383
Baldwin, Ricardo	1842	475–246
Baley, Fernando	1842	475–321
Benson, Juan J.	1843	476–334
Bentley, Santiago	1842	475–130
Brundied, Benjamin	1842	475–219
Brus, Henrique	1843	476–409
Cooper, Juan S.	1843	476–333
Creemer, Juan J.	1842	475–332
Danache, Carlos	1843	476–97
Daniels, Mateo	1843	476–364
Davis, Guillermo R.	1842	475–388
Davis, Luis	1843	476–145
Dirgan, Tomas	1843	476–226
Doan, Handley	1842	475–38
Douvillen, Jules L.	1842	475–379
Dutton, Luis	1843	476–227
Epps, Guillermo E.	1842	475–132
Ferris, Tomas D.	1842	475–460
Fristoe, Juan	1843	476–411
Gookin, Juan	1842	475–385
Green, Dennipen	1842	475–381
Hanna, Roberto	1843	476–146
Hardy, Tomas	1842	475–390
Harks, J. D.	1842	475–351
Henry, Juan	1842	475–333
Hervin, Cristobal	1842	475–387
Hevenson, Hugo	1843	476–225
Hollbrook, Carlos	1842	475–389
Howard, Juan	1842	475–245
Johnson, D. Tomas	1843	475–5
Johnson, Guillermo A.	1842	476–314
Kelley, Tomas O.	1842	475–339
Kerr, Washington	1842	475–411
Kinney, Enrique	1843	476–421
Langstroth, Alejandro	1842	475–378

Name	Year	Legajo
Laxton, Jorge	1842	475–323
Le Grand, Eduardo	1842	475–4
Logan, Juan	1842	475–384
Lowrce, Daniel	1842	475–350
McElhose, Santiago A.	1843	476–365
McKinney, Santiago C. A.	1842	475–374
McMonus, Francisco	1842	475–96
Mackeon, Eduardo	1842	475–340
Major, Santiago	1842	475–129
Maning, Carlos	1843	476–407 & 475–464
Marsh, Pedro A.	1842	475–247
Moffett, Guillermo E.	1843	476–211
Newberry, Jacobo	1843	476–519
Nicholls, Isaac	1842	475–218
Osborn, Eduardo	1842	475–6
Packarell, Alberto	1843	476–147
Palton, Juan S.	1843	476–410
Pell, Gilberto	1842	475–332
Pettigrew, Juan	1843	476–363
Remer, Simeon	1842	475–380
Riddells, Benito	1842	475–183
Ridelles, Casnille B.	1842	475–448
Ripley, D. Santiago B.	1842	475–37
Rogers, Samuel	1842	475–410
Rois, Juan J.	1842	475–462
Wright, D. A. S.	1842	475–95

(3) *Libreta de Consulta:*

Year	Subject	Reference (ramo)
1826	*Justicia Eclesiástica*, various and New Mexico	00091
1842	Passports	00475
1831	Register of Correspondence	01744
1824–25	*Aduanas*	01973
1845	*Aduanas*	01971
1827	*Aduanas*	01975
1728–1866	Militia—troop movements, salaries, supplies, etc.	02030
1846	Militia—judgments, general	02031
1830–40	*Aduanas*	02059

Year	Subject	Reference (ramo)
1840–43	*Aduanas*	02060
1844–49	*Aduanas*	02061
1847	*Aduanas*	02062
1820–39	*Alcabalas*	02072
1840–45	*Alcabalas*	02073
1817–1905	Militia	02080
1822–47	Militia	02289

The reader should bear in mind that the above lists are samples of only some of the many references pertaining to the economic life of all the states and territories. Goods which could be imported duty free, coins minted in Chihuahua, and records of taxes, forced loans, lists of goods moving in interstate commerce, agricultural productivity, state monopolies on tobacco and gunpowder, plus a great variety of information not documented above, await the diligent researcher in the *Hacienda* archives.

C. JUSTICIA.   More correctly referred to as *Justicia y Negocios Eclesiásticos,* this ministry was frequently joined to the *Secretaría de Relaciones Interiores* during the Mexican period. *AGN* holdings reflect the broad nature of this ministry's function and reveal the extent to which matters of church and state remained interrelated even during the process of mission secularization.

Finding aids are inadequate. Herbert Eugene Bolton's *Guide to Materials for the History of the United States in the Principal Archives of Mexico* is a good place to begin,[19] even though the *AGN* staff feels that organizational changes may have invalidated his references. For *Justicia,* his citations are accurate, and several of the *ramos* in *Justicia* have been or are in the process of being indexed. For the Mexican period, researchers will have to go beyond the finding aids to the manuscripts, where a large volume of New Mexico material is waiting to be used. Some examples of these holdings follow:

(1) Vol. 138, pp. 149–67. Three letters written to Bishop Don José Antonio de Zubiría from Antonio José Martínez, Fernando Ortiz, and Juan de Jesús Trujillo. In addition to church matters, these letters chronicle the events of 1837 when New Mexico was racked by revolution. The bishop's response is to write the *Ministro de lo Interior* implying that North Americans are somehow responsible. In another group of letters which deals with the Cebolleta uprising of 1839, Manuel Armijo and Guadalupe Miranda discuss the instigators and how the revolt was suppressed.

(2) Vol. 48, pp. 29–62. In these documents, petitioners from Sandía Pueblo argue that they have not received title to lands they settled on in 1748 with three hundred "Moqui" Indians. Correspondence with the *jefe político* between

1829 and 1841 resulted in finding the appropriate deed in the New Mexico archive. Additional problems dealing with the administration of justice in New Mexico are discussed by Governor Manuel Armijo in a letter of December 31, 1828, in which he laments the absence of lawyers, the ignorance of the *alcaldes,* and the length of time necessary for the appeal process to reach Mexico City. Additional complaints were voiced against him by the *ayuntamiento* of New Mexico for alleged violations of election laws.

(3) Vol. 28, pp. 186–200. Correspondence between *Justicia* and several citizens of New Mexico describes the bankrupt condition of New Mexico's treasury *(comisaría)* and suggests that Agustín Durán, *subcomisario,* mismanaged the public funds. Sixteen-thousand pesos belonging to the *Hacienda Nacional* disappeared. The implications are that Durán was in league with José María Alarid and that both were involved in deals with the "estranjeros," thus depriving New Mexico of income from taxes. The outcome of this correspondence in 1833 was that Antonio Barreiro was sent to New Mexico to put the administration of justice in order.

(4) Vol. 159 1/3, pp. 303, 331. The first item is a letter from the *Comandante General* of Chihuahua to the *Ministro de lo Interior* warning of the consequences of North American merchants entering Mexico in large caravans in 1840. Other letters in this volume have to do with the relationship between Manuel Armijo and Manuel Alvarez in 1839. Alvarez asked Armijo for a letter of recommendation supporting his claim to rights as a Mexican citizen. Armijo's letter to the *Ministro de lo Interior* praised Alvarez as a capable and distinguished servant of Mexico. Alvarez then received a permit to act as U.S. Consul in Santa Fe without losing his Mexican citizenship. Included in this *legajo* is a discussion by Armijo of the mineral riches of New Mexico. The *Ministro de lo Interior* responded by saying that he had permission to develop the deposits in *Real de los Dolores* (June 18,1840).

These examples illustrate the variety of documentation extant in the *ramos* of *Justicia.* Ecclesiastical matters comprise another significant segment of the documents. One can learn about the Franciscans from New Mexico who participated in a Mexico City reunion in 1821; details of mission secularization; correspondence concerning New Mexico's exemption from taxes on their "*frutos decimales*"; and permits, licenses, indulgences, and other matters relating to the supervisory role of the Church in the lives of its religious. This *unidad* contains a potpourri of information valuable to research on the Mexican period.

D. GUERRA Y MARINA.   In contrast to *Justicia,* the fourth *unidad, Guerra y Marina,* offers very few possibilities for productive research on New Mexico in the Mexican period. The move to Lecumberri and recent efforts to modernize the indexes to the *ramos Archivo de Guerra* and *Operaciones de Guerra* have stimulated organizational activities, however, bringing to light heretofore unclassified materials.[20] To date, nothing of substance has appeared on New Mexico. The *sumarias* in *Archivo de Guerra* involve a few soldiers from Chihuahua and Durango, but the vast majority of these charges concern military courts in other parts of the country. *Operaciones de Guerra* relates largely to military affairs prior to 1821.

Indiferente de Guerra is the one *ramo* which might prove useful for research on New Mexico. It has been cataloged chronologically. Very general information is contained on cards in a *fichero*. In addition, a two-volume unpublished guide was prepared on the pages of which various archivists have written sometimes conflicting information. A lot of work is needed on this *ramo* to make it useful for research. Information in the documents themselves includes military budgets, the fighting strength of different units, order books, service records, legal proceedings, supply problems, and correspondence between civil and military authorities. Many dates between 1821 and 1848 reveal the importance of this *ramo* to the Mexican period.

E. RELACIONES EXTERIORES.   The final *unidad* of the *AGN* that coincides with the existence of Mexican period ministries is *Relaciones Exteriores*. It is composed of four *ramos*. The largest, *Cartas de Seguridad,* is made up of 221 volumes which include letters from the states and the minister of *Relaciones Exteriores* regarding requests from Mexicans and foreigners to travel or take up residence in Mexico. *Expulsión de Españoles* and *Pasaportes* both have published guides (see comments in this chapter regarding *AGN* publications), and *Historia, Notas Diplomáticas* contains some diplomatic correspondence. Most diplomatic correspondence, as well as documents relevant to Mexico's affairs with other nations, are to be found, however, in the archive of *Relaciones Exteriores* located on the ground floor of the Antiguo Claustro Franciscano de Tlatelolco at the Plaza de Tres Culturas. The collection is described later in this chapter.

Remarkable improvements have been made by the *AGN* in support services and specialized resources for researchers interested in more than manuscript collections. As with the improvements made in the organization and accessibility of the *unidades,* these new departments have made noteworthy progress during the *sexenio* of President López Portillo. Researchers of the Mexican period should be familiar with the following:

(1) *Hemeroteca.* Not to be confused with the *Hemeroteca Nacional* described in the beginning of this chapter, the *AGN*'s *Hemeroteca* is located in the section of the old prison which used to serve as administrative offices and prisoners' court for appeals and paroles (facing on Calle Albañiles). The *Hemeroteca* has ample space for newspapers transferred there from the basement of the old *AGN* in the Palacio Nacional. Under the aggressive leadership of a new director, future acquisitions from all government ministries will be archived under the same roof.

Dr. Gerald L. McGowan began work on this project in 1977 when Dr. Alejandra Moreno wooed him from El Colegio de Mexico after he had already established himself as an expert in *periodismo*.[21] His goals for the *Hemeroteca* are to collect, classify, and microfilm all official newspapers created in the capital and provinces of Mexico.[22] Emphasis is on searching for newspapers from the nineteenth century. Although his objectives parallel those of the *Hemeroteca Nacional*, McGowan's experience with newspaper research combined with conspicuous organizational skills suggest the possibility that the *AGN* could become equally useful to scholars doing research in Mexican periodicals.

Newspapers in the *AGN* have been separated into two main categories: official and privately published. They have been further organized by place of origin and thematic interest. To facilitate research, McGowan published the first *Lista de Fichas Hemerográficas* in 1979. It is organized in five sections:

(a) *Periódicos de la Capital*
(b) *Periódicos Oficiales* (includes newspapers from all branches of federal and state government)
(c) *Periódicos de Provincia*
(d) *Revistas Generales* (includes publications from Mexico and other countries)
(e) *Folletos*

In addition to the years of the newspaper, the *Lista* shows if it has been cataloged, if illustrations are registered, if an index exists, and if supplements and extras are available.

As of the summer of 1981, the *Hemeroteca* had processed 1,018 titles. At that time the third edition of the *Lista* was ready for publication, incorporating all titles registered in the first two editions. Official Mexico City newspapers in the *AGN* which are useful for Mexican period research are listed as follows:[23]

Gaceta Imperial de Mexico	1822
Gaceta del Gobierno Imperial de Mexico	1822–23
Gaceta del Gobierno Supremo de Mexico	1823
Gaceta del Supremo Gobierno de la Federación Mexicana	1824–25
Gaceta Diaria de Mexico	1825–26
Gaceta del Gobierno Supremo de la Federación Mexicana	1826
Registro Oficial	1830–33
Telégrafo	1833–34
Diario del Gobierno de los Estados Unidos Mexicanos	1835
Diaro del Gobierno	1835–37
Diario del Gobierno Del. [sic]	1838
Diario del Gobierno	1839–41
Boletín Oficial	1841

Diario del Gobierno	1841–46
Boletín de Noticias	1846
Diario Oficial	1846
Diario del Gobierno	1847
Correo Nacional, El	1847–49

Research in provincial (state) newspapers for the Mexican period will have to be done in the *Hemeroteca Nacional* or in the respective frontier states.

(2) *Departamento de Registro Nacional.* Recognizing the need to identify and assist in the preservation of state and local manuscript collections, Dr. Alejandra Moreno created the *Departamento de Registro Nacional* in 1976, choosing for its head Dr. Stella González Cicero from El Colegio de Mexico. With her husband Mstro. Jorge Garibay, Dr. González developed a six-step approach to improving conditions in both civil and ecclesiastical archives of the states:

Step 1: *Registro* (With the assistance of local universities, identify existing document repositories.)

Step 2: *Diagnóstico* (Analyze the status of the collection, its location, general conditions, accessibility, etc.)

Step 3: *Coordinación del Gobierno:* (Working with local people, hold regional conventions, classes dealing with document preservation, and other functions designed to maintain the archives in the best possible condition.)

Step 4: *Asesoría y Capacitación* (Provide supplies and training for archivists.)

Step 5: *Inventarios* (Take inventory of all documents.)

Step 6: *Publicación* (Publication of inventories and *archivalias.*)[24]

Dr. González had planned at first to concentrate on collections containing the oldest documents, but when she discovered that the access of her staff was occasionally blocked due to political problems and local jealousies, she decided to shift the emphasis of her work to those localities most receptive to *AGN* assistance. Consequently, the *Departamento de Registro Nacional* has done some work in all states of the republic except Morelos, Tamaulipas, Chiapas, and Sonora. The last mentioned was neglected only because it had already been surveyed by Enrique Florescano's Instituto Nacional de Antropología e Historia (INAH). Although Dr. González's staff has increased slightly in size, the task at hand is almost overwhelming. The goal for the end of 1982, the end of President López Portillo's *sexenio,* was to register twenty percent of all the nation's municipal archives.

The *Departamento de Registro Nacional* has made progress in the civil and ecclesiastical archives of Juárez, Chihuahua, Parral, and Durango as follows:

(a) *Juárez.* Three government archives have been visited. The *Archivo Gen-*

eral de la Presidencia Municipal located in the Biblioteca Municipal y Archivo is the one whose archive has been filmed by UTEP. No inventory has been prepared, but the documents are already cataloged and finding aids are available. In addition to municipal *actas, informes, boletines, permisos, mapas, and estadísticas,* researchers will find copies of the *Diario Oficial* and a *Registro de Extranjeros* for the Mexican period. This archive is sometimes referred to as the *Archivo de la Presidencia Municipal de Juárez.* Another archive, the *Registro Civil,* is located in the Palacio del Gobierno. Documents span the 1866–1890 period. The *Departamento de Registro Nacional* has also located private archival collections belonging to Professor Armando B. Chávez M. and Lic. Clemente Bolio.

(b) Ciudad Chihuahua. Approximately one-half of the *parroquias* have been registered since work began in 1978. A *diagnóstico eclesiástico* has been prepared showing the content of these archives.

More progress has been made in the municipal archives. Approximately seventy-five percent have been registered, and inventories have been prepared for Jimenez, Villa Aldama, Aquiles Serdán, Rosales, General Trias, and Cuahetemoc. A *borrador* (rough draft) of the *archivalia* for Chihuahua has been prepared.

(c) Parral. In addition to listing the boxes and dates for those municipal records located in the Benjamin Franklin Library, the *Departamento de Registro Nacional* plans a future inventory of these materials.

(d) Durango. Initial steps have been taken to visit existing civil and ecclesiastical archives. A preliminary list has been prepared showing the location of existing collections, their inclusive years, and their general condition. A great deal of work remains to be done in the state of Durango.

(3) *Mapoteca.* Some research topics require the use of maps, plans, and illustrations. Several map archives in Mexico City should be consulted. Examples are: the *Sociedad de Geografía y Estadística;* the *Instituto de Geografía* at the Universidad Nacional Autónoma de Mexico; the *Centro Histórico de Ayuntamiento;* and the *Mapoteca de la Defensa Nacional.* There are others. The *AGN* also has a *mapoteca,* the advantage of which is that more than ten catalogs have been published providing descriptions and easy access to illustrative materials in its many *ramos.* Each volume contains references to materials in a specific *ramo.* Although sources on New Mexico are scattered, information available on such matters as irrigation projects, weapons and armaments, military and civilian dress styles, missions, presidios, jails, and Indians reveals the importance of this archive.[25]

(4) *Dirección de Difusión y Publicaciones.* Publications of the *AGN* are useful for many research topics. Some are out of print, but an attempt is being made to reprint those items most frequently requested. Additionally, the staff of each *unidad* assigns personnel to revise existing publications in order to reflect changes taking place in individual *ramos.* Available from the *AGN* is a

pamphlet entitled *Catálogo de Publicaciones* (1982). It lists a number of publications useful to research on the Mexican period, including the following:

(a) *Inventario de Guías e Indice actualizado al mes de marzo de 1978.* Organized by *unidades* and then by *ramos,* this inventory of *AGN* holdings lists volumes and in some cases *legajos* along with information regarding indexes and other finding aids. It is useful but dated.

(b) *Guía descriptiva del Archivo General de la Nación.* The *ramos* of the *AGN* are listed alphabetically, not by *unidades.* Descriptions include an overview of the content of each *ramo,* the approximate time period covered by the documents, and the number of volumes. This work, prepared by Miguel Civéira Taboada and María Eleiva Bribiesca, should be used in conjunction with the *Inventario.* Although presently out of print, the authors are working on an updated version.

(c) *Guía general de los fondos que contiene el Archivo General de la Nación,* 1981. This guide reflects the *AGN*'s move to Lecumberri. It describes the contents of each *galería* and lists finding aids.

(d) *Vocabulario de Terminos en documentos históricos.* The focus of this work is on colonial and ethnohistoric word usage. Words are listed alphabetically with an explanation of their meaning. Many, such as "acta," "alcabala," "alcalde," "arbitrios," "aduana," "departamento," "derechos," "diligencia," "juez," are terms also used in the Mexican period. Out of print.

(e) *Ramo Provincias Internas,* 2 vols. Eighteenth- and early nineteenth-century documents are indexed in this guide. It should also be used for assistance in locating lost collections from Durango and Chihuahua. Out of print.

(f) *Ramo Expulsión de Españoles,* 2 vols. Heretofore studied only briefly, the socio-economic impact of congressional legislation expelling Spaniards from Mexico can be traced with the help of this two-volume calendar. Seventy-two volumes are organized chronologically; each entry is a brief summary of correspondence relevant to this issue. Many references to New Mexico and Chihuahua and a biographical-geographical index make the calendar very easy to use.

(g) *Ramo Pasaportes.* Researchers will be disappointed that this guide covers only the years 1821–1827. Of the fifty-eight volumes in this *ramo,* only eight have been referenced. Information deals with passport applications, government orders regarding frontier restrictions, *cartas de seguridad,* import restrictions, and complaints from foreign legations.

(h) *Guía documental del Archivo Histórico de Hacienda, tomos* I and II. The latest guide to the relatively unknown contents of the *Hacienda* archive. This is new.

5. ARCHIVO DE LA SECRETARIA DE LA DEFENSA NACIONAL:

Located on the ground floor of the military complex known as the *Defensa Nacional,* the *Archivo Histórico Militar* consists of two separate entities, both of which are contained in the same complex: *Archivo Histórico (Operaciones Militares)* and *Archivo de Cancelados*. The former embodies data on military campaigns; the latter contains service records of the regular army. Access to the *Defensa* is from the Periférico via Ejército Nacional into Colonia Lomas de Sotelo. Permission to work at this archive must be requested from the *Secretaría del Estado Mayor*, and a minimum of six weeks should be allowed for a decision. Documents describing the exact nature of research, previous publications, and letters of support from supporting institutions will speed the process. Even with all the correct documents, permission to do research at the *Defensa* can be difficult to obtain even for Mexican citizens.

A. ARCHIVO HISTORICO (OPERACIONES MILITARES). Although Bolton's *Guide* dedicates forty-seven pages to materials of the *Defensa Nacional* and the *Secretaría de Guerra y Marina*, the most useful finding aid for Mexican period materials is Volume I of the *Guía del Archivo Histórico Militar de Mexico*, published by the *Defensa* in 1948. Listing those *expedientes* which deal with the 1821 to 1847 period, complete with an index by subject, geographical site, and personal names, the *Guía* provides easy access to New Mexico materials.

Two additional volumes which were never published are available for consultation at the Bancroft Library. Both are carbon-copy typescripts, Volume II covering the years 1848 to 1855, Volume III, 1855 to 1859. Volume II contains a few items of significance to the Mexican period, but Volume III concentrates on the Ayutla uprising, the overthrow of Santa Anna, and the opening of the War of the Reform. The following references are a sampling of information found in Volumes I and II dealing with New Mexico:

Volume I[26]

(1) Exp. XI/481.3/1220. *Partes relativos al pronunciamiento de la población de Nuevo Mexico, E.U.A. Año de 1837.* 9 pages.

(2) Exp. XI/481.3/1221. *Partes del Coronel Manuel Armijo, Gobernador y Comandante General Militar de Nuevo Mexico, E.U.A., dando cuenta de las operaciones efectuadas con motivo del pronunciamiento de la población. Año de 1838.* 25 pages.

(3) Exp. XI/481.3/1222. *Socorro de tropas con destino a Nuevo Mexico, E.U.A. Año de 1838.* 2 pages.

(4) Exp. XI/481.3/1223. *Partes relativos al pronunciamiento de la población de Nuevo Mexico, E.U.A. Año de 1838.* 9 pages.

(5) Exp. XI/481.3/1224. *Indice de documentos relativos al pronunciamiento de la población de Nuevo Mexico, E.U.A. Año de 1837.* 9 pages.

(6) Exp. XI/481./3/1225. *Partes relativos al pronunciamiento de la población de Nuevo Mexico, E.U.A. Año de 1837.* 86 pages.

(7) Exp. XI/481.3/1226. *Partes relativos al pronunciamiento de la población*

de Nuevo Mexico, E.U.A. Año de 1837. 27 pages.

(8) Exp. XI/481.3/1227. *Partes relativos al pronunciamiento de la población de Nuevo Mexico, E.U.A. Año de 1837.* 56 pages.

(9) Exp. XI/481.3/1228. *Partes relativos al pronunciamiento de la población de Nuevo Mexico, E.U.A. Año de 1837.* 16 pages.

(10) Exp. XI/481.3/2199. *Correspondencia del Ministerio de Relaciones Exteriores, relacionada con la ocupación de las plazas de Monterey, Nuevo León y Tampico, por fuerzas norteamericanos. Asuntos diversos de la Administración General de Correos y de las Comandancias Generales de . . . Durango, Sinaloa, Chihuahua y Nuevo Mexico. . . . Información hecha en la villa de El Paso, Chih., el 7 octubre de 1846, en que se menciona la actuación del General Manuel Armijo, con motivo de la ocupación de la plaza de Santa Fe, Nuevo Mexico por fuerzas norteamericanas. Año de 1846.* 1,014 pages.

(11) Exp. XI/481.3/2201. *Asuntos diversos. . . . Instancia de la Asamblea Departamental de Nuevo Mexico para que se establezca Comandancia General, siendo designado el General Manuel Armijo. Año de 1848.* 134 pages.

(12) Exp. XI/481.3/2204. *Partes de las Comandancias Generales de Tamaulipas y Nuevo Mexico, dando cuenta de la campaña desarollada en la Alta California y ocupación de Nuevo Mexico, por fuerzas norteamericanas. Año de 1846.* 107 pages.

(13) Exp. XI/481.3/2588. *Formación de causa al General Manuel Armijo, por su actuación política y militar en la ocupación del territorio de Nuevo Mexico, por fuerzas norteamericanas. Años de 1846–47.* 57 pages.

Volume II

(14) Exp. XI/481.3/3092. *Incidentes relacionados con la sumaria formada al Gral. Manuel Armijo por su comportamiento como Comandante General del Depto. de Nuevo Mexico, asi como durante la ocupación de la Villa del Paso, Chih. por fuerzas norteamericanas. Años de 1849–50.* Pages 77–121.

(15) Exp. XI/481.3/3504. *Partes del Comandante General del Edo. de Chihuahua, Don Angel Frías, dando cuenta de los abusos cometidos por el Presbítero D. Ramón Ortiz, en su comisión de Traslador de familias de Nuevo Mexico a la República. Año de 1853. Transcripción de un artículo publicado en el periódico San Antonio Ledger relativo a una colisión ocurrida en la Mesilla, Chihuahua, entre las autoridades Mexicanas y Norteamericanas. Año de 1853.* Pages 4–7.

(16) Exp. XI/481.3/4433. *Incidentes relativos a la acusación presentada en contra del Gral. Manuel Armijo, por abandono del mando político y militar de Nuevo Mexico, durante la invasión norteamericana.* Pages 6–10.

   B. ARCHIVO CANCELADOS. This archive contains in alphabetical order the *expedientes* of all the generals, *jefes*, and officers who, having served in the army, no longer form a part of it either because of their death or their separation from the service. Those who die while in the service, and whose families receive a pension by law, have their records in another section, *Pensionados*, but a notation is supposed to be on file in alphabetical order in the *fichero* pertaining to *Cancelados*. No guide is available to *Cancelados*. Names are requested from attending military personnel who bring the service records to researchers for perusal. In addition to military history, these records contain personal information on a soldier's family, prizes and awards, correspondence, petitions, and complaints, and a valuable reference number showing where further information on the individual can be encountered in the *Archivo Histórico*. The following examples illustrate the content of typical records in *Cancelados:*

(1) José María de Arce, *Teniente Coronel de Infantería.*[27]

    (a) Promotion list showing dates each rank attained, followed by time in grade, duty assignment, etc.

    (b) Military actions listing seven campaigns, several skirmishes against the Indians, pursuit against North Americans entering the country with contraband, service in maintaining civil order in Chihuahua and Durango, and other actions in support of various plans of the federal government.

    (c) Non-combat assignments such as reconnoitering New Mexico in search of the best places to place fortifications; defining the jurisdictional limits of pueblos in the Río Abajo; effecting peace treaties with the Indians, etc.

    (d) Personal characteristics such as bravery, health, leadership, education received, civil and military conduct, and natural abilities.

    (e) Leaves of absence, special requests, awards, etc.

(2) Albino Pérez, *Teniente Coronel de Caballería.*[28]

    (a) Correspondence between *Guerra y Marina* and the widow of Albino Pérez in which she shows proof of her legitimate marriage and asks repeatedly for the pension she is supposed to receive from the government.

    (b) Service record showing time in grade, units in which service was performed, military campaigns, personal characteristics, and general conduct.

    (c) Correspondence in which Pérez notes that he was taken prisoner when he pronounced against the Iturbide government; appointment papers naming him *Comandante Principal del Territorio de Nuevo Mexico y Gefe Superior Político;* orders for his arrest in Veracruz in 1834 and communications from Pérez denying his participation in the revolution; letters from Pérez while governor of New Mexico, etc.

In 1954–55 the Bancroft Library was permitted to have microfilmed selected documents of the *Archivo Militar*. Selections were made with primary emphasis on California and the American Southwest with dates from the 1820s to the 1850s. Ninety-three reels of 16 mm film are now available for consultation only in the Bancroft Library. Although some of it is difficult to read, its value as a source material for the Mexican period of New Mexico is even greater given the difficulties of gaining entrance to the manuscripts themselves in the *Defensa Nacional.*

6. ARCHIVO DE LA SECRETARIA DE RELACIONES EXTERIORES (TLATELOLCO):

This archive, which is now housed in the Antiguo Claustro Franciscano, adjacent to the modern building used as headquarters by *Relaciones Exteriores,* was first organized in 1923. At that time, documents were collected from different dependencies as well as from an archive for *Relaciones Exteriores* located in the *AGN.* A classification system was adopted based on the use of alphabetical and decimal cataloging supported by chronological and geographical finding aids. This system, while greatly extended, has not been altered in the past sixty years. Some of the original groupings relevant to New Mexico are as follows:[29]

(1) *Colección completa de decretos, circulares y disposiciones del Ministerio de Relaciones Exteriores,* 1820–1900.
(2) *Sucesos entre Mexico y Estados Unidos, relacionados con Texas y los estados limítrofes,* 1821–1845.
(3) *Cartas de naturalización expedidas por la Secretaría de Relaciones Exteriores,* 1830–1953.
(4) *Reclamaciones entre Mexico y Estados Unidos,* 1840–1871.
(5) *Sucesiones de estranjeros en Mexico,* 1843.

In 1973 the Antiguo Claustro, officially known as the *Dirección de Archivo, Biblioteca y Publicaciones,* was opened for archival and library usage. This charming building, once a monastery, has become one of the most delightful places to do research in Mexico.

After occupying the building in 1976, the staff continued to classify documents, so that what is essentially historical material is now almost entirely accessible for research. Two main *ficheros* for the nineteenth and twentieth centuries provide easy entry to document reference numbers. A third *fichero* is available for twentieth-century newspaper research. Six additional indexes are supposed to contain a year-by-year listing of documents and a decimal classification number. Unfortunately, some have been lost while others provide duplicate information.

Permission to work in the archive is relatively easy to obtain if visiting scholars present a letter of recommendation from an academic institution. Photoduplicating facilities are available, but the budget has not yet permitted microfilming. Although by law all of these materials should eventually return to the *AGN,* it is more than likely that they will remain at Tlatelolco because of the amount of time and money already invested in this archive, its convenient location next to the *Secretaría de Relaciones Exteriores,* and the immense amount of work expected by the *AGN* in establishing itself at Lecumberri.[30]

Samples of entries in the *fichero* for the nineteenth century are:

(1) 1–1–34. *Decreto de 18 de enero declarando que los departamentos fronterizos son Chiapas, Nuevo Mexico, Alta California y Texas.* 1845.

(2) 3–3–4061. *El Ministro del Interior inserta el dictamen del Consejo del Gobierno sobre la solicitud de varios ciudadanos de los Estados Unidos para abrir un camino.* 1839.

(3) 6–17–94. *Informes y determinación de la Junta de Fomento de las Californias sobre el Camino que Estados Unidos trata de construir.* 1829.

(4) 2–3–2135. *El Ministro de la Guerra transcribe oficio del . . . sobre depredaciones de los Indios Bárbaros de los Estados Unidos a los que dirige al paisano Antonio Vigil.* 1826.

(5) 2–3–2338. *Documentos relativos a las expediciones comerciales a Nuevo Mexico y otras provincias Mexicanas del Norte.* 1825.

(6) 1–2–515. *Se comunica a los gobernadores de los Departamentos que el Congreso extraordinario autoriza al Ejecutivo para repelar la invasión Norteamericana.* 1846.

(7) 1–11–1143. *Correspondencia de Chihuahua relativa a la invasión Norteamericana.* 1847.

(8) 1–11–1148. *Consulta del Gobernador de Chihuahua sobre planes de defensa y medidas que deben tomarse contra los extranjeros sospechosos que se introduzcan en el Estado dada la guerra que existe con los E.U.A.* 1846.

(9) 3–14–5137. *El gobernador de Durango comunica que las tropas norteamericanas que tomaron Nvo. Mexico han ocupado la población de Doña Ana cerca de El Paso.* 1846.

(10) 1–2–532. *El gobierno de Chihuahua comunica que los norteamericanos han invadido Nvo. Mexico y propone que se invite a Inglaterra para que ayude a Mexico.* 1846.

(11) 3–14–5174. *La Asamblea de Nuevo Mexico informa sobre la ocupación de aquel departamento por los invasores norteamericanos y la conducta que observa el Gobernador y Comandante Gral. Manuel Armijo.* 1848.

(12) 1–2–474. *Invasión a Nuevo Mexico por aventureros de E.U.A. Información y datos sobre los mismos que son apoyados y enviados por aquel país.* 1838.

(13) 6–2–58. *Diversos documentos relacionados con una invasión de Nuevo Mexico por E.U.A.* 1843.

(14) 1–1–295. *Comunica que en San Luis Missouri y Territorio de Arkansas, se fabrica moneda mexicana para introducirla en la República.* 1832.

(15) 2–13–2971. *El Gobernador de Chihuahua se refiere a la traslación de*

familias mexicanas de Nuevo Mexico de acuerdo con el Tratado de Guadalupe Hidalgo. 1849.

(16) 12–1–6. *Reclamación contra varios americanos por haberse introducido al territorio mexicano a dedicarse a la caza de nutria.* 1828.

(17) 40–11–1. *Orden del 6 de febrero que trata de los efectos prohibidos de comercio extranjero.* 1822.

(18) 16–3–31. *El ministro del Interior informa sobre el tráfico comercial que hacen los americanos del norte en las fronteras de Sonora y Chihuahua.*

Additional references, not included in this sampling, provide evidence of North American activities with the Indians of Chihuahua and other frontier states. Other collections contain correspondence concerning New Mexican families returning to Mexico after the Mexican War; correspondence between the U.S. Consul in Santa Fe and the Secretary of Foreign Relations; circulars to state governors on assorted subjects; information on treaties, passport restrictions, and reclamations against the Mexican government; and assorted legal matters involving international relations. The archive is rich in source material, well organized and staffed, and a genuinely pleasant place in which to work.

7. BIBLIOTECA DE HACIENDA:

Now located on Rep. El Salvador a few blocks from the old *Biblioteca Nacional,* this library was in the Palacio Nacional until 1973. As the library for Mexican legislation, it is an excellent source for state and federal laws and decrees. Most of the books and pamphlets are government publications. They deal with Indian activities, population statistics, mining and agriculture, foreign trade, and other topics of importance to the northern frontier. The library also contains a collection of newspaper articles dealing with the government's fiscal and economic policies. The *fichero* is not normally available to the public, but special permission is obtainable upon presentation of letters of recommendation. Collections specialize in the twentieth century.

8. CENTRO DE ESTUDIOS DE LA HISTORIA DE MEXICO (CONDUMEX):

This private library and archive was founded in 1953 by Anaconda Wire and Cable Company. It was located on the northern edge of Mexico City at Avenida Poniente 140 until late in the 1970s, when everything was moved to the old *capilla* Chimalistac, Plaza Federico, which had been converted to satisfy the needs of a research library. The new location, just off Insurgentes Sur and a short distance from UNAM, is much more convenient for both visiting and resident scholars. The facilities are appropriate for research and they are professionally staffed.

Manuscript acquisitions have concentrated on the Colonial period, War for Independence, Empire of Maximilian, *Reforma,* and Revolution, 1910–20.[31] Nineteenth-century material is made up largely, but not exclusively, of decrees, circulars, *memorias,* and other government publications. Along with some contemporary printed materials, books and pamphlets, researchers will also find an almost complete run of the *Diario Oficial.* A guide to the *AGN*'s *ramo Civil (unidad Justicia)* was prepared by Luis Orozco Chávez. His file cards, located in the main *fichero,* suggest that this *ramo* of 2,378 volumes contains items of interest for New Mexico in the nineteenth century. References are made to mines, local government, land grants, Indians, taxes, criminal proceeding, uprisings, names of towns, *villas,* and cities, religious matters, maps, publications, and a potpourri of miscellaneous items.[32]

Some examples of Mexican period materials as listed in the main *fichero* are as follows:

From the chronological Index:

(1) L.G.C. I–2. *Carpeta* 12–38. Doc. No. 87. Circular, 17 de enero de 1822, *Remite ejemplares del Bando, concediendo a las Provincias Internas de Oriente libre comercio de mulas por tierra con los Estados Unidos.*

(2) L.G.C. I–2. *Carpeta* 12–38. Doc. No. 931. Decreto Imp. Mexico el 8 de mayo de 1822, *Informe que el Congreso Constituyente decreta que a falta de Jefe Político e Intendente propietarios, preside la Diputación provincial el vocal mas Antiguo de ella.*

(3) L.G.C. I–2. *Carpeta* 12–38. Doc. No. 947. Circular Imp. Mexico, 12 de Junio de 1822, *Hace saber que los Ayuntamientos y Diputaciones Provinciales deberán comunicarse con el gobierno y éste con ellos por medio de los Jefes Políticos.*

(4) L.G.C. I–2. *Carpeta* 14–38. Doc. No. 1114. Circular, Mexico 14 de abril de 1823, *Remite decreto relativo al reglamento provisional para la milicía cívica y que expidió el Congreso Constituyente.*

(5) L.G.C. I–2. *Carpeta* 14–38. Doc. No.1115. Decreto, Mexico 16 de abril de 1823, *Transcribe decreto del Congreso Constituyente Mexicano sobre el establecimiento de la Milicía Nacional.*

From the alphabetical index:

(1) 1826. *Discurso del diputado Abreú sobre la situación en Nuevo Mexico.* Aguila Mexicana *27 de enero de 1826,* p. 4, col. 1.

(2) 1826. 2132. *El Ministro de la Guerra transcribe queja del Jefe Político de Nuevo Mexico.*

(3) 1832. Barreiro, Antonio. *Ojeada sobre Nuevo Mexico. . . .*

(4) 1835. *Nuevo Mexico, Situación de . . . (El Sol,* 14 de marzo de 1835, pag. 166, misc. 17).

(5) *Nuevo Mexico: Historia y descripción de Nuevo Mexico.* Vol. I de la Col. [Collección] de Estadística de la Subdirección.

(6) Pino, Pedro Bautista. *Noticias Históricas y estadísticas de la antigua provincia de Nuevo Mexico.*

(7) *Circunstancias agrícolas e industriales de Chihuahua.* Reg. [Registro] Oficial, 5 de marzo de 1831, fol. 254.

(8) 1834. *Memoria de Gobernador presentada el 3 de julio de 1834. El Tiempo,* 9 de dic. de 1834, pag. 658. Misc. Vol. 12.

(9) 1835. *Comunicación dirigida al Sr. Comandante General del Estado de Chihuahua por él de la segunda sección de operaciones contra los indios bárbaros. El Sol,* 10 de feb. de 1835, pag. 38, Misc. Vol. 17.

(10) 1835. *Proposiciones hechas por el Diputado López de Vergara sobre facilitar recursos al Estado de Chihuahua y discursos que se produjeron en el debate de la sesión de 17 de feb. de 1835. El Sol,* 22 de feb. de 1835, pag. 85, Misc. Vol. 17.

(11) 1835. *Sobre paces con los apaches. El Sol,* 11 de marzo de 1835, pag. 156, Misc. 17.

As with many manuscript collections in Mexico, those in *Condumex* are undergoing reclassification. The discovery of errors in the numbering system prompted a complete review of all manuscript holdings. Initiated in 1981, this task was approximately fifty percent completed by the end of the year. Its significance to future research is that the archival staff will soon have a far more sophisticated grasp of all holdings.

9. MISCELLANEOUS:

Archives mentioned above constitute the principal repositories containing collections on the Mexican period. Thorough research, however, will require the pursuit of additional items in private and public collections which may eventually prove to be of equal importance. For contemporary printed books, for example, one will need to review the collection of the *Museo de Antropología.* The library of this museum has the works of Lucas Alamán, Carlos María de Bustamante, José Fernando Ramírez, José María La Fragua, and many others who wrote about Mexico during the 1821–1848 period. Archives of the Senate and Chamber of Deputies need to be searched. Both contain records dating back to the First Congress. Although many have been lost or destroyed since then, the search is a necessary part of a thorough investigation. By the same token, records at the *Instituto Nacional de Antropología e Historia (INAH)* may prove useful. Most of the materials observed by the author were twentieth-century economic records, but some Mexican period sources are referenced. Furthermore, the possibility exists that some of the lost Franciscan records will be found here.[33] If the reader will bear in mind that research in Mexico is still a pioneering endeavor for the Mexican period, documents are likely to be found in the most unlikely places.

10. A SUMMARY OF DESCRIPTIVE REFERENCES AND FINDING AIDS EXCLUDING UNPUBLISHED INDEXES AND INVENTORIES:

(1) Bolton, Herbert Eugene. *Guide to Materials for the History of the United States in the Principal Archives of Mexico.* Washington: Carnegie Institution, 1913 (Kraus Reprint, 1965). Although dated, Bolton's contributions to an understanding of manuscript collections in Mexico City are pioneering efforts which still have value to researchers.

(2) Carrera Stampa, Manuel. *Archivalia Mexicana.* Publicaciones del Instituto de Historia, Número 27. Mexico: Universidad Nacional Autónoma de Mexico, 1952. The second part of this study discusses archives in the city of Mexico and is organized according to those which depend on the Executive branch of government, those under the Distrito Federal and other government agencies, and those which are controlled by the church and the national university.

(3) *Catálogo de Ilustraciones.* 10 vols. Mexico: Centro de Información Gráfica del Archivo General de la Nación, 1979–82. These volumes are organized by *ramos* in the *AGN*. Each is a guide to one or more *ramos* in which is listed the maps, *planos*, and other kinds of illustrative information known to exist in the archives.

(4) *Centro de Estudios de Historia de Mexico.* Mexico: Condumex, S.A., 1972. The information on this archive and library is general, but the pamphlet provides a brief history of how it was formed and lists the principal collections.

(5) Civéira Taboada, Miguel, and María Eleiva Bribiesca. *Guía descriptiva de los ramos que constituyen el Archivo General de la Nación.* Mexico: *AGN*, 1977. An annotated listing of all *ramos* in the *AGN* with a brief explanation of the contents of each. This volume should be used in conjunction with the *Inventario de Ramos.*

(6) Del Río, Ignacio. *Guía del Archivo Franciscano de la Biblioteca de Mexico.* Mexico: Universidad Nacional Autónoma de Mexico, Instituto de Investigaciones Bibliográficas, 1975. Most references on New Mexico are to the colonial period.

(7) Greenleaf, Richard E., and Michael Meyer. *Research in Mexican History: Topics, Methodology, Sources, and a Practical Guide to Field Research.* Lincoln: University of Nebraska Press, 1973. Although out-of-date in some details, this guide to research in Mexico contains much valuable information on collections and how to use them.

(8) *Guía del Archivo Histórico de Hacienda, Siglos XVI a XIX,* 2 volumes. Mexico: Secretaría de Hacienda y Crédito Público, 1940–45. Originally published as a series of *Boletines* under the direction of Agustín Hernández, this guide provides some assistance in gaining entry to one-half of the materials pertaining to *unidad Hacienda.*

(9) *Guía del Archivo Histórico Militar de Mexico.* Tomo I. Prólogo de Vito Alessio Robles. Mexico: Taller Autográfico, 1949. This is the only published

guide to the historical archive in the *Defensa Nacional*. It covers the Mexican period listing military actions, activities, and communications with both the *Secretaría de Guerra y Marina* and civilian authorities. Indexes list names and places.

(10) *Guía general de los fondos que contiene el Archivo General de la Nación,* 1981. The newest addition to descriptive guides on *AGN* holdings, this one reflects advances made since the *AGN* moved to Lecumberri.

(11) Gómez Canedo, Fray Lino. *Indice de Documentos Franciscanos existentes en la Sección de Manuscritos de la Biblioteca Nacional,* 2 volumes. Washington: The Academy of American Franciscan History, n.d. Volume two has a few items on New Mexico in the Mexican period.

(12) *Inventario de Ramos, Guías e Indices Actualizado al mes de marzo de 1978.* Mexico: Departamento de Publicaciones del Archivo General de la Nación, 1978. Although changes have been made since this was put together, it is valuable for understanding the *unidad-ramo* organization of the *AGN*. Volumes contained in each *ramo* are listed along with notes regarding finding aids.

(13) Ker, Annita Melville. *Mexican Government Publications.* Washington: U.S. Government Printing Office, 1940. This useful volume is a guide to publications of the Mexican government from 1821 to 1936. It includes the official gaceta *(Diario Oficial),* annual and semi-annual messages of the president to Congress, *memorias* (annual reports) of the cabinet members of Congress, and the transactions of Congress itself. Before each section listing publications, the author has included a brief description of the issuing agency.

(14) McGowan, Gerald L. *Lista de Fichas Hemerográficas.* Mexico: *AGN,* 1981. This is the third volume of information on *AGN* newspapers containing data from the first two lists. It organizes and archives newspapers by geographical area and provides information on supplements, illustrations, and extras. A distinction is made between official and unofficial newspapers.

(15) Millares Carlo, Agustín. *Repertorio bibliográfico de los archivos mexicanos y de los europeos y norteamericanos de interés para la historia de Mexico.* Mexico: Instituto Bibliográfico Mexicano, 1959. Although somewhat broad in its sweep, this volume does have some information on archives in Mexico and the states. See particularly pages 108–61.

(16) Moreno Valle, Lucina. *Catálogo de la Colección La Fragua de la Biblioteca Nacional de Mexico, 1821–1853.* Mexico: Universidad Autónoma de Mexico, Instituto de Investigaciones Bibliograficas, 1975. The author describes items in this collection, most of which are government reports, newspaper articles, and manifestos on a variety of subjects. More than a few references to New Mexico.

(17) Rodríguez de Librija, Esperanza. *Indice analítico de la guía del Archivo Histórico de Hacienda.* Mexico: *AGN,* 1975. This is an index to the *Guía del Archivo Histórico de Hacienda* mentioned above.

(18) Rubio Mañe, Jorge Ignacio. *El Archivo General de la Nación, Mexico, D.F*. Mexico: Editorial Cultura, 1940. Also published in *Revista de la Historia de America* 9(1940): 63–169. The history and contents of the *AGN* are the focus of this excellent study by a man who was its director for many years.

EVOLUCION DE LAS DEPENDENCIAS CENTRALIZADAS DE
LA ADMINISTRACION PUBLICA FEDERAL A PARTIR DE 1821*

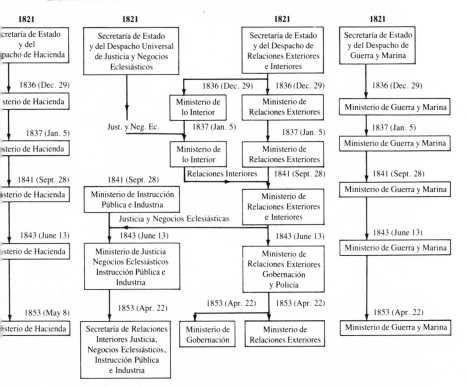

*Chart copied from *anexo* attached to the *Ley Orgánica de la Administración Pública Federal*. Mexico: Secretaría de la Presidencia, 1977.

NOTES

1. Mexican historians working in the Mexican period in spite of the difficulties have concerned themselves mostly with the Texas revolt or with diplomatic relations leading to the Mexican War. Students of the former include José C. Valadés, Pablo Herrera Carrillo, Miguel A. Sánchez Lamego, and Carlos Sánchez-Navarro. The best diplomatic studies are by Carlos Bosch García and Luis G. Zorrilla. Vito Alessio Robles' two-volume study of Coahuila and Texas is one of the few interpretive works published by Mexican historians. Josefina Vázquez and Moisés González Navarro, both of the Colegio de Mexico, are both very familiar with the sources for this period. Publications of the above mentioned scholars are cited in David J. Weber, ''Mexico's Far Northern Frontier, 1821–1854: Historiography Askew,'' *Western Historical Quarterly* VII (1976): 283, n.10.

2. Zaragoza-Observatorio Line; station stop: San Lázaro. The *AGN* is a ten-minute walk from the Metro along Calle Eduardo Molina.

3. Opening day was September 30, 1900, according to the newspaper *El Imparcial* of the same date.

4. The *AGN* is presently organized into fifteen *unidades: Secretaría del Virreinato, Hacienda, Tierras, Eclesiástica, Ayuntamientos, Fomento y Obras Públicas, Instrucción Publica, Salubridad, Justicia, Guerra y Marina, Gobernación, Presidentes, Relaciones Exteriores, Trabajo, Fondos Incorporados y provisionalmente Historia y Segundo Imperio.* See *Inventario de Ramos, Guías e Indices Actualizado al mes de marzo de 1978* (Mexico: Departamento de Publicaciones del Archivo General de la Nación [AGN], 1978), and *Guía General De Los Fondos Que Contiene El Archivo General De La Nación* (Mexico: Dirección de Difusión y Publicaciones del Archivo General de la Nación, 1981). Dr. Moreno had in mind the seven non-administrative *unidades*. The *crujías* are now referred to as *galerías*.

5. Richard E. Greenleaf and Michael C. Meyer, *Research in Mexican History: Topics, Methodology, Sources, and a Practical Guide to Field Research* (Lincoln: University of Nebraska Press, 1973). I have the highest praise for the Greenleaf-Meyer study even though specific parts may be outdated.

6. A more exact description of these entries can be found in the *''Indice Analítico''* of Lucina Moreno's *Catálogo* under the headings ''Nuevo Mexico'' (p. 1132) and ''Chihuahua'' (p. 1006).

7. Letter from Manuel de Jesús Rada to Fray José Antonio Guisper, March 31, 1829, in which he points out the shortage of clergy in the New Mexico missions and the risk that the Indians might return to paganism. *Guía,* p. 266.

8. Ibid., *Indice,* p. 145.

9. Professor Ramón A. Gutierrez, Pomona College, who has also looked for

Franciscan materials, agrees with this assessment and further suggests a search of the Vatican Archives if nothing turns up in Mexico. Conversation with the author, April 22, 1981.

10. Dr. Alejandra Moreno, Director of the *AGN*, placed so much importance on the need to understand bureaucratic structure that she organized seminars on the subject for her staff. The most recent manual on modern Mexican bureaucracy is *Manual de Organización del Gobierno Federal,* Publicaciones de la Dirección General de Estudios Administrativos de la *Secretaría de la Presidencia* (Mexico: Imprenta Madero, 1976). See also Annita Ker, *Mexican Government Publications* (Washington: U.S. Government Printing Office, 1940), and Manuel Dublán and José María Lozano, *Legislación Mexicana . . . ,* 19 vols. (Mexico: Imprenta del Comercio, 1846–90), vol. 9, pp. 88–90.

11. See, for example, José Rogelio Alvarez, *Enciclopédia de Mexico,* Tomo V 3ª ed. (Mexico: Enciclopédia de Mexico, S.A., 1978). Under the heading, *"Gabinetes,"* are fourteen pages filled with names, pictures, and dates of tenure of men appointed to head the nation's ministries.

12. Index No. 1: *"Inventario Gobernación* I: *Inventario de los Fondos documentales del Archivo llamado 'Casa Amarilla'."* This inventory indexes *legajos* numbered 150–1293. Of these, eighty-seven are missing according to the previously cited *Inventario de Ramos,* p. 64. Index No. II, *"Inventario de los Fondos documentales del Archivo llamado 'Casa Amarilla' (Secretaría de Gobernación)."* This inventory indexes *legajos* numbered 1 to 149. Index No. III, *Ramo Gobernación: Catálogo Original,* leg. no. I, lists *legajos* numbered 1 to 9 followed by 9 BIS and 200 to 205. These three indexes were prepared at different times for different purposes.

13. In addition to the indexes mentioned above, an overview of *Gobernación's* holdings can be found in a report signed by Ana Laura Delgado Rannauro and presented to Dr. Alejandra Moreno on January 15, 1979.

14. A complete listing of *Hacienda's ramos* appears in *Inventario de Ramos,* pp. 14–19.

15. As of the summer of 1981, the head archivist, Irene Portillo R. de E., was working on *caja* no. 2518. Her estimate of unorganized material is consistent with that of others who have seen the documents.

16. *Inventario de Ramos,* p. 14.

17. Esperanza Rodríguez de Lebrija, *Indice Analítico De La Guía Del Archivo Histórico De Hacienda,* Colección Documental, Número 2 (Mexico: *AGN,* 1975).

18. This list is supposed to represent those *norteamericanos* who entered Mexico in 1842 and 1843. Surnames suggest that it might include other nationalities. The list is not complete.

19. Herbert Eugene Bolton, *Guide to the Materials for the History of the Principal Archives of Mexico* (Washington: Carnegie Institution, 1913). Kraus reprint, 1965.

20. *Archivo de Guerra* is comprised of 1,463 volumes. Entry to these materials used to be through a five-volume index and a five-page list showing the *legajo* numbers and years included in each *legajo*. Gilberto Martínez Bribiesca has prepared an *Indice Provisional* that arranges documents in different categories. Some of these are "Desertion," "Insubordination," "Criminal," "Conspiracy," "Wounds," "Uprising," "Opposition," "Sedition," "Theft," etc. Each *sumaria* (verbal process) is identified by the class of offense, the year, and a number showing the *legajo, expediente,* and pages. Martínez has also made a chronological list of the volumes in the *ramo Operaciones de Guerra.*

21. Gerald L. McGowan, *Prensa y Poder, 1854–1857* (Mexico: El Colegio de Mexico, 1978). This publication is a revised version of McGowan's doctoral thesis for El Colegio de Mexico.

22. From 1820 to the death of Benito Juárez, official newspapers used basically the same format. They printed no editorials, no daily news, and no criticism. Published by either a government or private press, they were mouthpieces of those in power. They printed laws, decrees, government circulars, and notifications of personnel changes in the bureaucracy. Important to the history of New Mexico in the Mexican period is the abundance of official correspondence which appears in newspapers. Letters from northern *comandancias* were selected for publication if they included good news or treated a subject about which the government wished the people to read. Because some official correspondence has been lost, the newspapers are an excellent alternate resource for researchers. McGowan is looking into new technologies for electronically preserving copies of the newspapers, since the predicted life of microfilm is only seventy-five years.

23. Gerald L. McGowan, *Lista de Fichas Hemerográficas,* 3ª ed. (Mexico: AGN, 1982), pp. 64–66.

24. As of January 1983, the *AGN* has published the following inventories:

Civil: *Archivo Municipal de Chihuahua, Chih.*
              Archivo Municipal de Julines, Chih.
              Archivo Municipal de Tecuala, Nay.
              Archivo Municipal de Santa María del Oro, Nay.
              Archivo Municipal de Rosamorada, Nay.
              Archivo Municipal de Ruiz, Nay.
              Archivo Municipal de Compostela, Nay.

Ecclesiastical: *Archivo Parroquial del Santo Angel Custodio Analco, Pue.*
              Archivo Parroquial del Ixtacamaxtitlán, Pue.
              Archivo Parroquial del Sagrado Corazón Sta. Barbara, Chi.
              Archivo Parroquial del Sagrario, León, Gto.
              Archivo Diocesano de Zacatecas, Zac.
              Archivo Parroquial del Real de Catorce, S.L.P.

Inventories awaiting publication include the municipal archives of Jalisco and Tepic in Nayarit; Jalpade Méndez, Jalapa, Centla, Teapa, E. Zapata, and Paraiso in Tabasco; Tinún, Telcanto, Maxcanu, and Alcil in Yucatán. Ecclesiastical archives awaiting publication include the *Archivo Diocesano of Puebla,* Siglo XVI and XVIII; and the parroquial archives of La Soledad in Puebla, Santo Cristo de Burgos in Cd. Jimenez, San José in Parral, Santa Cruz in Rosales, Hermosillo and Cd. Obregón, San Antonio Julimes, San Juan Bautista de Analco, Santa Ana, and La Sagrada Familia in Durango.

The *Departamento de Registro* will continue to prepare and publish civil and ecclesiastical archival holdings as funds become available.

25. Each *Catálogo de Ilustraciones* is published by the Centro de Información Gráfica del Archivo General de la Nación. *Ramos* represented in the first ten volumes are arranged as follows:

Volume I:	Caminos y Calzadas	Historia
	Desague	Casa de Moneda
	Correspondencia de Virreyes	Marina
	Provincias Internas	
Volume II		
through		
Volume V:	Tierras	
Volume VI:	Operaciones de Guerra	Escribanos
	Obras Públicas	Padrones
	Minería	Real Caja
	Misiones	Intestados
	Acordada	Vínculos y Hospital
	Correos	de Jesús
Volume VII:	Indiferente de Guerra	Carceles
	Correspondencia de Autoridades	Censos
	Justicia	Clero Regular y Secular
	Justicia Archivo	Colegios y Universidades
	Justicia Eclesiástica	Justicia Instrucción
	Justicia Imperio	Pública
	Templos y Conventos	Mercados
	Temporalidades	Presidios y Carceles
	Bandos	Fomento Calzadas
	Californias	Fomento Caminos
Volume VIII:	Fomento Camino Cuentas	Oficio de Soria
	Fomento Correos	Policía
	Fomento Desague	Real Acuerdo
	Fomento Ferrocarriles	Río y Acequias
	Fomento Puentes	Traslado de Tierras
	General de Parte	Real Fisco de la Inquis.

Consulado
Real Audiencia
Filipinas
Corresp. de Diversas Autoridades
Intendentes
Criminal
Civil
Industria y Comercio

Volume IX: Documentos Oficiales para la
Historia de Mexico
Reales Cedulas
Salinas
Renta de Tabaco
Ayuntamientos
Oficios Vendibles
Propios y Arbítrios
Pólovora

Volume X: Universidad
Inquisición
Tabaco
Archivo Bulnes
Subdelegados

Hospitales
Lotería
Bulas y Santa Cruzada
Bines de Difuntos
Protomedicato
Notas Diplomáticas
Arzobispos y Obispos
Infidencia
Monte de Piedad
Impresos Oficiales
Archivo de in Guerra
Alcabalas
Archivo de Buscas
Bienes Nacionales
Infidencias
Universidad

Fondo Reservado
Fondos Incorporados
Gobernación
Californias

26. Examples selected are some of the references relating to the rebellion in 1837 and the occupation of New Mexico by North American forces in 1846. They were chosen from entries under Manuel Armijo in the *Indice Onomástico*. Researchers should consult the *Guía* directly for a complete reference to many other New Mexico items. In addition to military information, many of the *informes* provide details on Indians, movements of North Americans, Santa Fe trade data, activities of New Mexicans, copies of newspaper articles, correspondence with several ministries in Mexico, and the political factions which aired their views of one another in official missives.

27. See file number D/111–5/7056, 12 *fojas*. Arce's service spanned the years 1803 to 1826. He served in various posts in Santa Fe, Carrizal, Chihuahua, and Durango.

28. See file number D/111–5/54988, 17 *fojas*. Pérez was the only governor of New Mexico who was appointed to that post without having been nominated by the citizens of New Mexico. He was killed during the Revolution of 1837. His military service spanned the years 1808 to 1837.

29. See Berta Ulloa, *Revolución Mexicana, 1910–1920*. Guías para la Historia Diplomática de Mexico, No. 3 (Mexico: *Secretaría de Relaciones Exteriores*, 1963), pp. 3–4.

30. Interview with Subdirectora de Archivo Lic. María Eugenia López de Roux, Mexico, June 12, 1981.
31. Library and archival collections are briefly described in *Centro de Estudios de Historia de Mexico* (Mexico: Condumex, S.A., 1972).
32. The resident specialist on Luis Orozco Chávez is Evelia Trejo de Kent.
33. Conversation with Dr. Ernesto de la Torre Villar, Mexico, July 1, 1981.

Governor Manuel Armijo, transmittal of the orders of the Alferes *Tomas Martinez and Antonio Sena to the* Gefe Superior de Hacienda, *May 27, 1840.* (Mexican Archives of New Mexico, *Governors Papers, Communications Sent by Governor and Comandante General to Authorities within New Mexico. New Mexico State Records Center and Archives.) Photograph by Daniel Martinez.*

BIBLIOGRAPHY OF PRINTED SOURCE MATERIALS

T he following annotated list of sources is intended to supplement document citations in this book. Entries are arranged alphabetically and contain information regarding various editions of several printed works. Some entries are cross-referenced between the editor and the individual(s) who prepared the diary, journal, or firsthand account of New Mexico in the Mexican period. References to "Becker" draw the reader's attention to the fourth edition of Henry R. Wagner and Charles L. Camp, *The Plains and the Rockies. A Critical Bibliography of Exploration, Adventure and Travel in the American West, 1800–1865*. Revised, enlarged and edited by Robert H. Becker (San Francisco: John Howell-Books, 1982).

This bibliography does not pretend to be complete. The works listed are those primary sources most frequently cited and available in the United States. Additional contemporary printed sources will be found in the microfilm publication, *Western Americana: Frontier History of the Trans-Mississippi West, 1550–1900* (Woodbridge, Conn.: Research Publications, Inc., 1977), which contains the Everett D. Graff Collection (Newberry Library) and the William Robertson Coe Collection (Yale University Library) on 617 reels. Research Publications, Inc. has also filmed the Thomas W. Streeter Collection under the title, *Texas as Province and Republic, 1795–1845*, 125 reels (RPI, 1980). For the many sources that describe or refer to the Santa Fe Trail, an indispensable tool is Jack D. Rittenhouse, *The Santa Fe Trail, A Historical Bibliography* (Albuquerque: University of New Mexico Press, 1971).

Rittenhouse's bibliography provides cross-referencing to government publications many of which were privately reprinted under different titles. A great number of U.S. government publications not included in this work can be located by reference to the *U.S. Serial Set Index, Part I*, American State Papers, and the 15th–34th Congresses, 1789–1857. The subject index contains a variety of entries dealing with New Mexico, including: military expeditions; reports on depredations committed against United States citizens; protection of the Santa Fe trade; numbers and characteristics of Indians in New Mexico; land claims; customs problems relative to fur traders and merchants; correspondence regarding United States–Mexican relations; decrees from Mexico regarding New Mexico; and a great number of communications and reports concerning the Mexican War. No one has compiled a list of materials in the *Serial Set* similar to that prepared by Donald H. Powell for the 1846–1861 period. Powell's publication can be found in two issues of the *New Mexico Historical Review:* Vol. XLIV (Oct. 1969), pp. 315–42; and Vol XLV (Jan. 1970), pp. 47–82. Accomplishment of this task would be a great service to scholars interested in the Mexican period of New Mexico.

Abert, James William. *Report of an Expedition led by Lieutenant Abert, on the Upper Arkansas and Through the Country of the Comanche Indians, in the Fall of the Year 1845.* U.S. 29th Cong., 1st Sess., vol. 8, Sen. Doc. 438 (Serial 477). Washington, June 16, 1846. There are two reprints. The full text was published with notes by H. Bailey Carroll in *Panhandle-Plains Historical Review*, vol. 14, 1941. The latest reprint edition by John Galvin, which appeared under the title, *Through the Country of the Comanche Indians in the Fall of the Year 1845. The Journal of a U.S. Army Expedition led by Lieutenant James W. Abert of the Topographical Engineers Artist extraordinary whose paintings of Indians and their Wild West illustrate this book,* was published by John Howell-Books, 1970. Becker #120 includes a list of the plates.

Abert was sent by John Charles Fremont to investigate the country south of Raton Pass to the Canadian River when Fremont was on his third expedition to the West. Abert made the first astronomical observations of this area and produced an important map.

————. *Report of the Secretary of War, Communicating, in Answer to a Resolution of the Senate, a Report and Map of the Examination of New Mexico, made by Lieutenant J. W. Abert, of the Topographical Corps.* U.S. 30th Cong., 1st Sess., Sen. Exec. Doc. 23 (Serial 506). Washington, February 10, 1848. Also published as House Exec. Doc. 41 (Serial 517). It is included in William H. Emory, *Notes of a Military Reconnoissance . . . ,* reprinted as *Abert's New Mexico Report, 1846–47,* Horn and Wallace, 1962; and published as *Western America in 1846–1847; The Original*

Travel Diary of Lieutenant J. W. Abert who mapped New Mexico for the United States Army, edited by John Galvin. San Francisco: John Howell-Books, 1966. Becker #143 includes a list of the plates.
Abert's diary describes his trip from Fort Leavenworth over the Santa Fe Trail via Bent's Fort, his survey of the northern part of New Mexico, and his return.

Allison, William H. H. "Recollections of Col. Francisco Perea." *Old Santa Fe* II (1915): 392–406.
Perea comments on the changes which had taken place in New Mexico since the arrival of the North Americans. He concludes that United States sovereignty was the "greatest blessing" ever bestowed on the people of New Mexico. A list of merchants doing business in Santa Fe in 1849 is included.

———. "Santa Fe as It Appeared During the Winter of the Years 1837 and 1838." *Old Santa Fe* II (1914): 170–83.
Col. Francisco Perea recalls certain events associated with the uprising of 1837. His remarks must be judged by the fact that he was only eight years old at the time, but he makes some interesting comments about Manuel Armijo and the activities in Santa Fe.

Armijo, Antonio. "Armijo's Journal of 1829–30: The Beginning of Trade between New Mexico and California." Edited by LeRoy R. Hafen. *The Colorado Magazine* 27 (1950): 120–31. The journal also appears as, *"Camino Descubierto Desde el Pueblo de Abiquiú en el Territorio de Nuevo Mexico, Hasta La Alta California,"* Registro Oficial de Gobierno de los Estados Unidos Mexicanos, June 1830. A translated version appeared in the *Huntington Library Quarterly* II (1947): 87–101; Hafen again published the journal in Archer B. Hulbert's *Southwest on the Turquoise Trail.* Denver: The Steward Commission of Colorado College and the Denver Public Library, 1933. The French translation appears as, *"Itineraire Du Nordmexico A La Haute-Californie, Parcouru en 1829 et 1830 Par Soixante Mexicains."* *Bulletin de la Societe de Geographie* (Paris), Second Series, vol. III, 316–23. The Armijo journal is #39a in Becker.
The journal is a record of Armijo's trip along what later would be known as the Old Spanish Trail. His trip is significant because it opened up trade between California and New Mexico, and also because the route was an extension of earlier probes in that direction by Spanish explorers.

Barreiro, Antonio. "Antonio Barreiro's 1833 Proclamation on Santa Fe City Government." Edited by Marc Simmons. *El Palacio* 76 (1970): 24–30.
Barreiro's "Proclamation on Maintenance of Order and Good Government" is a descriptive account of conditions in Santa Fe.

———. *Ojeada Sobre Nuevo-Mexico, Que da Una Idea de Sus Producciones*

Naturales, Y de Algunas Otras Cosas Que Se Consideran Oportunas Para Mejorar Su Estado. E Ir Proporcionando su Futura Felicidad. Formada Por El Lic. Antonio Barreiro, Asesor de Dicho Territorio. A Petición Del Ecsmo. Señor Ministro Que Fue de Justicia Don José Ignacio Espinosa. Y Dedicada Al Ecsmo. Señor Vice-Presidente de los Estados Unidos Mexicanos Don Anastacio Bustamante. Puebla, Mexico: Imprenta de Ciudadano José María Campos, 1832. It was first published in English in the *New Mexico Historical Review* III (1928): 73–96; 145–78. The Historical Society of New Mexico reprinted Lansing Bloom's translation as part of its *Publications in History,* vol. 5. It is also translated in H. Bailey Carroll, *Three New Mexico Chronicles.* Albuquerque: The Quivira Society, 1942. Reprinted by Arno Press, New York, 1967. Becker #45a. Barreiro was sent to Santa Fe in 1831 as a legal advisor. He was asked to prepare a formal report of his observations. The result is a Mexican's view of New Mexico in the 1830s.

Becknell, Thomas. "The Journals of Capt. Thomas Becknell from Boone's Lick to Santa Fe and from Santa Cruz to the Green River." *Missouri Intelligencer,* April 22, 1823; June 25 and September 2, 1825. Reprinted in *Missouri Historical Review* 4 (1910): 65–84. A. B. Hulbert includes the journal in his *Southwest on the Turquoise Trail.* Denver: The Steward Commission of Colorado College and the Denver Public Library, 1933. Becker #30a.

Descriptions of Becknell's travels during 1822 and 1823, in which he discusses various forms of wildlife, the countryside, and the art of survival. See also Marmaduke, Meredith Miles.

———. "Thomas Becknell as a Mountain Man: Two Letters." Edited by David Weber. *New Mexico Historical Review* 46 (1971): 253–60.

These letters from Becknell, one to Governor Bartolomé Baca and the other to Mr. Patten, are an account of a trapping expedition in northern New Mexico and southern Colorado. The letter to Governor Baca was never before published in its entirety. The letter to Mr. Patten appeared in the *Missouri Intelligencer* at Franklin, June 25, 1825. The date of the letter to Baca is October 29, 1824; the second letter describing the tour is not dated.

Becknell, William. See Hulbert, Archer Butler.

Bell, John R. *The Journal of Captain John R. Bell, Official Journalist of the Stephen H. Long Expedition to the Rocky Mountains, 1820.* Edited by Harlin M. Fuller and LeRoy R. Hafen, The Far West and the Rockies Historical Series, 1820–1875, vol. IV. Glendale, Calif.: The Arthur H. Clark Co., 1957.

Until this journal was found in 1932, it was believed that the only extant account of the Yellowstone Expedition was that of Edwin James. Bell chronicles the return of one group by way of the Arkansas River in the summer of 1820.

Bent, Charles. "The Charles Bent Papers." Edited by Frank D. Reeve. *New Mexico Historical Review* 29 (1954): 234–39, 311–17; 30 (1955): 154–67, 252–54, 340–52; 31 (1956): 75–77, 157–64, 251–53.
The text includes correspondence from December 1837 to early 1846. Written mostly to Manuel Alvarez in Santa Fe, these letters contain comments on most leading figures of the time plus observations about the Santa Fe trade. The same letters are contained in the first of four reels of the Alvarez Papers available on microfilm at the Coronado Room, University of New Mexico Library, and at the History Library, Museum of New Mexico. The originals are located at the New Mexico State Records Center and Archives. See also Hyde, George.

Benton, Thomas Hart. *Thirty Years' View; or, a History of the Working of the American Government from 1820 to 1850.* 2 vols. New York: D. Appleton and Co., 1854. Reprinted by Greenwood Press, New York, 1968.
Benton played a leading political role in developing the Santa Fe Trail and trade. These two volumes have ample material on the struggle to get a road to Santa Fe as well as a discussion of the conquest of New Mexico in 1846.

Bieber, Ralph P., ed. *Marching with the Army of the West, 1846–1848.* Southwest Historical Series, vol. IV. Glendale, Calif.: Arthur H. Clark Co., 1936.
Contains the diaries of Philip Gooch Ferguson, Marcellus Ball Edwards, and Abraham Robinson Johnston, who entered New Mexico with U.S. forces in 1846. Includes many comments on Mexican culture, fights with Navajo Indians, and experiences with the Army of the West.
See also Cooke, Philip St. George; Gibson, George Rutledge; and Webb, James J.

Bigler, Henry W. "Extracts from the Journal of Henry W. Bigler." *Utah Historical Quarterly* 5 (1932): 35–64, 87–102, 134–60.
Bigler, a Mormon, passed through Santa Fe to California with the Mormon Battalion. He comments on various aspects of his trip.

Bliss, Robert S. "The Journal of Robert S. Bliss, with the Mormon Battalion." *Utah Historical Quarterly* 4 (1931): 67–96, 110–28.
Bliss also passed through Santa Fe on his way to California with the Mormon Battalion.

Boggs, William M. "The W. M. Boggs Manuscript about Bent's Fort, Kit Carson, the Far West and Life Among the Indians." Edited by LeRoy R. Hafen. *The Colorado Magazine* 7 (1930): 45–69.

Written in 1905, this manuscript describes Bent's Fort, the Indians, and traders who visited the fort. Other comments pertain to certain Mexican laws and the trade in general.

Bork, William Albert. *"Nuevos Aspectos del Comercio entre Mexico y Misuri, 1822–46."* Ph.D. dissertation, Universidad Nacional Autónoma de Mexico, 1944.

A summary of the Santa Fe trade, this dissertation includes texts of many Mexican archival documents, reports from Santa Fe customs, manifests of caravan freight, and lists of caravan members.

Bustamante, Carlos María de. *Apuntes para la Historia del Gobierno del General D. Antonio López de Santa-Anna, desde Principios de Octubre de 1841 Hasta 6 de Diciembre de 1844, En Que Fué Depuesto del Mando por Uniforme Voluntad de la Nación, Escrita por el autor del cuadro histórico de la revolución mexicana . . .* Mexico: Impr. de José María Lara, 1845.

The author reviews the principal domestic and international events significant to Santa-Anna's presidency. Included are several sections dealing with Texas problems, the attempted ''invasions'' of New Mexico, Mexico's relations with the United States and several European nations, the political fortunes of key figures, plans, and constitutions of the period, and miscellaneous social, political, and economic matters debated by Congress.

———. *"Diario de lo.Especialmente Ocurrido en Mexico."* Elias Amador Library of the state of Zacatecas MSS. Microfilm copies available in the library of the Anthropological Museum in Mexico City and at the Latin American Collection of the University of Texas.

Bustamante was an active participant in almost every Congress from Independence to his death. He knew figures from all phases of Mexican society. He daily recorded the principal events he witnessed, heard, or read about, and often included pamphlets and newspaper clippings. This work provides perspective on events taking place in New Mexico during the Mexican period.

———. *Diario Histórico de Mexico.* Mexico: J. Ortega, 1896.

This volume relates the major political events occurring in Mexico City and in other parts of the country between 1822 and 1841. Included are a number of biographical sketches and comments on diverse subjects.

———. *El Gabinete Mexicano Durante el Segundo Período de la Administración del Exmo. Señor Presidente D. Anastasio Bustamante Hasta la Entrega del Mando Al Exmo. Señor Presidente Interino D. Antonio López de Santa-Anna, Y Continuación del Cuadro Histórico de la Revolución Mexicana.* Tomo II. Mexico: Imprenta de José Maria Lara, 1842.

The title page appears as follows: *"Quien lo dedica al Exmo. Sr. general y gobernador del departamento de Nuevo-Mexico D. Manuel Armijo.''* Other subjects discussed by the author reveal his interest in and knowledge of affairs in New Mexico.

Carroll, H. Bailey, and J. Villasana Haggard, trans. and eds. *Three New Mexico Chronicles: The Exposición of Don Pedro Bautista Pino, 1812; The Ojeada of Licenciado Antonio Barreiro, 1832; and the additions by Don José Agustín de Escudero, 1849.* Albuquerque: The Quivira Society, 1942. Reprinted by Arno Press, New York, 1967. Becker #45a.

This work contains the 1812 comments of Pedro Bautista Pino and the additions of José Agustín de Escudero and Lic. Antonio Barreiro. Many of Escudero's opinions credit Josiah Gregg as the source. For nineteenth-century New Mexico, the three *Chronicles* provide valuable material about life in New Mexico.

Chávez, Fray Angélico. "New Names in New Mexico, 1820–1850." *El Palacio* 64 (1957): 291–318, 367–80.

Includes important data about Americans in New Mexico drawn from Church records.

Connelley, William, ed. "A Journal of the Santa Fe Trail." *Mississippi Valley Historical Review* 12 (1925–26): 72–98.

A journal by Philip St. George Cooke of a trip he made in 1843 which includes many comments on Manuel Armijo and North American traders such as Charles Bent and Ceran St. Vrain. Cooke had been assigned to lead a detachment of dragoons to accompany the annual Santa Fe caravan across the Plains.

———. "The Magoffin Papers." Historical Society of New Mexico, *Publications* 24 (1921): 42–63.

Correspondence between Magoffin and Secretary of War W. L. Marcy contains Magoffin's itemized account of expenses incurred while effecting the "Bloodless Conquest" of New Mexico. The file includes testimonial letters from William Connelley, Philip St. George Cooke, and others. Typescript copies of these papers are in the Twitchell Collection at the New Mexico State Records Center and Archives.

Cooke, Philip St. George. *The Conquest of New Mexico and California, an Historical and Personal Narrative.* New York: G. P. Putnam's Sons, 1878. Reprinted by Horn and Wallace, Publishers, Albuquerque, 1964; and by Rio Grande Press, Inc., Chicago, 1964.

This is a companion volume to Cooke's earlier *Scenes and Adventures in the Army.* The author arrived in Santa Fe in 1846 with the Army of the West and then took command of the Mormon Battalion, which he led to California. Cooke's remarks on meetings with Mexican officials prior to the army's entry into Santa Fe are particularly interesting. He also comments on Manuel Armijo and Santiago Magoffin, as well as many Mexican customs.

————. *Exploring Southwestern Trails, 1846–54: Cooke's Journal.* Edited by Ralph P. Bieber. Glendale, Calif.: The Arthur H. Clark Co., 1938.
Cooke's journal of the March of the Mormon Battalion, 1846–47, describes the author's extensive travel in New Mexico. He mentions the Mormon settlements at Pueblo, Santa Fe, Bernalillo, Albuquerque, and El Paso, and the Armijo and Chávez families and discusses difficulties encountered while requisitioning supplies.

————. *Scenes and Adventures in the Army; or, Romance of Military Life.* Philadelphia: Lindsay and Blakiston, 1856. Reprinted by Arno Press, New York, 1973.
Includes an account of Kearny's 1845 expedition to the Rockies. This is Cooke's first book about his experiences in the West. He describes his services with the 2nd Dragoons along the Santa Fe Trail.

Coombs, Franklin S. "Santa Fe Prisoners: Narrative of Franklin Coombs." *New Mexico Historical Review* 3 (1930): 305–14.
This account of the Texan Santa Fe expedition of 1841–42 supplements the accounts of George Wilkins Kendall and Thomas Falconer. It discusses the problems encountered by the Texans after arriving at Palo Duro and details the experiences of the expedition after it was intercepted and the Texans taken prisoner by Governor Armijo's New Mexicans. This account was printed in *Niles National Register,* March 15, 1842, and also in Thomas Falconer's book, *Letters and Notes on the Texan Santa Fe Expedition, 1841–1842* (1930).

Covington, James W. "Correspondence Between Mexican Officials at Santa Fe and Officials in Missouri: 1823–1825." *Missouri Historical Society Bulletin* 16 (1959): 20–32.
Correspondence between José Antonio Vizcarra and Governor Alexander McNair of Missouri illuminates problems resulting from Indian raids by tribes who resided in New Mexico and others that crossed over from the United States.

[Craig, James S.] "Letter from Dr. James S. Craig, formerly of Little Rock, Arkansas, dated Santa Fe, New Mexico, Jan. 2, 1831." *Arkansas Gazette,* June 8, 1831. Becker #42.
Craig was a member of Col. Robert Bean's expedition from Arkansas to Taos. On reaching New Mexico, the party was ordered out of the country by the Mexican governor.

Cutts, James Madison. *The Conquest of California and New Mexico.* Philadelphia: Carey and Hart, 1847. Reprinted by Horn and Wallace, Publishers, Albuquerque, 1965. Becker #131.

Although this volume is similar to others which describe New Mexico during the Mexican War, its use as a primary source is limited by the fact that much of the writing is copied from Lt. William H. Emory's *Notes*.

Davis, William Watts Hart. *El Gringo; or, New Mexico and Her People*. New York: Harper and Brothers, Publishers, 1857. Reprinted by Rydal Press, Santa Fe, 1938, and by Rio Grande Press, Chicago, 1963.
Although Davis did not arrive in New Mexico until 1853, he was appointed U.S. district attorney in Santa Fe, where he served for several months as acting governor. He was a literate man, whose views of New Mexico are appropriate even though Davis' Anglo-American bias is strong.

Dunham, Harold H., ed. "Sidelights on Santa Fe Traders, 1839–1846." *Westerners Brand Book, Denver Annual* 6 (1950): 263–82.
Despatches from Manuel Alvarez to Secretary of State Daniel Webster discuss problems encountered by traders in New Mexico, the character of Governor Manuel Armijo, and the coming of war. The original letters are in the National Archives, General Records of the Department of State, Record Group 59, Consular Despatches, Santa Fe.

Dye, Job F. *Recollections of a Pioneer, 1830–1852: Rocky Mountains, New Mexico, California*. Early California Travels Series II, Los Angeles, Calif.: Glen Dawson, 1951.
Dye traveled to New Mexico from Arkansas as a member of Col. Robert Bean's expedition.

Edwards, Frank S. *A Campaign in New Mexico with Colonel Doniphan*. Philadelphia: Carey and Hart, 1847. Also published by James S. Hudson, London, 1848. Reprinted by University Microfilms, Ann Arbor, Michigan, 1966. Becker #132:1 and #132:2.
This is a personal account of a man who was attached to Doniphan's Missouri Mounted Volunteers. According to Henry Raup Wagner, it is "the most entertaining account of the expedition."

Edwards, Marcellus Ball. See Bieber, Ralph P.

Emory, William H. *Notes of a Military Reconnoissance, from Fort Leavenworth, in Missouri, to San Diego, in California, including part of the Arkansas, Del Norte, and Gila Rivers. By Lieut. Col. W. H. Emory. Made in 1846–47, with the advanced guard of the "Army of the West."* 30th Cong., 1st Sess., House Exec. Doc. 41 (Serial 517). Washington: Wendell and Van Benthuysen, Printers, February 9, 1848. Reprinted as *Lieutenant Emory Reports*, edited by Ross Calvin. Albuquerque: University of New Mexico Press, 1951. Becker lists eleven editions.
The basic document, first released in 1848, includes the reports of Lt. J. W. Abert Emory and Philip St. George Cooke. The document also appeared as Sen. Exec. Doc. 7 (Serial 505) but without some of the appended reports.

Emory's comments on New Mexico, through which he passed in 1846 with the Army of the West, are a classic statement of the views of conquering North Americans.

Escudero, José Antonio. *Noticias Estadísticas de Chihuahua*. Mexico City: J. Ojeda, 1834.

As noted in Colton Storm's *Catalogue* to the Graff Collection, item no. 3297 appears as: "Pino, Pedro Bautista, Antonio Barreiro, and José Agustín de Escudero, *Noticias Históricas y Estadísticas de la Antigua Provincia del Nuevo-Mexico . . . Adicionadas Por El Lic. D. Antonio Barreiro en 1839 [!]; Y Ultimamente Anotadas Por El Lic. Don José Agustín de Escudero . . .* Lara, 1849."

Falconer, Thomas. *Expedition to Santa Fe. An Account of its Journey from Texas through Mexico with Particulars of its Capture*. New Orleans: Lumsden, Kendall and Co., 1842. Reprinted with notes and introduction by F. W. Hodge as *Letters and Notes on the Texan Santa Fe Expedition, 1841–42*. New York City: Dauber and Pine Bookshops, Inc., 1930. The most recent edition was printed by The Rio Grande Press, Inc., Chicago, 1963. The Rio Grande Press edition contains Falconer's *Notes of a Journey through Texas and New Mexico in the Years 1841 and 1842*. It was published originally in the *Journal of the Royal Geographical Society* 13 (1844): 199–222. Becker #90 and #106a.

Falconer, an Englishman, accompanied the Texan-Santa Fe expedition, but was released when his government exerted influence on the Mexicans. He read a paper on his experiences in which he included a description of being taken prisoner by the Mexicans and the treatment he received.

Farnham, Thomas Jefferson. *Travels in the Great Western Prairies, the Anáhuac and Rocky Mountains, and in the Oregon Territory*. Poughkeepsie, N. Y.: Killey and Lossing, Printers, 1841. Reprinted by Plenum Publishing Co., New York, 1968; and in the Early Western Travel Series, vols. 28 and 29. Cleveland: The Arthur H. Clark Co., 1906. Becker #85:1 and #85:4.

Farnham traveled the Santa Fe Trail in 1839. His descriptions of the route and Indian tribes met on the way were prepared with care.

Ferguson, Philip Gooch. See Bieber, Ralph P.

Field, Matthew C. *Matt Field on the Santa Fe Trail*. Collected by Clyde and Mae Reed Porter, and edited by John E. Sunder. Norman: University of Oklahoma Press, 1960. Becker #104.

The Arkansas Valley in 1839 and various aspects of the Santa Fe Trail are themes of Matt Field's recollections. His comments about Governor Manuel Armijo and other New Mexicans reveal that he was not completely taken in by contemporary North American biases.

―――. *Prairie and Mountain Sketches*. Collected by Clyde and Mae Reed

Porter, edited by Kate L. Gregg and John Francis McDermott. Norman: University of Oklahoma Press, 1957.
Field was with the Stewart expedition. This work includes material on the expedition from Field's unpublished journals.

Folsom, George F. *Mexico in 1842: A Description of the Country, Its Natural and Political Features; With a Sketch of its History, Brought Down to the Present Year; To Which is added an Account of Texas and Yucatan; and of the Santa Fe Expedition.* New York: C. J. Folsom, 1842. Becker #91.
This narrative covers a wide range of subjects, including history, agriculture, political structure, geography, population, and New Mexico statistics. There is considerable information on place names and the distances of travel along routes throughout the region of Mexico.

Fowler, Jacob. *The Journal of Jacob Fowler Narrating an Adventure from Arkansas through the Indian Territory, Oklahoma, Kansas, Colorado and New Mexico to the Sources of the Rio Grande Del Norte, 1821–22.* Edited by Elliot Coues. New York: Francis P. Harper, 1898. Reprinted by University of Nebraska Press, Lincoln, 1970.
Fowler traveled to Taos in 1821 with a party of twenty men under Hugh Glenn. They followed the Arkansas River to the present-day site of Pueblo, Colorado, and then struck out for Taos. The party returned east in 1822.

Garrard, Lewis Hector. *Wah-to-Yah, and the Taos Trail, or Prairie Travel and the Scalp Dances, with a look at Los Rancheros from Muleback, and the Rocky Mountain Campfire.* Cincinnati: H. W. Derby and Co., 1850. Reprinted as vol. IV of the Southwest Historical Series, The Grabhorn Press, San Francisco, 1936, and University of Oklahoma Press, 1955. Becker #183.
Garrard left Westport in 1846 with a Santa Fe caravan. His very readable account of New Mexico gives a vivid description of the people, their way of life, and the shock of culture clash.

Gibson, George Rutledge. *Journal of a Soldier under Kearny and Doniphan, 1846–47.* Southwest Historical Series, vol. III. Glendale: The Arthur Clark Co., 1935.
Gibson, a newspaperman, enlisted in the Army of the West under Kearny and marched over the Santa Fe Trail. He stayed in Santa Fe long enough to become editor of the Santa Fe *Republican* before returning home in 1848.

———. *Over the Chihuahua and Santa Fe Trails, 1847–1848; George Rutledge Gibson's Journal.* Edited and annotated by Robert W. Frazer. Published in cooperation with the Historical Society of New Mexico. Albuquerque: University of New Mexico Press, 1981.
The second portion of the Gibson journal, not previously published,

describes the trip from Santa Fe to Chihuahua, the return to Santa Fe, and the journey from Santa Fe to Leavenworth.

Gilliam, Albert M. *Travels Over the Table Lands and Cordilleras of Mexico.* Philadelphia: John W. Moore, 1846. Reprinted as *Travels in Mexico During the Years 1843 and 1844.* Aberdeen, Scotland: George Clark and Son, 1847. Becker #120c:1.

Gilliam was Consul in California. This book deals with his travels in 1834–1844 in a star-spangled-banner approach that demeans an "inferior" Mexican society.

Gregg, Josiah. *Commerce of the Prairies: or the Journal of a Santa Fe Trader, During Eight Expeditions Across the Great Western Prairies, and a Residence of Nearly Nine Years in Northern Mexico.* 2 vols. New York: Henry G. Langley, 1844. Also published in Reuben Gold Thwaites, *Early Western Travels: 1748–1846,* vols. XIX and XX. Glendale, Calif.: The Arthur H. Clark Co., 1905. Reprinted by AMS, New York, 1966. Becker lists sixteen publications before 1900 and six after 1900. Perhaps the most useful edition is that edited by Max Moorhead. Norman: University of Oklahoma Press, 1954. It is also available in paperback from the University of Nebraska Press, Lincoln, 1967. Another edition was edited by Milo Milton Quaife. New York: The Citadel Press, 1968.

Gregg made his first trip to Santa Fe in 1831. In the next nine years he crossed the Plains four times. First published in 1844, his book has been a classic on the Mexican period for its detailed observations of the Santa Fe trade, the Mexican people, and the useful statistics he provides.

―――. *Diary and Letters of Josiah Gregg.* Edited by Maurice Garland Fulton; introduction by Paul Horgan. Norman: University of Oklahoma Press, 1941 (vol. I), 1944 (vol II).

These volumes provide useful supplementary material to *Commerce of the Prairies.* Volume I deals with Gregg's Southwestern enterprises, 1840–47; volume II deals with his excursions to Mexico and California, 1847–50.

Gregg, Kate Leila, ed. *The Road to Santa Fe: the Journal and Diaries of George Champlin Sibley and Others Pertaining to the Surveying and Marking of a Road from the Missouri Frontier to the Settlements of New Mexico, 1825–1827.* Albuquerque: University of New Mexico Press, 1925.

This work deals with the first survey of the Santa Fe Trail. It includes a number of documents which reflect North American attitudes toward New Mexico at that time.

Hardy, R.W.H. *Travels in the Interior of Mexico in 1825, 1826, 1827 and 1828.* London: Colburn & Bentley, 1829. Reprinted by The Rio Grande Press, Inc., Glorieta, N. M., 1977.

Robert William Hale Hardy, a Lieutenant in the British Royal Navy, traveled throughout the interior of Mexico at a time when foreign travelers were still new to the area. His views are clearly those of a nineteenth-century Englishman in a land unlike any in which he had ever traveled.

Hobbs, James. *Wild Life in the Far West: Personal Adventures of a Border Mountain Man, Comprising Hunting and Trapping Adventures with Kit Carson and others; Captivity and Life Among the Comanches; Services Under Doniphan in the War with Mexico.* Hartford: Wiley, Waterman and Eaton, 1872. Reprinted by The Rio Grande Press, Glorieta N.M., 1969.
Hobbs went over the Santa Fe Trail in 1835 and again in the 1840s. He knew James Kirker, Albert Speyer, and Kit Carson.

House, E. *A Narrative of the Captivity of Mrs. Horn and her two Children, with Mrs. Harris, by the Camanche [sic] Indians, after They had Murdered their Husbands and Travelling Companions; with a Brief Account of the Manners and Customs of that Nation of Savages, of whom so little is Generally known.* St. Louis: C. Keemle, Printer, 1839. Another edition was printed in Cincinnati, 1851. Becker #74:1.
Mrs. Horn and Mrs. Harris were captured in Texas and taken to Santa Fe, where they were ransomed in the fall of 1837. Mrs. Horn then spent some time near San Miguel with an American trader before returning to Independence, Missouri.

Hughes, John T. *Doniphan's Expedition; Containing an Account of the Conquest of New Mexico; General Kearny's Overland Expedition to California; Doniphan's Campaign Against the Navajos; His Unparalleled March Upon Chihuahua and Durango; and the Operations of General Price at Santa Fe: With a Sketch of the Life of Col. Doniphan.* Cincinnati: J. A. and U. P. James, 1848. Reprinted as 63rd Cong., 2nd Sess., Sen. Exec. Doc. 608, 1916; and by The Rio Grande Press, Inc., Chicago, 1936. Becker includes six entries for the Hughes document.
This is an excellent account of the journey from Fort Leavenworth to Santa Fe and then to Chihuahua with extensive comments on the countryside, Mexican morals and laws, and the activities of Indians in New Mexico.

Hulbert, Archer Butler, ed. *Southwest on the Turquoise Trail: The First Diaries on the Road to Santa Fe.* Overland to the Pacific Series, no. 2 Denver: Stewart Commission of Colorado College and the Denver Public Library, c1933.
This book is composed of the diaries and journals of Pedro Vial, William Becknell, M. M. Marmaduke, George Sibley, Alphonso Wetmore, and others. It also includes documents dealing with the establishment of com-

merce with New Mexico. Opinions regarding the nature of Mexicans are freely given.

Hyde, George E. *Life of George Bent: Written from His Letters*. Edited by Savoie Lottinville. Norman: University of Oklahoma Press, 1968.
George, the son of William Bent, was born in 1843. His correspondence with Hyde discusses Bent's Fort, the St. Vrain-Bent business, and the Cheyenne Indians. Although tangential to New Mexico in the Mexican period, it contains important firsthand information on trade with New Mexico.

Isaacs, Robert. "Perils of a Mountain Hunt." *Missouri Republican*, September 4, 1832. Reprinted in Columbia *Missouri Intelligencer* and *Boon's Lick Advertiser*, October 6, 1832. Becker #45b.
This article is an abstract of part of Robert Isaac's journal. He was from Howard County, Missouri, and came to New Mexico to trap the Gila River. The trapping party left Santa Fe on August 25, 1831.

James, Thomas. *Three Years Among the Indians and Mexicans*. Waterloo, Ill.: Printed at the Office of the "War Eagle," 1846. Reprint edited by Walter Douglas. St. Louis: Missouri Historical Society, 1916. Edited by Abraham P. Nasatir.Chicago: Donnelly, 1953; and Philadelphia: J. B. Lippincott Co., 1962. Becker #121.
James went overland to Santa Fe in 1821 with one of the first trade caravans to arrive there from the United States.

Johnston, Abraham Robinson. See Bieber, Ralph P.

Jones, Nathaniel V. "Extracts from the Life Sketch of Nathaniel V. Jones." Edited by Rebecca M. Jones. *Utah Historical Quarterly* 4 (1931): 3–23.
Jones, a sergeant in the Mormon Battalion, marched overland to California via Santa Fe.

Kendall, George Wilkins. *Narrative of the Texan Santa Fe Expedition, Comprising a Description of a Tour through Texas, and Across the Great Southwestern Prairies, the Camanche [sic] and Cayuga Hunting-Grounds, with an Account of the Suffering from Want of Food, Losses From Hostile Indians, and Final Capture of the Texans, and Their March as Prisoners, to the City of Mexico*. 2 vols. New York: Harper and Bros., 1844. Many reprints, including a facsimile reprint of the first edition by Steck Co., Austin, 1935, and another by University Microfilms, Ann Arbor, 1966. Becker #110:1–#110:10.
Kendall was a reporter for the New Orleans *Picayune*. He decided to take a trip for his health at the same time that the Texans were putting together a "commercial" expedition to Santa Fe. He was captured with the rest of the expedition, and when released, he returned to the United States to dip his pen in gall. His commentary on New Mexicans has long been

considered an accurate reflection of New Mexico in the Mexican period, but Kendall's nineteenth-century prejudices need to be put into proper perspective.

Kirker, James. "Don Santiago Kirker the Indian Fighter." *Santa Fe Republican,* November 20, 1847. Reprinted by Glen Dawson, Los Angeles, 1948. Becker #135.
    Kirker was in Santa Fe in 1824. From 1824 to 1827 he was involved in various adventures which caused the Mexicans to put a price on his head. He later became involved with Col. Alexander Doniphan.

Lester, Thomas Bryan, M.D. "Notes by the Wayside," [his diary] in Thomas B. Hall, M.D., *Medicine on the Santa Fe Trail.* Dayton, Ohio: Morningside Bookshop, 1971, pp. 24–27.
    Lester's comments include information on General Manuel Armijo's whereabouts after being taken prisoner and then released on parole by order of General Sterling Price.

Magoffin, Susan Shelby. *Down the Santa Fe Trail and into Mexico: The Diary of Susan Shelby Magoffin, 1846–1847.* Edited by Stella M. Drumm. New Haven: Yale University Press, 1926. Reissued in paperback, Yale University Press, 1962.
    Trader James Magoffin, asked by Secretary of War Marcy to pave the way for Kearny's army, came to New Mexico in 1846. Susan was the wife of brother Samuel Magoffin who brought a trade caravan into New Mexico behind the Army of the West. Susan, Samuel's bride of eight months, kept a journal of her trip with the caravan to Santa Fe and Chihuahua.

Marmaduke, Meredith Miles. "Santa Fe Trail: M. M. Marmaduke Journal." Edited by Francis A. Sampson. *Missouri Historical Review* 6 (1911): 1–10. Also printed as a separate pamphlet by the *Missouri Historical Review* and in Hulbert's *Southwest on the Turquoise Trail* (c1933).
    Marmaduke arrived in Santa Fe in 1824. He found it difficult to sell his trade goods because of a shortage of money, so he stayed for ten months. His account of New Mexicans reflects an acute ethnocentrism. See also Becknell, Thomas, and Hulbert, Archer Butler.

Martínez, Antonio José. See Weber, David.

Martínez, Severino. See Minge, Ward Alan.

Mayer, Brantz. *Mexico as It Was and As It Is.* New York, 1844.
    Written as a journal when Mayer was Secretary of the U.S. Legation to Mexico, 1841–42, this work comments on the Texan-Santa Fe expedition, the Mexican War, and other related matters.

Meriwether, David. *My Life in the Mountains and on the Plains: The Newly*

Discovered Autobiography by David Meriwether. Edited by Robert A. Griffen. The American Exploration and Travel Series, vol. 49. Norman: University of Oklahoma Press, 1955.

Meriwether went to Santa Fe in 1820. He was arrested and then released to make his way back east. He returned to New Mexico, serving as governor from 1853–57. This volume contains information on Manuel Armijo's death and other matters of significance to the Mexican period.

Minge, Ward Alan. "The Last Will and Testament of Don Severino Martínez." *New Mexico Quarterly* 33 (1963): 33–50.

This document is important for many words relating to New Mexico's material culture. Minge is the translator.

Moorhead, Max L. "Notes and Documents [Mexican Report on American Invasion of New Mexico]." *New Mexico Historical Review* 26 (1951): 68–82.

These are three reports presenting different views of the American invasion in 1846. One is from Santa Fe signed by 105 New Mexican citizens; another is by Manuel Armijo from Chihuahua; the third was drawn up by the New Mexico assembly.

Nidever, George. *The Life and Adventures of George Nidever, 1802–1883*. Edited by William Henry Ellison. Berkeley: University of California Press, 1937.

While most of Nidever's adventures were in California, there are accounts of Arroyo Seco and San Fernando [Taos] as bases for trapping operations from 1831 to 1833. He makes reference to the good treatment the trappers always received from the Mexicans. Nidever orally presented the account of his adventures to E. F. Murray in September 1878.

Olmstead, Virginia L., trans. and ed. *Spanish and Mexican Censuses of New Mexico, 1750–1830*. Albuquerque: The New Mexico Genealogical Society, Inc., 1981.

This collection of censuses, together with the first volume cited below, gives the researcher a century of New Mexico families before the area came under the jurisdiction of the United States.

———. *Spanish and Mexican Colonial Censuses of New Mexico: 1790, 1823, 1845*. Typescript published by the New Mexico Genealogical Society, Inc., Albuquerque, 1975.

Data include names, ages, and marital status of heads of households and spouses. Of related interest is the Antonio Narbona count of 1827 published in *Three New Mexico Chronicles*.

Ortega, Melquiades Antonio. See Potash, Robert A.

Parraga, Charlott Marie Nelson. "Santa Fe de Nuevo Mexico: A Study of a

Frontier City Based on an Annotated Translation of Selected Documents (1825–1832) from the Mexican Archives of New Mexico.'' Ph.D. dissertation, Ball State University, Muncie, Ind., 1976. Available on Microfilm from University Microfilms International, Ann Arbor, 1977. This dissertation purports to provide translation, transcription, and facsimiles of eight Mexican period documents dealing primarily with the fur trade, administration of justice, and Juan Bautista Vigil y Alarid. Translations should be used with care.

Pattie, James Ohio. *The Hunters of Kentucky; or the Trails and Toils of Trappers and Traders, During an Expedition to the Rocky Mountains, New Mexico, and California.* New York: Wm. H. Graham, 1847. A summary of the narrative appeared in *Harpers Magazine* 21 (June 1860): 80–93. This account records Pattie's second journey across the country to California.

———. *The Personal Narrative of James Ohio Pattie of Kentucky, Being an Expedition from St. Louis, through the Vast Regions between that Place and the Pacific Ocean, and Thence Back through the City of Mexico to Vera Cruz, During Journeyings of Six Years; in Which He and His Father, Who Accompanied Him, Suffered Unheard of Hardships And Dangers, Had Various Conflicts with the Indians, And Were Made Captives, in Which Captivity His Father Died; Together With A Description of the Country, and the Various Nations Through Which They Passed.* Edited by Timothy Flint. Cincinnati: John H. Wood, 1831and 1833. Pattie's account was reprinted in vol. XVIII of Rueben Gold Thwaites, *Early Western Travels.* Cleveland: The Arthur H. Clark, Co., 1905. This series was reprinted by the AMS Press, New York, 1966. Pattie's narrative was also published by R. R. Donnelley, Chicago, 1930, and J. B. Lippincott, Philadelphia, 1962. Becker #45:1 and #45:2. Pattie reached Santa Fe on a trading expedition in 1824. He asked for a license to trap beaver and then spent the spring of 1825 at the Santa Rita copper mines. He returned to Santa Fe, lost his furs to Mexican authorities, then departed with a new license to trap the Gila River. His comments about New Mexico are extensive but raise questions about their veracity.

Perea, Francisco. See Allison, William H. H.

Pérez, Demetrio. See Read, Benjamin M.

Perrigo, Lynn I., trans. ''New Mexico in the Mexican Period as revealed in the Torres Documents.'' *New Mexico Historical Reveiw* 29 (1954): 28–40. Commentary on the political religious functions of officials shows the relationship between church and state in the Mexican period. Juan Gerónimo Torres was a militia lieutenant, farmer, and deputy alcalde at Sabinal from 1819 to 1827.

————., trans. "The Personal Interests of Juan Gerónimo Torres." *New Mexico Historical Review* 26 (1951): 159–64.

Included in these "Notes and Documents" is a translated sale contract for a piece of land in Sevilleta. The exchange of deed occurred in 1828. Another document attests to the election of Torres to lieutenant in the civil militia.

————., trans. "Provincial Statutes of 1824–1826." *New Mexico Historical Review* 27 (1952): 66–76.

These statutes consititute a schedule of regulations to which the alcaldes of the Territory of New Mexico were required to abide as legislated by the provincial legislature. Penalties for crimes are specified and individuals are encouraged to denounce violators of local codes.

Potash, Robert A., trans. and ed. "Notes and Documents [Answers from Tucson and Santa Fe to a Questionaire, from the Banco de Avio, 1831]," *New Mexico Historical Review* 24 (1949): 332–40.

The responses by Teodoro Ramírez and Melquiades Antonio Ortega to the thirty-one questions of the Banco de Avio provide some information on economic conditions of the two towns. The Ortega account of Santa Fe was published in the *Registro Oficial*.

Rada, Manuel de Jesús. See Weber, David.

Ramírez, Teodoro. See Potash, Robert A.

Read, Benjamin M. "In Santa Fe During the Mexican Regime." *New Mexico Historical Review* II (1927): 90–97.

These are translated recollections of Don Demetrio Pérez collected by Read in 1913. Pérez recalls the arrival of Governor Mariano Martínez in 1844 and comments on what he did for Santa Fe.

Richardson, William H. *Journal of William H. Richardson, a Private Soldier in Col. Doniphan's Command.* Baltimore: Jos. Robinson, 1847. Reprinted in *Missouri Historical Review* 22 (1928): 193–236, 331–60, 511–42. Becker #137:1 to #137:4.

Another of several journals of the soldiers who came to New Mexico with Col. Alexander Doniphan.

Ruxton, George Augustus Frederick. *Adventures in Mexico and the Rocky Mountains.* London: John Murray, 1847 and 1861; Boston: "Star Spangled Banner," 1847; New York: H. Long & Brother, 1847; Philadelphia: T. B. Peterson, 1847; New York: Harper & Brothers, 1848 and 1855. Partly reprinted in 1916 as *Wild Life in the Rocky Mountains;* some sections also included in Clyde and Mae Porter's *Ruxton of the Rockies,* University of Oklahoma Press, Norman, 1950. Becker entries #139:1–#137:7.

Ruxton was an Englishman who traveled from central Mexico to Chihuahua and Santa Fe in 1846. His opinions of Mexicans are not very flattering, but because he comments on so many different aspects of the people and their way of life, his views are valuable.

Sage, Rufus B. *Scenes in the Rocky Mountains, and in Oregon, California, New Mexico, Texas, and the Grand Prairies; or Notes by the Way, during an Excursion of Three Years, with a Description of the Countries Passed through, including Their Geography, Geology, Resources, Present Condition, and the Different Nations Inhabiting Them; by a New Englander.* Philadelphia: Carey and Hart, 1846. The most useful of several editions is the 1956 two-volume set published by Arthur Clark Co., Glendale, Calif., which includes the full text annotated by LeRoy R. and Ann W. Hafen together with many of Sage's letters. A facsimile of the first edition recently has been reprinted by University of Nebraska Press, Lincoln, 1982. Becker #123:1.
Sage, a member of Charles A. Warfield's command which was after booty on the Santa Fe Trail, traveled to Pueblo, Colorado, and Taos, New Mexico, in 1843. His narrative is accurate and intelligent. It discusses several encounters with Mexicans and his experiences in Taos.

"Santa Fe and the Far West." *Niles Register* 61 (December 4, 1841): no. 209. Also published in *New York Tribune*, November 31, 1841. Becker #86. Reprinted in *New Mexico Historical Review* 5 (1930); 299–304.
This is a reprint of a letter dated July 29, 1841, which appeared originally in the Evansville, Indiana *Journal*. It is a social commentary on New Mexico and her people with most of the usual observations that one finds in the accounts of ethnocentric Santa Fe traders.

Sibley, George C. *The Road to Santa Fe: the Journal and Diaries of George Champlin Sibley and Others Pertaining to the Surveying and Marking of a Road from the Missouri Frontier to the Settlements of New Mexico, 1825–27.* Edited by Kate Leila Gregg. Albuquerque: University of New Mexico Press, 1925.
This work deals with the first survey of the Santa Fe Trail. It includes a number of documents which reflect North American attitudes toward New Mexico at this time.
See also Hulbert, Archer Butler.

"Some Laws and Legal Proceedings of the Mexican Period: Collection of Tithes." *New Mexico Historical Review* 26 (1951): 244–47.
This is a set of instructions for tithe collectors written by Pedro Armendarís on January 1, 1820.

Storrs, Augustus. *Answers of Augustus Storrs, of Missouri, to Certain Queries upon the Origin, Present State, and Future Prospect, of Trade and Intercourse between Missouri and the Internal Provinces of Mexico, Pro-*

pounded by the Hon. Mr. Benton. U.S. 18th Cong., 2nd Sess., Sen. Doc. 7 (Serial 108). Washington: Gales and Seaton, January 3, 1825. Reprinted in *Niles Register,* January 15, 1825; by Stagecoach Press, Houston, 1960; and in A. B. Hulbert's *Southwest on the Turquoise Trail.* Also in *The American Scene* 6 (1965), theme issue, "Santa Fe Trade."

Storrs was a wagon-trail leader to Santa Fe in 1824. His detailed answers to twenty-two questions from Senator Thomas Hart Benton led to a survey of the Trail. His remarks on New Mexico are significant.

Taylor, Benjamin Franklin, ed. *Short Ravelings from a Long Yarn, or Camp March Sketches of the Santa Fe Trail; from the Notes of Richard L. Wilson.* Chicago: Geer and Wilson, *Daily Journal Office,* 1847. Reprinted by Fine Arts Press, Santa Ana, Calif., 1936, with an introduction by Henry Raup Wagner.

Wilson made this trip in 1841 or 1842. He discusses the social life of New Mexicans, the Mexican customs inspectors, the governor, and the people, whom he describes as indolent, shiftless, and treacherous.

Theisen, Gerald, ed. "Opinions on the Newly Independent Mexican Nation: Documents from the Archdiocese of Santa Fe, New Mexico, 1820–1843." *Revista de Historia de América* 72 (1971): 484–96.

Four documents which reflect the attitude of the Church in Santa Fe towards the independence of Mexico.

Thompson, Waddy. *Recollections of Mexico.* New York and London: Wiley & Putman, 1846.

Thompson went to Mexico in 1842. His recollections describe the manners and customs of the Mexicans.

Torres, Juan Gerónimo. See Perrigo, Lynn I.

Turner, Henry Smith. *The Original Journals of Henry Smith Turner, with Stephen Watts Kearny in New Mexico and California, 1846–1847.* Edited by Dwight L. Clarke. Exploration and Travel Series, vol. 51. Norman: University of Oklahoma Press, 1966.

A good companion to Emory's *Notes,* this journal reflects the thoughts of a man who was more of a loner than most. He recorded his impressions of travel through New Mexico and California in a more personal manner than other chroniclers, and commented on New Mexicans in a reasonably balanced fashion.

Tyler, Daniel. "The Personal Property of Manuel Armijo, 1829." *El Palacio* 80 (1974): 45–48.

Responding to a Congressional decree placing a five percent tax on incomes of one to ten thousand pesos, Armijo listed his property and the income he received from it. The document also reveals the workings of the *partido* system.

Waldo, William. "Recollections of a Septuagenarian." *Missouri Historical Society Glimpses of the Past* 5 (1938): 59–94.
William Waldo made his first trip over the Santa Fe Trail in 1829. He was the brother of David Waldo, noted Santa Fe trader.

Walker, Joel P. *A Pioneer of Pioneers: Narrative of Adventures thro' Alabama, Florida, New Mexico, Oregon, California, etc.* Early California Travels Series, vol. XVII. Los Angeles: Glen Dawson, 1953.
These are firsthand memoirs from a manuscript in the Bancroft Library. Walker went with a party of thirty men to Santa Fe in 1822.

Waugh, Alfred S. *Travels in Search of the Elephant: the Wanderings of Alfred S. Waugh, Artist, in Louisiana, Missouri, and Santa Fe in 1845–46*. St. Louis: Missouri Historical Society, 1951.
The author makes several references to Manuel Armijo and Doña La Tules. He has a heavy "gringo" bias and condemns Mexicans for their immorality. Waugh reached Santa Fe in June of 1846. A letter is appended, written July 14, 1846, telling of the situation in Santa Fe just before Kearny arrived.

Webb, James Josiah. *Adventures in the Santa Fe Trade, 1844–1847*. Edited by Ralph P. Bieber. Southwest Historical Series, I. Glendale: The Arthur H. Clark Co., 1931. Reprinted by Porcupine Press, Philadelphia, 1974.
Webb was a Santa Fe trader. His account begins in the same year that Gregg's ends and therefore makes excellent companion reading. His eighteen trips to Santa Fe and numerous contacts in the business make this an important account of New Mexico in the Mexican period.

———. "The Papers of James J. Webb, Santa Fe Merchant, 1844–1861." Edited by Ralph P. Bieber. *Washington University Studies* XI (1924): 255–305.
Webb, a Connecticut-born Missouri trader, entered the trade after the Mexican government had imposed many restrictions and then reopened it in 1843. He made trips in 1844, 1845, and 1846 and took some of his goods to Chihuahua. He comments on Governor Manuel Armijo and the state of affairs in New Mexico. Bieber notes that the most interesting of the Webb Papers are "Memoirs of James J. Webb, 1844–1847," in possession of the New Mexico Historical Society. (Now in the Museum of New Mexico. See entry in Chapter I.)

Weber, David J., ed. "*El Gobierno Territorial de Nuevo Mexico. La Exposición del Padre Martínez de 1831.*" *Historia Mexicana* 24 (1975): 302–15.
This document is Martínez' declaration before a legislative committee regarding the circumstances and conditions pertaining to the lack of authority of a committee on which he serves by appointment. Martínez read the statement in Santa Fe, and a copy was sent to Mexico City.

———. "A Letter from Taos, 1826." *New Mexico Historical Review* 41 (1966):

155–64.

A letter from William Workman to his brother asks for stills and complains of the difficulty of selling anything in New Mexico.

―――. *Northern Mexico on the Eve of the United States Invasion: Rare Imprints Concerning California, Arizona, New Mexico and Texas, 1821– 1846.* New York: Arno Press, Inc., 1976.

Included in this volume is a report of Manuel de Jesús Rada published in 1829. Rada gives an account of conditions in New Mexico to the General Congress. The other documents included in this volume were collected from several archives and libraries.

―――, trans. and ed. *The Extranjeros: Selected Documents from the Mexican Side of the Santa Fe Trail, 1825–1828.* Santa Fe: Stagecoach Press, 1967.

These documents consist of some Mexican records of the Santa Fe trade from 1825 to 1828.

Wetmore, Alphonso. "Major Alphonso Wetmore's Diary of a Journey to Santa Fe, 1928." *Missouri Historical Review* 8 (1914): 177–97. Also published as a chapter in A. B. Hulbert's *Southwest on the Turquoise Trail.*

This diary is about an 1828 trip to New Mexico. Wetmore sent this information along with a letter to Secretary of War Lewis Cass in 1831. In the letter he comments on other trips to Santa Fe from 1821 to 1829 and provides opinions of New Mexico.

See also Hulbert, Archer Butler.

―――. *Petition of Sundry Inhabitants of the State of Missouri, Upon the Subject of a Communication Between the Said State and the Internal Provinces of Mexico, with a Letter from Alphonso Wetmore upon the Same Subject.* U.S. 18th Cong., 2nd Sess., Sen Doc. 79 (Serial 116). Washington: Gales and Seaton, Feb. 14, 1825. Becker #30.

This is a request from Missourians for protection of the Santa Fe Trail. Wetmore's comments on travel between 1821 and 1824 suggest that the journey to Santa Fe was relatively easy.

Wilson, Benjamin David. "Benjamin David Wilson's Observations on Early Days in California and New Mexico." Foreword and Explanatory Notes by Arthur Woodward. *Historical Society of Southern California Annual Publications* 16 (1934): 74–150. Printed privately by Miss Anne Wilson Patton, Benjamin Wilson's great granddaughter; and by Robert Glass Cleland as the volume "Pathfinders" of the California Series, Los Angeles, 1929.

Wilson arrived in Santa Fe in 1833. He trapped in the Gila for a time and returned to Santa Fe in 1835. He worked for Gregg and later bought out Gregg's merchandise. His account provides considerable detail concerning the political atmosphere of New Mexico and California during the Mexican period.

Wilson, Richard L. *Short Ravelings from a Long Yarn, or Camp March Sketches of the Santa Fe Trail; from the Notes of Richard L. Wilson.* Edited by Benjamin Franklin Taylor. Chicago: Geer and Wilson, *Daily Journal* Office, 1847. Reprinted with an introduction by Henry Raup Wagner, by the Fine Arts Press, Santa Ana, Calif., 1936.
Wilson made this trip in 1841 or 1842. He discusses the social life of New Mexicans, the Mexican customs inspectors, the governor, and the people, whom he describes as indolent, shiftless, and treacherous.

Wislizenus, Frederick Adolphus. *Memoir of a Tour to Northern New Mexico, Connected with Col. Doniphan's Expedition, in 1846 and 1847.* U.S. 30th Cong., 1st Sess., Sen. Misc. Doc. 26 (Serial 511). Washington: Tippin and Streeper, Printers, 1848. Reprinted by Calvin Horn, Publishers, Albuquerque, 1969; and by The Rio Grande Press, Glorieta, N.M., 1969. Becker #159:1.
Wislizenus traveled over the Santa Fe Trail to Chihuahua with a caravan headed by Albert Speyer, just ahead of Kearny's Army of the West.

Workman, William. See Weber, David J.

INDEX

This index includes only *names* and *places* found in the main body of the text. The foreword, introduction, footnotes, and summaries of references have not been indexed. Because of its frequent use in the text, "New Mexico" has not been indexed. The author is grateful to Cyndy Erickson for her assistance in completing this chore.